THE AUTHOR

JOHN WALKER, who is a professor of Spanish in Queen's University in Kingston, Ontario, Canada, was born and brought up in Graham territory in Dumbarton, Scotland, where Don Roberto's name was a household word. In his Latin American studies at Glasgow University he encountered with increasing frequency the name of Cunninghame Graham, and what began as an interesting hobby ended as a major enterprise. He has published innumerable articles in scholarly journals and newspapers throughout the world and has recently spent his sabbatical leave in South America collecting further material on the English-speaking writers of the River Plate region, with special emphasis on R. B. Cunninghame Graham.

Portrait of Don Roberto by Sir John Lavery. Courtesy Museo Nacional de Bellas Artes, Buenos Aires, Argentina

THE
SOUTH AMERICAN
SKETCHES
of
R.B. Cunninghame Graham

Selected and edited, with an
Introduction, Notes, Glossary, and Bibliography by
JOHN WALKER

University of Oklahoma Press
Norman

Library of Congress Cataloging in Publication Data

Graham, Robert Bontine Cunninghame, 1852–1936.
    The South American sketches of R. B. Cunninghame
Graham.

    Bibliography: p.
    Includes index.
    1. South America—Social life and customs—Addresses,
essays, lectures.   2. South America—Description and
travel—Addresses, essays, lectures.   3. Pampas—Social
life and customs—Addresses, essays, lectures.
4. Graham, Robert Bontine Cunninghame, 1852–1936—
Addresses, essays, lectures.   I. Walker, John, 1933–
II. Title.
F2210.G72   980'.03   77–18604
ISBN 0–8061–1468–1

To my mother
and the memory of my father

EDITOR'S FOREWORD

The aim of this book is to reintroduce Robert Bontine Cunninghame Graham to the general reading public and to make at least some of his works available again to the specialist. Almost all of his books have long since been out of print, as also the two essential biographies by A. F. Tschiffely[1] and Herbert F. West,[2] which concentrate mostly on the man and his life. A comparatively recent book by Richard E. Haymaker,[3] which is a detailed study of Graham's writings, was published in 1967. Haymaker's excellent book presupposes a close knowledge of Graham's material, which is hardly likely since his works are no longer readily available. This present study is meant to bridge the gap between the two previous approaches. I have said something of the man and his life and his writing, and the reader can judge for himself in the sketches that follow. I have chosen the South American sketches for two reasons. First, he spent a long time there, and second, it happens to be the field of my speciality. I hope, however, that this collection will be the first of several, and Graham's sketches about Spain, Scotland, North Africa, Mexico, and Texas will follow.

[1] A. F. Tschiffely, *Don Roberto*.
[2] Herbert F. West, *Robert Bontine Cunninghame Graham—His Life and Works*.
[3] Richard E. Haymaker, *Prince Errant and Evocator of Horizons*.

This book is, in a sense, a labor of love. I was born and brought up in Graham territory in Dumbarton, Scotland, as a child playing in streets called Graham Road, Bontine Avenue, Ardoch Crescent, where Don Roberto's name was a household word. We simply accepted the Graham ambience without any deep knowledge of the man and his achievements. As an undergraduate in the Hispanic Department of Glasgow University, I encountered with increasing frequency in my Latin American studies the name of Cunninghame Graham as an authority in both the literary and historical field. What began as an interesting hobby ended as a major enterprise.

Robert Bontine Cunninghame Graham was a very prolific writer. Not counting histories and travel books, his sketches, tales, and essays amount to some two hundred, about fifty of which are about Latin America. When it comes to making a selection, the big problem is what to leave out. However, I have tried to give a representative selection, choosing the best and taking into account geographical and chronological considerations. To give some shape and uniformity to the work I have divided the sketches into groups, based on the different South American countries he visited and described. The reader will note that within the groups the sketches have been arranged in an order that will make sense, such as, for example, geographical background, the people, and their customs. Naturally, the preponderance will be about the region he knew best, the Argentine pampas. I have also selected examples of all the other countries he visited as a youth— Uruguay (as it is called now), Paraguay, Brazil, and the countries he visited in the twilight of his life, Colombia and Venezuela, which fittingly completes the cycle, for here it all began with the birth of Graham's mother. This geographical division might have produced a clash with the chronological sequence of the sketches, but fortunately in most cases they coincide. Where this is not the case, it is interesting to compare the early sketches—"A Vanishing Race," "A Jesuit," "In the Tarumensian Woods"—in which he is still trying to master his trade, with those written in the last years of his life, in which he is an accomplished evocator of horizons (to use Haymaker's phrase)—"Los Llanos del Apure" and "Charlie the Gaucho." The reader will have noted that I have omitted all sketches about Mexico, thus calling the collection South American and not Latin American sketches. Mexico, Texas, and the Southwest will provide the material for the next collection.

A complete collection of his South American sketches would have been desirable, but from the thirty chosen the reader will be able to paint a good picture of Robert Bontine Cunninghame Graham in the New World—not only Graham the writer, but also the man, for in his work he writes his own life story.

I should like to express my thanks to Admiral Sir Angus Cunninghame Graham for permission to reproduce the sketches of his uncle, and also for his encouragement and cooperation over the years; to the Museo Nacional de Bellas Artes, Buenos Aires, for permission to use the Lavery reproduction as a frontispiece; to my wife for her patience and help in reading the manuscript and proofs; to Inés Granda and Joanne Coe for valuable secretarial work; to Brock University, St. Catharines, which provided the research grant for the preparation of the manuscript; to Queen's University, Kingston, for a valuable research award; to the Canada Council for various travel grants.

The book has been published with the help of a grant from the Humanities Research Council of Canada, using funds provided by the Canada Council.

JOHN WALKER

Kingston, Ontario, Canada

CONTENTS

South American Sketches

INTRODUCTION
by John Walker

The Man and his Life

Robert Bontine Cunninghame Graham was by temperament, family background, and upbringing inevitably drawn toward the New World. His mother was born in 1828 on the British flagship *Barham* at La Guaira, off the coast of Venezuela, where she spent the first three years of her life. Her father, Admiral Elphinstone Fleeming, who had married Catalina Paulina Jiménez, the daughter of an old Spanish family of hidalgos, gained some fame and respect for his part in mediating between the liberator, Simón Bolívar, and one of his lieutenants, José Antonio Páez, when these two came to loggerheads after expelling the Spaniards in the wars of independence.

Robert was born in London on May 24, 1852, of a Scottish soldier-father and his half-Spanish mother. Brought up on his father's Scottish estates in Finlaystone and Gartmore, he soon acquired a passion for riding and horses that was to stay with him for the rest of his life. Visits to his Spanish grandmother on the Isle of Wight and his relations in Cádiz gave him an early feeling for the Spanish language and things Hispanic. He received the typical aristocratic education at Harrow and in Brussels, where he learned French and fencing, to add to his Spanish and horse riding. Thus, in his ancestry, education, and upbringing, was sown the seed of his cosmopolitanism that was to produce the kindly Scottish laird with the demeanor, dignity, and idealism of a Spanish noble.

His father had hoped that Robert would follow him into the army, but young Graham, already international in outlook as

3

well as by birth, preferred to seek adventure, and, not surprisingly, he chose the New World. In 1870, at the age of seventeen and with the connivance of his mother, he set out on a ranching adventure to Argentina. Though the venture failed, mainly because of the drinking habits of his partner, he gained valuable experience, the desired adventure, and material for his future writing. In the sketch "Cruz Alta"[1] he describes his early problems of ranching, selling horses, and cattle droving. Don Roberto, as he was affectionately called, found the life of the pampas cowboys, the gauchos, much to his taste. While living with them he wore gaucho dress and took part in all their activities—breaking in mustangs, throwing the *bolas*, racing horses, promoting cockfights, and organizing ostrich hunts. The gaucho in him never died, and in later life he always wore the gaucho belt, even when formally dressed. In company he often had the habit of crouching gaucho-fashion, and spent his leisure hours throwing the lasso. Once, when praised by an admirer as a poet and a gaucho, he replied, "more gaucho than poet."[2] He learned to know the pampas even better than the gauchos themselves, for he traveled more than they did. His great knowledge of the pampas and their inhabitants was recognized by his friend and fellow writer, W. H. Hudson. Hudson dedicated *El ombú* to Don Roberto, "the *singularísimo escritor inglés* who has lived with and knows (even to the marrow, as they would themselves say) the horsemen of the Pampas, and who alone of European writers has rendered something of the vanishing colour of that remote life."[3] Graham was later to lament the passing of these expert horsemen in his sketch "A Vanishing Race."[4] Their horses, separated from which they were only half-men, he praised in "The Horses of the Pampas" in the same book.

Though thirsty for adventure, young Robert could not have foreseen himself in the midst of a revolution. Like other innocents, he was swept away by wild riders who offered him the choice of joining the band of Reds or Whites or have a bloodthirsty captain "play the violin," a euphemism for slitting his throat. Thus Don Roberto became embroiled in the confused revolution of General López Jordán against the government of

[1] From his *Thirteen Stories*.
[2] A. F. Tschiffely, *Don Roberto*, 431.
[3] W. H. Hudson, *El ombú*.
[4] *Father Archangel of Scotland*.

President Sarmiento.[5] As well as the dangers of war, he had to combat natural enemies like the piranha, the cannibal fish, and the poison arrows of the Indians.

Out of the revolutionary army, Don Roberto's next adventure took him to Paraguay in 1873–74, where he obtained a concession for growing maté tea. When he arrived there the Paraguayans had just fought a losing war against the might of Argentina, Brazil, and Uruguay. What Don Roberto found there was a nation of old people, women, and children. The architect of the disaster was the infamous dictator, Francisco Solano López, known to the people as "Monkey Tiger"—one of the many despots who has plagued Latin America over the last century and a half since independence. López was killed while trying to flee with his French-Irish mistress, Madame Lynch.[6] It was in the New World that Don Roberto, seeing abuses and injustice everywhere, first acquired the spirit of radicalism, with the poor and oppressed at the mercy of unscrupulous dictators, both regional and national. These early travels motivated his later association with unlikely companions like the socialists, Keir Hardie, John Burns, H. M. Hyndman.

Two years later saw him in Uruguay with his friend George Mansel, a former naval officer. Here they bought horses to sell in Brazil. In spite of the attention of the jaguars and the desertion of their gauchos, they managed to smuggle them over the border for a not very profitable sale. Then they bought the Sauce Chico Ranch and raised cattle in the face of Indian attacks. In spite of the attacks, he still sympathized with the plight of the Indian, and in "A Hegira"[7] he describes with great sarcasm and pity an Apache hunt. This generous aristocrat was always on the side of the underdog, whether it be Zulu, Turk, Scottish miner, or English chainmaker, all of whose causes he defended vigorously at various times in his life.

Home again in 1878, he visited Spain and France, and it was in

---

[5] Domingo Faustino Sarmiento (1811–88), also the author of *Facundo* (1845), a study of the struggle between civilization and barbarity in nineteenth-century Argentina, as portrayed through the *caudillo*, Facundo Quiroga. Translated into English by Mrs. Horace Mann as *Life in the Argentine Republic in the Days of the Tyrants* (London, 1868; reprinted New York, 1960; Boston, 1961).

[6] Some sixty years later appeared Graham's history of Paraguay under López, entitled *Portrait of a Dictator*.

[7] *Thirteen Stories*.

Paris that he met Gabrielle de la Balmondière, his future wife, almost bowling her over, typically, with his horse. As one would expect, she proved to have been born in Chile of a French father and a Spanish mother. Finding her unhappy, he rescued his maiden in distress in true chivalrous fashion like Don Quixote, whom he also resembled in appearance, and married her on October 24, 1878. Becoming increasingly bored at Gartmore, they left for Texas, where they spent four years before losing everything in an Indian raid. Staying at San Antonio, he had another of his "profit-making" schemes—this time selling cotton in Mexico City. The hard life of the trail, the cold, and the constant presence of the Mescalero Indians on the warpath were described by Gabrielle in one of her first sketches, "The Waggon Train."[8] Graham's fencing education in Brussels, however, stood him in good stead, for he set up a fencing academy in Mexico City under the name of Professor Bontini, a name that greatly appealed to his sense of humor. When they had gathered enough money, they returned to San Antonio to find the ranch wrecked by Indians. Don Roberto was obliged to work as an interpreter, hunt buffalo, drive cattle, and school horses for the rich, whilst Gabrielle taught French and painting. During his stay in San Antonio, he came in contact with the famous Buffalo Bill at the Horsehead Crossing.

When his father died in 1883 and left him debts of £100,000, Don Roberto was obliged to return home. It was at this time that he acquired his most famous horse, Pampa, whom he found hauling trams in a Glasgow street. He paid £50 for this Argentine mustang which he was to ride for some twenty years. When he wrote *The Horses of the Conquest* (1930), he took the unusual step of dedicating the book "To Pampa, My black Argentine whom I rode for twenty years without a fall. May the earth lie on him as lightly as he once trod upon its face. Vale—or until so long—Don Roberto." Pampa, however, was not merely a leisure-time companion. When Don Roberto entered the political field, this great character always arrived at the Houses of Parliament on horseback.

Flamboyant, extravagant, and often exasperating, this latter-day Raleigh, this last of the Elizabethans, as he was known, entered Parliament in 1886, as Liberal M.P. for West Lanarkshire.

---

[8] *The Christ of Toro* (London, 1908).

For six years this *enfant terrible* was to achieve fame and notoriety for progressive ideas, fiery speeches, and a radical spirit that was born on the pampas of Argentina. Although disclaiming the Socialist label (John Burns called him "a social reformer"), he expressed progressive ideas that were the stuff of the twentieth century. He advocated universal suffrage, free secular education with a free meal, an eight-hour working day, nationalization of land, graduated income tax, triennial parliaments, abolition of the House of Lords, and prison reform, as well as opposing capital and corporal punishment. Ramsay MacDonald, onetime prime minister of Great Britain, said that "Graham's socialism was based on romantic ideas of freedom and his profound feeling for the bottom dog." [9] He shocked his own class by expounding democratic ideas and associating with socialists like Keir Hardie. Although humorous in his speeches, he was no eccentric playing at politics, nor an idealist tilting at windmills. If quixotic in appearance, he also had the Spanish knight's admirable quality of idealism, so essential for reform. That he was uncompromising in his fight against injustice is obvious from his famous "I never withdraw" to the Speaker. This breach of parliamentary etiquette (1887) was prompted by the case of the Cradley Heath workers against whose exploitation Graham was protesting. George Bernard Shaw was to take these words as the inspiration for his Bulgarian hero of *Arms and the Man*. [10]

Actions, of course, speak louder than words, and when spurred on by principles he held sacred, he was prepared to take vigorous action. On November 13, 1887, Don Roberto gained public notoriety and praise for his part in "Bloody Sunday." With the Irish Question very much in the air, some supporters of the imprisoned Irish M.P., William O'Brien, organized a meeting in Trafalgar Square. The banning of the meeting seemed to Graham a flagrant denial of the right of free speech. The blood flowed, he was arrested, and although he pleaded not guilty to "assault of the police (?)," he and John Burns were sent to prison for six weeks.

When he lost his seat in Parliament in 1892, the eccentric in him took him on a fruitless gold hunt to Spain, based on Pliny's

[9] Tschiffely, *Don Roberto*, 440.
[10] See notes to *Three Plays for Puritans* (Penguin, London, 1949), 342, and my article "Bernard Shaw and Don Roberto," *The Shaw Review*, XV, No. 3 (September 1972), 94–103.

description of ancient Lusitania. In 1897 he decided to try to reach Tarudant, the Forbidden City in Morocco, which had never been entered by a Christian. Unfortunately, he was captured by a *kaid*, or chief, suspected of being a British agent, and was finally released without reaching his objective. This adventure was recounted in *Mogreb-el-Acksa*, one of the most exciting travel books ever written. George Bernard Shaw unashamedly confessed that it had been the source of *Captain Brassbound's Conversion*.[11]

Though far from the New World, he was never totally isolated from it. As his experiences had been the basis for his political activity, so too were they the stuff of his literary output. On his return from Morocco, he settled down to do some writing, and during his "quiet period" from 1898 till 1914, he produced a book almost every year. They were mostly collections of stories, essays, and sketches, with South American themes and settings appearing in every book. Many of the Latin American histories were to emerge later out of these earlier shorter pieces, but as early as 1903 one history, *Hernando de Soto*, had already appeared. In the same year he suffered the first of two tragic losses—the sale of the family estate at Gartmore, followed by the death of his wife in 1906. However, history of a more modern kind was being made in 1914, and Don Roberto, now a man of 62, offered his services as a Rough Rider. This was an open rebuff to those who had doubted his patriotism because of the radical and anti-imperialist views that he had expressed, especially in his letters from the New World, on the Turkish question and the Zulu wars. Accepting as a poor substitute a distasteful mission to buy horses for the government, he returned to Argentina, which he found greatly changed. The monster Progress (which he constantly lambasted whether its manifestations appeared in South America, North Africa, or Ireland), in the shape of telephones, fenced tracks, and machinery, had rendered the gaucho almost extinct. With Progress, he also included Commerce, that many-tentacled beast, and so-called Civilization.

This visit was the seed of one of his best histories, *A Brazilian Mystic*, published in 1920, the story of Antonio Conselheiro, rebel, fanatic, prophet, and martyr. This messianic figure led a group of villagers (from Canudos) against the might of the Bra-

---

[11] *Three Plays for Puritans*, 341. See also my article referred to in note 10.

zilian government, ostensibly over a tax dispute.[12] This epic struggle of the *sertanejos* of the Brazilian backlands, a people "condemned to civilization," appealed to Graham. In 1917 he made another trip for the government, this time to Colombia to buy cattle. As always, adventure followed him, and he was torpedoed and shipwrecked twice. The literary result of this visit was the publication of two more histories, *Cartagena and the Banks of the Sinú* (1921), and *The Conquest of New Granada* (1922). With the end of the war, a last half-hearted political fling saw him defeated in 1918 as the Independent Liberal candidate for West Stirlingshire. Now in his seventies, he saw his friends Hudson and Conrad die, and finally, in 1925, his mother died at the age of ninety-seven. These deaths, all in the space of three years, left him an old man with no ties, and not surprisingly, he turned to the scenes of his youthful triumph.

In 1925 he set out on a sentimental journey to Venezuela and after going six hundred miles up the Orinoco in an old ship, he explored the *llanos* on horseback. The natural beauty of the places visited he described vividly in "The Plains of Venezuela."[13] During his visit he was invited to dine with the dictator Juan Vicente Gómez. True to his principles, he refused, saying: "He seemed to think that by increasing the population with a hundred and twenty children he could atone for the hundreds he massacred and the hundreds more he exiled."[14]

Don Roberto spent his last few years at the family home at Ardoch, on the banks of the River Clyde, and in London, dividing his time between his two great passions—writing and riding. Almost every year he produced a book, usually about South America, like the histories *Pedro de Valdivia* (1926), *José Antonio Páez* (1929), and *The Horses of the Conquest* (1930). Short trips to Ceylon and South Africa in 1934 and 1935 extended his field of travel. Then the "master of life," having partaken to the full, finally decided in 1936, at the age of 84, to make the final pilgrimage to his first love, Argentina. A year before, the real crisis of old age had overtaken him, and significantly, was reflected in his

[12] The incident had been treated earlier by Euclydes da Cunha (1866–1909), in *Os Sertões* (1902), from which Graham quotes; translated into English by Samuel Putnam as *Rebellion in the Backlands* (Chicago, 1944).
[13] This was Tschiffely's new title in *Rodeo* of a sketch originally entitled "Los Llanos del Apure" in *Redeemed*.
[14] Tschiffely, *Don Roberto*, 388.

inability to get into the saddle. In his last book, *Mirages*, published in 1936, he had written about the Englishman, Charlie the Gaucho, who had returned to the pampas to die with his boots on. As if impelled by his own creation, he set out on January 18, 1936, though obviously unwell. Always a lover of horses, he carried two bags of oats for Mancha and Gato, the horses of his friend Tschiffely, whose great achievement in making the famous journey from Buenos Aires to New York Graham had recorded in "Tschiffely's Ride."[15] A visit to *Los veinte y cinco ombúes*, the house near Buenos Aires where Hudson was born, was an emotional and final part of his pilgrimage.

By March he had contracted a serious attack of bronchitis, and died of penumonia in Buenos Aires on March 20, 1936. His body lay for twenty-four hours in the Casa del Teatro in Buenos Aires, where friends and admirers, including the president of the Republic, paid their last respects to this man of two worlds. On his death, the British Ambassador in Buenos Aires, Sir Neville Meyrick Henderson, paid tribute to "the lover of freedom, the friend of the common people, the champion of reform . . . the defender of the cause of small nations and of backward peoples. . . . His sympathies were with the gaucho rather than with the modern farmer, with the covered waggon and the bullock cart rather than with the train and the pullman . . . Aristocrat and Hidalgo, by birth as well as by nature. . . ."[16] When the funeral procession went through the streets of Buenos Aires, Mancha and Gato walked behind the hearse, led by two gauchos. The cycle was complete.

When they brought his body home to Scotland, they buried him beside his wife in the ruined Augustinian priory on the island of Inchmahome, on the Lake of Menteith. One can still see there carved on his tombstone, as he had requested, his old Argentine cattle brand. The following year, June, 1937, a monument to Don Roberto was unveiled on ground that he had given to the National Trust for Scotland. This monument, built of stones shipped from Argentina and Uruguay, stands not far from the family home at Ardoch, about a mile from Dumbarton. The Duke of Montrose performed the unveiling ceremony for Scotland, Dr. Alberto Guani represented Uruguay, and Graham's

---

[15] *Writ in Sand.*
[16] Tschiffely, *Don Roberto*, 439.

friend and biographer A. F. Tschiffely represented Argentina. It is fitting that Pampa should be remembered on this monument, by way of the tribute originally used as a dedication for *The Horses of the Conquest*, and a reproduction of its head. To commemorate Don Roberto, there is a fine medallion by Alexander Proudfoot, and an epitaph bearing these words:

ROBERT BONTINE
CUNNINGHAME GRAHAM
1852–1936
FAMOUS AUTHOR,
TRAVELLER AND HORSEMAN
PATRIOTIC SCOT
AND CITIZEN OF THE WORLD
AS BETOKENED
BY THE STONES ABOVE
DIED IN ARGENTINA
INTERRED IN INCHMAHOME
HE WAS A MASTER OF LIFE—
A KING AMONG MEN

The Writer

As a writer Robert Bontine Cunninghame Graham has never been fully appreciated by the reading public. This is partly due to the fact that some of his writing is now dated, since, in many cases, he was writing of, and for, his time. What he has to say of colonialism, imperialism, the abuses of commerce, civilization *appears* to have little relevance to the second half of the twentieth century. It was also due to his own modesty and the tendency of others to play down his literary talents in the face of his other qualities and enterprises. Writing home from the New World in the 1870's, he confesses, "I think I have no literary ability whatever. . . ."[17] Acquaintances like Frank Harris and Morley Roberts helped to propagate this misguided idea by labeling him "an amateur writer of genius." Some thirty books, not counting translations, pamphlets, and prefaces and a host of literary admirers like Conrad, Hudson, and Blunt did not quite manage to raise him, in the public eye, to the level of his more popular

[17]Ibid., 179.

associates. Admirers tended to emphasize more the "character," the politician, the reformer, the horseman, the traveler, the eccentric, to the detriment of the writer.

Graham contributed somewhat to this image of the talented amateur by his slapdash approach to his writing. Producing a book almost every year for some forty years, typically he scorned conventional practices like proofreading and polishing up his manuscripts. After praising *Mogreb-el-Acksa* as a masterpiece, Conrad reprimanded him: "You haven't been careful in correcting your proofs. Are you too *grand seigneur* for that infect labour? Surely I, twenty others, would be only too proud to do it for you." [18] He wrote with a spontaneity, a naturalness and a freshness reminiscent of the early romantics. This, however, can be a fault if carried to excess, and a little of the eighteenth century discipline would have improved his work greatly. Revision would have corrected the long-winded, intricate, and sometimes grammatically incorrect sentences that appear occasionally in his work, but, like many romantics, Graham was more interested in matter than in form. He has a tendency to repeat himself with images, proverbs and the like. "Life is a fandango," he says in both "La tapera" and in the preface to *Hope.* "Justice, but not in my house," he repeats several times. "God is not a bad man after all," several of his characters say at different times. This, however, is understandable, when one considers that he wrote some two hundred sketches over a period of forty years, often about the same region and the same people. He had an eye for images and an ear for speech, and his powers of observation were so acute that he was capable of reproducing conversations and natural descriptions sixty years after the event—a quality he shared with one of his subjects, Bernal Díaz del Castillo, the soldier-historian who was with Cortés at the Conquest of Mexico, and who chronicled the events in his *Historia verdadera de la conquista de Nueva España.*

Perhaps his lack of pretentiousness and sophistication as to the writer's status and trade detracted somewhat from his own position. Stating simply his own literary credo, he may have deprecated the writer's stock in the eyes of the public, who prefer to think of the writer as a man apart, who speaks a different lan-

[18] Ibid., 332.

guage and who has hidden sources of inspiration. Don Roberto destroyed that myth in his apologia to *His People* (1906). "Still I believe, that be it bad or good, all that a writer does is to dress up what he has seen or felt, and nothing real is evolved from his own brain, except the words he uses and the way in which he uses them. Therefore, it follows that in writing he sets down (perhaps unwittingly) the story of his life." This idea he repeated in 1909 in the preface to *Faith*: "All that we write is but a bringing forth again of something we have seen or heard about. What makes it art is but the handling of it, and the imagination that is brought to bear upon the theme out of the writer's brain." By merely recording what he has seen and felt, with *his* life and *his* imagination, his writings cannot fail to be interesting and are often artistic. Throughout his two hundred sketches he is writing his own autobiography, whether it be a description of a rodeo, a gaucho fight in a canteen, an attack on a farm, or a sunset. Everything is grist for his mill and is reproduced with accurate detail and a sureness of touch—a Spanish proverb, the botanical name of a rare plant, or some technical equine term.

Throughout the sketches certain themes keep recurring. With his regret for the passing of the gauchos and their way of life goes his bitter attack on the triple evils—progress, civilization, and commerce, "that vivifying force, that bond of union between all the basest instincts of the basest of mankind." [19] His anti-imperialism and anticolonialism, which served as an antidote to the views of Kipling and company, first evident in young Robert's letters from the Argentine in the 1870's, manifests itself at every opportunity, highlighting the exploitation of the natives (African or South American, Irish or Turkish, as the case may be). With progress and colonization goes the false morality and the hypocrisy of the European nations, especially in contrast with the people of the New World. He had no illusions, however, about the savage Indians, who did not use guns and modern weapons simply because they did not possess them. He was not persuaded by the Rousseauesque ideas of the natural goodness of the noble savage.

Linked with his ideas on false morality was his soft spot for, and sentimentalization of, prostitutes. These figures of the *de-*

---

[19] *Thirteen Stories*, "Calvary," 192.

mimonde keep flitting through the sketches in the brothels of Spain and North Africa and appear in the South American sketches as the *chinas*, the *quitanderas*, who are always at hand in the pampa store when required. His prostitutes are almost always tenderhearted, used, and discarded by men who are products of a civilized society. Always on the side of the underdog, the unfortunate, the *infeliz*, his sympathy is for the failures of this world, summed up in one of his most powerful sketches, "Success." "For those who fail, for those who have sunk still battling beneath the muddy waves of life, we keep our love, and that curiosity about their lives which makes their memories green when the cheap gold is dusted over, which once we gave success." [20] Kind by nature, humane in spirit, he was constantly appalled by man's inhumanity to man—and to beast. Although Spanish by temperament, he detested "the sordid butchery" of the bullfight, and never indulged in the sport of hunting. Always a horse lover, he links this theme and the attack on civilized society in sketches like "Calvary" (one of his most biting attacks) and "Bopicuá," in which we see man's cruelty and the fate of the horses in man-created war.

As well as having certain themes, Graham has certain literary techniques that he uses constantly, such as the story within the sketch. A group of characters are gathered together round a fire, on board a ship, in a hotel, on the pampas, and to while away the time someone is requested, or volunteers, to tell a story—"The Captive" and "Anastasio Lucena." Another technique is the flashback, in which a death prompts one person to tell the past life of the deceased— *"Animula Vagula"* or "Charlie the Gaucho." The memory or *recuerdo* technique, in which one set of circumstances sets the author off at a tangent recalling similar events in another time and place, he uses in "El Tango Argentino." [21] Another technique is the imaginative sketch, prompted by the finding or the sight of an object. The author allows his mind to wander, re-creating what might have been the past life of his subject—"The Botanist" [22] and *"Animula Vagula."*

Unorthodox in many ways, Don Roberto, a noted writer of prefaces for the works of others, uses prefaces not only to com-

---

[20] *Success*, 2.
[21] *Brought Forward.*
[22] *His People.*

ment, but also to tell a story, for example, in the preface to *Hope*. Throughout all his works, sketches, histories, and travel books, Don Roberto constantly uses the aside, the digression, to pass ironic judgment on human behavior and his times. These barbs are usually reserved for the morality, hypocrisy, and abuses of his day ("the philosophy of unutterable scorn," Conrad named it), when he attacks the crimes perpetrated by man in the name of progress, civilization, and religion. Recognizing that Graham has "the *saeva indignatio* but no sentimentality," Edward Garnett in his introduction to *Thirty Tales and Sketches* was aware of "his detestation of society's collective hypocrisy, whether of privileged classes or of masses of men, and of the cant of 'civilisation.'" These qualities can be seen spasmodically in all the sketches, but two, in particular, are classic examples of sustained, vitriolic irony against the Establishment and all it represents—"Niggers" [23] and "Success."

· Though romantic in temperament (let us remember that Ramsay MacDonald said that Graham's socialism was based on romantic ideals of freedom) and in his literary approach, he did not shrink from the realism so necessary to portray the cruel times in which he lived. His descriptions of the excesses of the bloody cruelty of the civil wars between *Colorados* and *Blancos* match the real thing. Obliged to take part in the López revolution against Sarmiento, he was present at the gory slaughter and murders, which he depicted in "A Silhouette," in the preface to *Hope*. Death was also realistically described, whether it be a drowning horse, eyes rolling with terror, or some unfortunate having his throat cut. Though romantic in his attitude to prostitutes he did not refrain from describing in earthy fashion, in "*Aurora La Cujiñi*," [24] the gypsy dancer whose "short sleeves slipped back exhibiting black tufts of hair under her arms, glued to her skin with sweat."

From a reading of the many sketches and histories of South America, it is clear that he knew his background. All the South American sketches are a mine of local color, and Don Roberto emerges as one of the most important costumbrist writers of that continent, especially of the pampas, a region he knew better than many of the natives. He knew the gaucho at first hand, his

[23] *The Ipané.*
[24] *Charity*, 268.

customs, his dress, his way of life, his folk lore, as well as the gauchesque literature like *Martín Fierro*[25] (which appeared in 1872 when Graham was on the pampas), *El Fausto*,[26] *Facundo*,[27] *Don Segundo Sombra*,[28] all written by literary men. If he does use a Spanish word that seems technical or uncommon, it is because it comes naturally to him, and is *le mot juste*. When he describes gaucho activities like ostrich hunts, cock fights, horse races, roundups, brawls in the pampa store, he uses automatically the gaucho term, and soon the reader comes to accept the *bolas*, *lazos* and *facones* as common, everyday objects. Even when he moves away from his beloved pampas to Paraguay, he provides a wonderfully detailed picture of life in a village on a feast day, an orchid hunt in Colombia, or a bullfight in Venezuela. Throughout the sketches he makes great use of figures of speech, especially the simile. To a man of his experience, with an eye for an image, similarities abounded everywhere, almost always drawn from nature—the prostitutes in "Un angelito" "sitting like swallows on a telegraph wire," or the dead cows, in "The Captive," stuck in the stream "with their legs sticking out grotesquely, just as a soldier's dead legs stick out upon the battlefield." He knew intimately the natural background, the animals, the plants, the insects, and the birds, almost as well as his naturalist friend Hudson. His description of the birds of the Plate Region in "La tapera" rivals the ornithological wonders of Hudson. The use of the Spanish terms, sayings, proverbs,[29] irksome for some readers

[25]José Hernández (1834–86). The best known epic poem of the gauchos, translated by Walter Owen as *The Gaucho Martín Fierro* (Oxford, 1935), in which is depicted the outlawed gaucho ruthlessly pursued by corrupt authorities, pushed farther and farther back, till forced to join the Indians at the frontier.

[26]Estanislao del Campo (1834–80). Translated by Walter Owen as *Faust* (Buenos Aires, 1943), the tale of a gaucho's reaction to the performance of Gounod's opera in the Teatro Colón in Buenos Aires.

[27]See Note 5.

[28]Ricardo Güiraldes (1886–1927). Translated by Harriet de Onís as *Shadows on the Pampas* (London, 1935; also Penguin, West Drayton, 1948), *Don Segundo Sombra* is an artistic re-creation of idealized gaucho life, praising the gaucho values of independence, strength, and liberty.

[29]In many cases Graham gives the impression of thinking in Spanish and translating into English, which accounts for odd-looking and strange-sounding sentences, and rare uses of words, for example, "affront" which he uses in the Spanish etymological sense of the word. See my article "Don Roberto and Cervantes," *Anales Cervantinos*, XI (1972), 129–37.

at first, contributes to the quality of authenticity which marks the South American sketches.

It is rather a pity that his contemporaries like Shaw, who used Don Roberto for inspiration, Conrad, who was encouraged by Graham in the early days, his fellow lovers of the Pampas, Hudson, Blunt, and others have all come into their own, while Don Roberto never achieved the same heights in the English-speaking world.[30] His works have been translated into Spanish, and his name is a household word in the Argentine where he is regarded as one of *Los tres clásicos ingleses de la pampa*,[31] whereas in Britain and North America he is known to a small but devoted circle of admirers. If this circle is widened even a little, this present volume will have been worthwhile. Success one does not crave for him, for he scorned that all his days. What one would like to see in the treatment of his works is that other quality to which he devoted his life—justice.

The Text

As Conrad and others so often complained (not least his editors and publishers), Graham was notoriously lax in the preparation and revision of his manuscripts. This is evident in the editions that are available, even those that have been reprinted, including

---

[30] Two stories are worth recalling here. The one that Frank Harris tells in his biography *Bernard Shaw* (Simon and Schuster, New York, 1931), 120, shows Shaw's reaction to a piece Graham had written on the funeral of William Morris: " . . . a little masterpiece, a gem of restrained yet passionate feeling; absolute realistic description lifted to greatness by profound poetry. Shaw too was overwhelmed with admiration of Graham's story." Uttering his usual cliché about an "amateur of genius," Harris goes on to comment: "It's a pity he hasn't to earn his living by his pen." "A good thing for us," cried Shaw, "he'd wipe the floor with us all if he often wrote like that."

The other story is the one Tschiffely tells in the introduction to *Rodeo* (p. xi), when he and some colleagues were discussing why Graham had not attained the popularity he deserved. The reason, according to one of the cynical friends, was "he writes too well."

[31] Enrique Espinoza (Santiago de Chile, 1951). The other two were W. H. Hudson and Sir Francis Bond Head. The latter's *Rough Notes Taken During Some Rapid Journeys Across the Pampas and Among the Andes* (London, 1826) was one of the first works of travel and gauchesque costumbrismo written by an English author.

the collections prepared by other editors like Tschiffely, Garnett, and Bloomfield.

In general, Graham showed little ·concern for the niceties of manuscript preparation and equally scant respect for formal grammatical details like quotation marks and italicizing. He uses capital letters and quotation marks willy-nilly, and shows no consistency in his spelling of proper names and foreign words. This is partly understandable when one remembers that he wrote his two hundred sketches over a period of forty years and often describes places, people, and events after an interval of several decades.

One of the major tasks in this study, therefore, was to try to introduce a degree of consistency into the sketches selected. Where obvious orthographic errors existed, I have corrected them, both in English and in Spanish. In English he is seldom wrong, even when he uses words that appear incorrect, such as "digged," "in despite of," and others. Checking with reputable dictionaries, one finds that these odd words and expressions do exist but are generally archaisms—a typical Graham gesture in his efforts to halt the abuses of "progress" and uphold the values of the past.

Punctuation can be a problem in Graham's works. Often I have judiciously inserted, or discreetly removed, a comma, a semicolon, or other mark, in the interest of clarity, when he becomes involved in a long, intricate sentence, further complicated by parenthetical asides. To intervene too much in the text would be to tamper with the artist's creativity. I have, therefore, made punctuation improvements only when essential to make Graham's vivid, evocative prose (sometimes lessened by minor formal defects) more effective.

In the case of italicization, capitalization, and quotation, I have tried to introduce some uniformity by removing many useless capitals, quotation marks, and other things that only clutter up his writing. When necessary, I have omitted italics if I consider the word sufficiently well known in English to stand by itself— gaucho, pampa, rancho, maté, estancia. Names of plants, trees, birds, and animals I have left unitalicized if they are native words with no direct English translation—carpincho, tapir, chajá, viudita (all explained in the glossary). Using this uniform method, I hope the sketches will read easily without too much visual distraction.

For the nonspecialist and those interested in the South American continent (language, flora, fauna), I have appended a glossary of words and expressions. This is not exhaustive and is not intended to be a technical or specialist catalog, but is simply an aid to the fuller enjoyment and appreciation of the sketches.

All the footnotes are mine and have been supplied to explain to the nonspecialist reader some of Graham's literary, historical, and linguistic allusions.

The curious reader may be interested in comparing this edition with the original sketches. To this end I have supplied a bibliography, that may help to locate copies of Graham's works, which are becoming increasingly difficult to obtain. This selection is intended to offset, to some extent, this lack.

THE
SOUTH AMERICAN
SKETCHES

ARGENTINA

Editor's Preface to the Argentine Sketches

The Argentinian sketches constitute half the total number of the selections, which would seem to be an equitable division, since Graham spent most time there and wrote most about this region. I have tried to use an orderly method of presentation, moving from the physical background of the pampas to the inhabitants, the gauchos, their horses, their customs. From the gaucho we move to his half brother, yet enemy, the Indian, portraying something of his spirit. Then we see something of the historical background, of the bloody revolutions, and death, realistically described by Graham. After the gauchos and the Indians, we meet the European settlers, who, like Graham, lived in this atmosphere—the English, the Germans, and the descendants of the Scottish immigrants. I have chosen to end with "Gualeguaychú," which contains a little of all Graham's themes—natural descriptions, horses, gaucho customs, plus the usual sardonic comments on prostitutes, morality, and progress, which we find throughout all his works.

LA PAMPA

All grass and sky, and sky and grass, and still more sky and grass, the pampa stretched from the *pajonales* on the western bank of the Paraná right to the stony plain of Uspallata, a thousand miles away.

It stretched from San Luis de le Punta down to Bahía Blanca, and again crossing the Uruguay, comprised the whole republic of that name and a good half of Río Grande, then with a loop took in the *misiones* both of the Paraná and Paraguay.

Through all this ocean of tall grass, green in the spring, then yellow, and in the autumn brown as an old boot, the general characteristics were the same.

A ceaseless wind ruffled it all and stirred its waves of grass. Innumerable flocks and herds enamelled it, and bands of ostriches ("Mirth of the Desert," as the gauchos called them) and herds of palish-yellow deer stood on the tops of the *cuchillas* and watched you as you galloped past.

Down in the south, the Patagonian hare, mataco, and the quirquincho scudded away or burrowed in the earth. Towards the middle region of this great galloping ground, the greatest that God made—perhaps He could not possibly have made a better, even had He tried—great armadillos and iguanas showed themselves, and in the north, around the deep metallic-toned *isletas* of hard-wood *montes*, flocks of macaws—red, yellow, and bright blue—floated like butterflies. Up in the north, anteaters (the tamandúa of the Guaranís) and tapirs wandered, looking as if they had escaped from out the Ark.

23

Over the whole extent the teru-tero hovered, screamed, whistled, and circled just above your horse's head. From every *monte* and from every maize field flew chattering flocks of parakeets.

Tigers and pumas inhabited the woods, right from the Estero Ñembuco, which I have crossed so often with the mud and water to my horse's cinch, down to the Antarctic beech forests of Sandy Point.

In all the rivers *nutrias* and *lobos* and the carpincho, with its great red teeth, swam with their heads awash, laid flat upon the stream, just like a seal at sea.

Vizcachas burrowed, and wise, solemn little owls sat at the entrance of their burrows making pretence to guard them, as does a sentinel before a palace door.

Locusts occasionally visited the pampa, blackening the sun, devouring all the crops, and disappearing just as they had come.

"Where is the *manga*?" was a familiar question on the plains, and grave and bearded men reined in their horses, their ponchos suddenly clinging to their sides, just as a boat's sail clings around the mast when it has lost the wind, and pointing with a lean, brown finger stained with tobacco juice, replied, "Por allacito, en los Porongos," [1] and then departed, just as ships speak to each other on the sea. The north wind filled the air with cottony filaments, and the *pampero*, roaring like a whole rodeo that had taken fright, levelled the houses and the grass. The air was full in summer of a perpetual twittering of insects that hung invisible, whilst in the winter the white hoarfrost in early morning silvered the grass, and hung congealed upon the tops of stakes, just as it did in the old world in which the poet-king penned the *Cantar de los cantares*[2] two thousand years ago.

All that, was what the pampa had inherited from nature. When I first knew it, it looked just as it must have looked on the morning of the seventh day in far-off Nabothea, that old-world Entre Ríos, when the Creator rested and, looking earthwards, saw that it was good.

Man had but little altered it, but for a peach grove here and there, a white estancia house or a straw-coloured ranchería or *pulpería*, built either at the pass of some great river or on a hill, as that at the Cuchilla de Peralta, by which the mule-trail, used since the Conquest, led, winding upon its way towards Brazil.

[1] "Over there in the Porongos" (a region of the pampas).
[2] "Song of Songs" of King Solomon.

Men passed each other seated upright on their *recaos*, driving their horses in a bunch in front of them, swinging their whips around their heads.

They passed, shouting a salutation, or if too far off to be heard, waving a hand, and sank into the plain just as a vessel sinks into the sea, the body of the horse first disappearing, then the man, poncho, and, last of all, his hat. The waves of grass appeared to swallow him, and as men rode they kept their eyes fixed on the horizon, or, if at night, upon a star. When the night caught them on the plains, after first hobbling the mare, they tied a horse to a long *soga*, making, if neither stick nor bone were to be found, a knot in the rope's end, stamping it in, and lying down upon it.

They smoked a cigarette or two, looked at the stars a little, and took good care to place their heads in the direction towards which they had to journey, for in the mists of sunrise nothing was easier than to mistake the point you aimed at, and wander back upon the trail.

In that green ocean, as the proverb said, "He who wanders from the trail is lost"; and it was true enough, as many a heap of bones, to which a shred of tattered cloth still clung, most amply testified, as you came on them on a gallop, looking perhaps for horses stolen or strayed. Your companion might or might not rein up his horse, but certainly would point in passing, and remark: "See where the grass grows rank around the bones; there has a Christian died."

"Christian" was used more as a racial than a religious term, the Indians usually being called *los bravos, los infieles, los tapes*, the latter usually applied either to the descendants of the Charruas in the Banda Oriental, or to the Indian Mansos of the Missions of the north. How much the aforesaid *infieles* and the *tapes* had left their impress on the speech and the life of the gauchos, might be seen by the national costume of the poncho and the *chiripá*. These, as the early writers tell us, were adapted from the "infidel we found dwelling in all these plains, when first Don Pedro de Mendoza came with his following to conquer for his lord,[3] and to proclaim the glory of the name of Him who, though born in a stable, is higher than all kings." In the current pampa speech the words *bagual, ñandú, ombú* and *vincha, tatú, tacuará,* and *bacaray,* with almost all the names of plants, of shrubs and trees, recalled the

[3] Pedro de Mendoza (1487–1537), one of the first Spanish explorers of the River Plate region, founder of the city of Buenos Aires.

influence of the Indians, the Quichuas, and Guaranís, the Pampas and Pehuelches, Charruas, and the rest of those who once inhabited the land.

Las boleadoras, known to the gauchos as *las tres Marías*, was the distinctive weapon of the southern plains. With them the Indians slew many of Don Pedro de Mendoza's men at the first christianising of the River Plate, and with them also did the fierce gaucho troops who rose under Elio and Liniers crash in the skulls of various English, *luteranos*—for so the good Dean Funes styles them in his history[4]—who under Whitelock had attacked the town.[5] Only upon the pampa, in the whole world, was this tremendous weapon ever known. None of the pampa tribes used bows and arrows, for with them the *bolas*, and in especial the single stone, fixed to a plaited thong of hide and called *la bola perdida*, quite supplied their place.

In fact, for no land but the pampa, that is, in the Americas (for it could well be used in Africa and Asia), are *las tres Marías* fit. In North America the plains are bushy or the grass is long as hay, conditions which would militate against the throwing of a weapon which, often thrown a yard or two behind the quarry's legs, sprang from the ground and then entangled them.

Nothing could be more typical of the wild life of forty years ago upon the plains than was the figure of a gaucho dressed in his poncho and his *chiripá*, his naked toes clutching the stirrups, his long iron spurs kept in position by a thong of hide dangling below his heels, his hair bound back by a red silk handkerchief, his eyes ablaze, his silver knife passed through his sash and *tirador*, and sticking out just under his right elbow, his *pingo* with its mane cut into castles and its long tail floating out in the breeze as, twisting *las tres Marías* round his head, he flew like lightning down a slope, which the mere European horseman would have looked on as certain death, intent to "ball" one of a band of fleet *ñandús* all sailing down the wind.

Letting the *bolas* go, so easily, it seemed as if his will and not his hand directed them, they hurtled through the air, revolving

---

[4]Gregorio Funes, *Ensayo de la historia civil del Paraguay, Buenos Aires, y Tucumán*. 3 vols. (Buenos Aires, 1816–17).

[5]Graham is talking here of the abortive British attempt in the early nineteenth century to get a foothold in Buenos Aires. Under the leadership of Elio and Liniers, the Argentinian people expelled the British intruders, Popham, Beresford, and Whitelock, and went on to gain their independence from Spain.

on their own axis sixty or seventy yards, and, when the *sogas* met the ostriches' neck, the centrifugal force being averted, the balls fell down and, wrapping tightly round the legs, soon threw the giant bird upon its side. Ten or twelve bounds brought up the hunter, who, springing from his saddle, his huge iron spurs clanking like fetters on the ground, either put hobbles on his horse, or if he felt quite sure of him, threw the long reins upon the ground, confident that it, trained by experience to know a step upon the reins involved a pull upon the mouth, would stand obediently.

Then, drawing his *facón*, the gaucho either stuck it deeply into the bird, low down upon the breast, or if occasion served, drawing a spare set of *boleadoras* from around his waist, or taking them from underneath the *cojinillo* of the *recao*, crashed in his victim's skull. Sometimes, indeed, with a *revés* of the *facón* they used to cut the ostrich's head off at a blow; but this wanted a sharp and heavy knife, and an arm with which to wield it, strong beyond ordinary.

I have seen a gaucho, hunting wild colts or ostriches, in the very action of swinging the *bolas* round his head, have his horse fall with him, alight upon his feet, and without losing the command of the direction of his swing, catch his own horse as it, springing to its feet, was just about to leave him helpless afoot upon the plains.

Afoot upon the plains—that was indeed a phrase of fear upon the pampas of the south. No mariner afloat upon the waves, his mainstay but a little boat, was in a worse condition than the man who, from some cause or other, found himself horseless in the vast sea of grass.

From having been as free as a bird, he instantly became as helpless as the same bird with a wing broken by a shot.

If cattle saw him, they not infrequently attacked him, when his one chance of safety (on the open plains) was to lie down and, simulating death, to let them smell him, which when they had done, if he lay still enough, they turned and went away. When the pedestrian approached a house, the troop of dogs that every gaucho kept surrounded him like wolves, barking and snapping at his legs if it were daytime, or falling on him literally like wolves if it should happen to be dark. Small streams, which generally had muddy bottoms, and through which his horse had plunged, sinking down to the cinch, but always getting through, to the man afoot became impassable, making him wander up and down their banks, perhaps for miles, till he could find a "pass."

If by an evil chance he lost his way, his fate was sealed, especially upon that portion where distances were great between estancias, and where marauding Indians on a *malón* would kill him if they saw him, just as a boy kills a young bird when it runs fluttering across his path. To lose one's horse and saddle was worse than bankruptcy; in fact, was so considered, as in the story of a Frenchman who seeing a gaucho standing idly about, inquired why he did not go out and work.

"Work, *madre mía*," said the man, "how can I work when I am bankrupt?"

"What then," the Frenchman said, "you have been in commerce, and fallen upon a bad affair; poor man, I pity you." The gaucho stared at him, and answered, "In commerce—never in my life, but at a *pulpería* some infidel or other stole my horse and saddle, with *lazo*, *bolas*, and a *cojinillo* that I bought up in Rioja, and left me without shade."

Poor man, how could he work, afoot and saddleless? No doubt before the Conquest men crossed the plains afoot; but painfully, taking perhaps long years to go from the Atlantic to the Andes, groping along from stream to stream, as the first navigators felt their way from cape to cape, coasting along the bays.

The coming of the horse gave a new life to the vast plains; for nature seemed to welcome horses once again, from the long interval between the times in which the Tertian eight-footed horse roamed on the pampas, which now are populated by the descendants of the thirteen mares and the three stallions that Pedro de Mendoza left behind when he sailed back to Spain, after his first attempt to colonise.

This is the way I recollect it. First came short grasses, eaten close down by sheep, then thistles that grew as high as a man's head, a wilderness, through which the cattle had made a labyrinth of paths; then coarser grasses, and by degrees wiry, brown bents, until at length almost all sign of grass was lost, where the pampas joined the stony plains of Patagonia in the south.

Northwards, the waving grasses also grew sparser, till in the Jesuit Missions, clumps of yatays encroached upon the plains, which ended finally in the dense woods of Paraguay.

Silence and solitude were equally the note of north and south, with a horizon bounded by what a man could see when sitting on his horse.

There were few landmarks, but in the southern and the middle districts a dark ombú, standing beside some lone *tapera* and whose shade fell on some rancho or estancia, although the proverb said, "The house shall never prosper upon whose roof is thrown the shade of the ombú."

Well did the ancient Quichuas name the plains, with the word signifying "space," for all was spacious—earth, sky, the waving continent of grass, the enormous herds of cattle and of horses, the strange effects of light, the fierce and blinding storms and, above all, the feeling in men's minds of freedom, and of being face to face with nature, under those southern skies.

PAJA Y CIELO

Now, the whole pampa from the Romero Grande to Nahuel-Huapi and far Patagones is cut into innumerable chess-boards of wire fencing, and railways puff across it, taking up wool and corn and hides and other merchandise, to send to Europe, that Europe from which once came all the few luxuries the dwellers on the pampa ever knew.

But it was not so always, and where now wave interminable crops of corn, once waved the long brown virgin grasses, which made the pampa a sort of ocean, to the eye.

Nothing but grass and sky and sky and grass, and then more grass and still more sky. Nothing, for pampa means "the space" in Quichua. A vast and empty space, empty, that is, of man and all his works; but full of sun and light, and of the sweetest air imaginable, so sweet that merely to think of it keeps the lungs fresh amongst the reek of towns, and makes the soul rejoice, even when petrol-belching motor-cars fly past carrying their goggled freights.

It was the home of deer and ostriches, and of wild horses, dappled and pied, slate-coloured, roan, blood-bay, sorrel and dun, spotted like pudding-stone, calico, paint, buckskin, clay-bank, cream, and some the colour that the Arabs call "Stones of the River," they all were there, tossing their manes and whinnying for joy, leading their lives in that great grassy space, where there was nothing to be seen but grass and sky.

Nothing but deer and ostriches were there, with swiftly whirling teru-teros, the mining tucotucos, and the mysterious mataco, the quirquincho, the Patagonian hare, chajás with their great horny wings, flocks of flamingoes, and marching columns of the black-headed Patagonian swans, with the wind ever rustling in the grass, sounding the dirge of the fair Eden so soon to be defiled. Wind waved the surges of the grass, lifting the loose hair on the necks of animals, and on the sand-hills bending the plants, and making them draw patterns on the sand, just as in colder countries they trace figures in the snow.

Something there was about the pampa, almost unearthly, so natural it was that in a world where all is artificial, and man appears a giant, controlling everything, it seemed impossible he should be relegated back to his position as but one of the many animals, with but a little more intelligence than theirs.

A grassy sea, in which the landmarks were the stars, so that a man rode straighter in the night than in full noontide, if he had lost his way. A green illimitable sea, in which the horse was ship; a desert without camels, but as terrible to wander in as is the Sahara, in which the horseman who had lost his trail was swallowed up and never heard of, except some traveller chanced to find his skull, just sticking out of a dark tuft of grass, which had grown rank and vigorous, as his decaying flesh laid bare the bones.

This pampa, that now seems to be a dream, so far away it is, and so defiled by pestilential and beneficent progress, was above all an insects' paradise.

All day the hum of unseen wingéd things hung in the air, just as if millions of Eolian harps had been set everywhere—perhaps they were—and the long filaments that used to stretch from grass to grass, in a north wind, may have been good conductors of their song. All kinds of flies buzzed, hummed, and whirred, and made themselves a nuisance or a pleasure, just as you looked at them. Grasshoppers sprang into the air, just as a salmon springs up in a weir, and settled down again into the grass, in the same way the fish slips back into the water after leaping—even the splash was paralleled by the stirring of the grass the insect made, and the sharp breaking noise his wings caused in the stems. Crickets sang ceaselessly, seeming to be just at your horse's feet, but, if you stopped and looked for them, chirruped again behind you, making a sort of will-o'-the-wisp of sound. Locusts in myriads used to pass, high up, in search of cultivated land, making a noise as of an army in the air, darkening the sky, and followed by a multitude of birds, hanging upon their ranks.

The dwellers on the plains put all the tribe together under the name of *bichos*, and only thought of them as dangerous to crops, or disagreeable to the skins, although no doubt they would have missed them vaguely had they disappeared, just as a man bred in the country, though born without imagination, still misses something in a town, that he cannot describe.

Birds, from the ostrich, which the old Quichuas called the "Desert's Mirth," down to the little black and white viudita, swarmed in their millions. Vultures and crows hung almost out of sight like specks, and yet, when a tired animal was left to die, appeared as if by magic and waited, just as an heir waits with resigned impatience for a rich uncle's death. Along the streams the pink flamingoes fished, or rising in the sun looked like a flock which had strayed out of some old picture, lovely and yet unnatural to eyes accustomed to see birds, all grey or brown, flying through air as thick as blotting-paper.

All these were of the nature of exterior graces, but the interior vision of the pampas as revealed to one who writes of it, as of some personal friend, lost, but still recollected vividly, always lamented, and to be called again to memory by an effort of the will, was something that enflamed the heart with joy. Mountains and woods, snows, sands, and the illimitable vision of the sea, all have their moments when they seem to smile. Green woods in spring, mountains at sunrise, the deceitful sea when on the beach of some fair island it ripples in, as innocently as if it never drowned a mariner, or beat a ship to matchwood in its destroying surge; even the desert sands, for the brief season when the camel-thorn turns green, or when the setting sun flushes the sand-hills, all seem to smile. The keynote of them all is sadness, sadness and melancholy, which spreads a sense of cloud over the heart—tightening its strings and turning back the soul upon itself.

In the wide ocean of the pampa, where the waves seemed to roll without advancing or receding, tideless but for the ebb and flow of winter and of summer, all was joy. Even a storm obscured its smile but for a moment, and the wise saying that joy cometh in the morning—almost incomprehensible in other countries where each day brings care—might have been written by a gaucho prophet, or a philosophising Manzanero chief, or skin-clad Patagonian seer, with the strange emblems that they used to paint upon their *guillapices* of guanaco skin. Perhaps the being near to nature made all lightsome, for looking down below the surface, all was as horrible as it is elsewhere, man preying on the animals, they on each other, Indian on gaucho, and in the then small isolated towns the conquering European was just setting out on his career to enslave them all and make them miserable.

That it was near to nature was seen at once, both by man's attitude to man and to the animals. So ruthless was he in his dealings with them that he was scarcely cruel, that is unless a tiger be so when he strikes down an ox. Life was so joyous that it was taken without thought and rendered up without a tear; and when the taker, having wiped his knife upon a tuft of grass, sat down to smoke a cigarette, certain it is no qualm of conscience troubled him, more than it does a wolf. The little air that comes at sunset ruffled his hair as he pushed back his hat, and stirred the poncho of his victim lying huddled on the ground, and it may be he muttered, if indeed he thought at all about the matter, *"pobrecito,"* as if he felt he had accomplished both their destinies, almost against his will.

In the thick *montes* fringing the river banks, an air, as of a temple in which to worhip nature, stole on you as you entered them on horseback, following strayed animals, whilst birds in their degree seemed to sing greetings as they sat about, too unaccustomed to man's presence even to move away. The ceaseless wind which either howled or rustled on the plains was broken, and animals were fatter and less wild than those outside the woods. They moved amongst the trees, just as they must have done in the dim Nabothean Entre Ríos where they all took their birth. The parrots chattered joyously, the monkeys howled, myriads of frogs raised their metallic note, and sitting sideways on your horse, rolling a black Brazilian cigarette, you saw at once that it was love of nature, not want of faith, that made the Israelites propose to rear two tabernacles for their own wandering chiefs.

Deeper within the *monte* flowed some stream, set thick with camalote, as thick as is a piece of cloisonné enamel, with the same coloured flowers. Beneath them ran the water, and to cross you cut down branches, the horses treading gingerly along, their riders shouting when they gained the bank, out of the joy of life, and being answered back antiphonally by the sage cormorants seated upon the trees.

Over the plain and *monte* the same air of natural joy hung equally, making the darkest woods seem bright, and the wide pampa brighter still, to the interior vision of the man attuned to them and their primeval air. Railways may cut the one into vast chess-boards, on which the pawns are human lives, and in the darksome glades of the thick woods of espinillo and of ñandubay, sawing-machines, fed by pale, sweating men, may whirr and clatter, giving a foretaste of a hell compounded of the simples we ourselves have deified; but the bright recollections of the days of ostriches and deer will still remain and become legendary. Perhaps at daylight, or better, just at the false dawn, when the white mist enshrouds the *pajonales* making the ghostly heads of *paja brava* loom gigantic, all may be blotted out and purified, and the vast sea of grass and sky take for a moment its old aspect of a great inland ocean on which the ostriches appear just as a nautilus looks, blown by the north-east Trades.

That is the way in which I see it.—Adiós, pampa—or perhaps, until so long.

A VANISHING RACE

A melancholy interest attaches to anything about to go for ever. Especially so to a people who with their customs, superstitions, and mode of life are doomed. So with the gauchos of the pampa. Pampa, in the Quichua tongue, signifies the "space." In truth the pampa gives a good idea of space. Perhaps the loneliness, the immensity of it, has given the melancholy tinge to the gauchos, which is their chief characteristic. Civilised enough to have (sometimes) a picture of a saint in his house, to cross himself if he hears a sudden noise at night, still savage enough to know by the foot-print if the horse that passed an hour ago was mounted or running loose. A strange compound of Indian and Spaniard, of ferocity and childishness, a link between ourselves and the past. A centaur never to be seen on foot, apt at a bargain, yet careless of money, an inveterate smoker, long-sighted, a poet withal, a singer and improviser of melancholy wild songs. Clearly for such a type civilisation reserves no place. He must go. Already, I am told, he is hardly to be met with, except on the frontiers and in the upper provinces of Catamarca, Corrientes, and Santiago del Estero.

I knew him but twenty years ago, a force, a maker and unmaker of presidents, a stirrer up of revolutions, a very turbulent fellow. He and his horse—the untiring, angular, long-maned, fiery-eyed horse of the American desert—must be replaced by the heavy-footed Basque, the commonplace Canary Islander, and the Italian in his greasy velveteen suit. As the gaucho replaced the Indian, the European colonist will replace him, one more type will have faded from the world, one more step will have been made to universal ugliness. It becomes important therefore to preserve, however imperfectly, any characteristics, any customs that to the next generation will seem strange and incomprehensible, as those of the heroes of the *Nibelungenlied*.[1] In that generation the *gaucho haragán*, the wandering gaucho, with his lean horse and rusty spurs, never settled, always wandering, restless-eyed, will have disappeared, perhaps has done so already.

He would ride up to your house, ask for a glass of water, without dismounting pass a leg over his horse's neck, and sit talking; perhaps make a cigarette the while, chopping the tobacco from a lump with a knife a foot long, holding his cigarette paper between his bare toes till the tobacco was fine enough cut, cursing his horse if it moved, yet annoyed if it stood still, his glance fixed on nothing apparently, yet conveying to you somehow that it took in everything of value. "Did he want work?" "No, señor." "Was he going anywhere?" "Nowhere in particular." "Where would he sleep?" "Where the night caught him." "Had he no arms except that knife?" "No, señor. God is not a bad man." I can see him ride off, carrying a piece of meat tied to his saddle, his horse cantering like a wolf. I can see his torn poncho fluttering in the air, hear the rattle of his iron spurs, catch the gleam of sun falling on the handle of his knife stuck through his sash, and sticking out on both sides like the lateen of a Levantine boat, and reflect that usually the morning after his visit a good horse had disappeared, or a fat cow would be found dead—killed for his supper.

Let him go with God, if go he must.

His long hide reins, his broken saddle, covered with a dirty sheepskin, his ragged black hair, tied up in a red handkerchief, the two bags of maté and sugar tied to his belt, the tin kettle hanging from his horse's headstall, his brown bare legs shoved into top-boots (the skin of a horse's leg, the hock forming the heel), and his general look of contented villainy, will not fade easily from my memory. How he lived no one knew. Where he slept only the thickest woods and most desolate watercourses could tell you.

Present at every race; though a fine horseman, always riding a

[1] *The Lay of the Niebelungs*, a German heroic poem written around 1200 by an anonymous poet.

broken-down horse; at Bahía Blanca one month, and on the frontiers of Paraguay the next; feared by all, yet welcome for the news he brought, the *gaucho haragán* was indeed a type of a past order of things.

The *rastreador*, the tracker who looked for strayed animals, found thieves, and performed feats that Europeans would look on as impossible, is, I suppose, also going or gone. Generally he was a little taciturn *arribeño* from the upper provinces. He would arrive when horses had been stolen, dismount, seat himself by the fire, smoke a cigarette, get up, and walk out, peering at the ground, and say, without apparently looking, "Your horses were driven off about three this morning. Two men took them, they went to the southward, one of them riding a lame horse." "A lame horse?" "Yes, look at this sandy place, the horse did not put his off fore-foot down firmly." You wondered, thinking it was chance, but saddled your horse, and followed your men, the *rastreador* every now and then pointing apparently to nothing, and saying, "They changed horses here. Look where a saddle has been laid on the ground," or something of the sort. Eventually he generally brought you to where the horses were, or the trail was lost in a town; for nothing but riding through a town ever threw the human bloodhound off the track. Sometimes even then he would take up the track on the outskirts, and start off afresh. Indeed, sometimes he has been known to lead the search for stolen goods to the house of the chief magistrate of some little town, point at it and say, "Your things are there." This generally ended the day's sport, as Justice was, of course, blind and deaf in such cases (as in most others).[2]

"Why do you not work?" said Darwin to the gaucho. "I cannot, I am too poor," was the answer. Astonishment of the great naturalist. However, the answer was most obvious to all who knew the gaucho. The man had no horses. God had left him on foot. A gaucho never worked except on horseback. On horseback, no matter if seventy years of age, he always appeared young. On foot he waddled like an alligator. Whether herding sheep or cattle, marching, hunting, drawing water from a well, the gaucho always worked on horseback. He even drew a net on horseback; or churned butter by galloping about with a hide bag of milk tied

[2]The passage devoted to the *rastreador* episode echoes rather closely Sarmiento's description of the pampa tracker in *Facundo*, Part I.

to the end of a *lazo*. He lived on horseback, climbing when a child on to the back of an old horse, putting his little bare toes on the animal's knee and scrambling like a monkey to his seat. On the march he slept on horseback, never falling off. Coming from the *pulpería* drunk, but quite the gentleman, he swayed backwards and forwards but kept his seat. In death, too, not seldom has a horse been found straying about with his rider, the hand that guided dead, but the sinewy legs maintaining the wild horseman seated in the saddle as in life.

The beggars, what few of them existed, begged on horseback, extending a silent hand as you passed by them. In an alarm at night every one ran to his horse, and, mounting, was ready for what might betide. We thought a horse or gaucho was but half complete separated from each other. To be on foot was his idea of the greatest misery. A paternal government sentenced murderers, horse thieves, and other miscreants, not to death—why rob the Republic of a man?—but to serve so many years with infantry. Miserable enough that infantry sometimes was, and those who served in it comparable as to fortune with the Christian captives who, in the Middle Ages, rowed in Turkish galleys.

The poorest man usually had at least one *tropilla* of horses and a hundred mares.

Every horse was branded with the marker of his owner—a hat, a spur, a letter, a device. The marks were the books of the gauchos. On summer evenings they sat talking and "painting marks" in the dust. "Sí, señor," I once saw this mark on a horse ten years ago in Entre Ríos. If you came upon a group of gauchos talking, ten to one it was about horses' marks. The subject was ever new, as different marks were taken out nearly every day. When a horse was sold the owner put his mark on him twice. Thus, if the horse was marked B, the addition of another B rendered the horse unmarked—*orejano*, as it was called. The seller placed his mark on him, and he became his property. Good horses were frequently found with six or eight marks upon them. The *lazo* and the *bolas* were the tools the gaucho worked with. With the *lazo* he caught horses or cattle, then threw them down and killed or branded them. With the *bolas* he caught wild or runaway horses, and ostriches or deer. To go upon the *boleada*— that is, to go out to catch ostriches with the *bolas*—was the great sport of rich and poor.[3]

---

[3] See Graham's sketches "The Lazo" and "The Bolas" in *The Ipané*.

The twilight ride to the hunting places (many a time have I ridden it in agony of fear on a half-wild horse) resembled a procession of shadows, the light going, unshod horses hardly brushing the dew from the grass, the greyhounds led carefully for fear of startling the game. Arrived at the places where ostriches had been seen the day before, the company spread out in the shape of fans, striving to encircle the birds. Then a rush forward at full speed was made, and the *bolas* commenced to whistle through the air. Sometimes an old ostrich or two would dash through the line and be madly pursued by an eager horseman twisting the *bolas* round his hand, his horse rushing like a deer, himself sitting like a statue of bronze upon his horse. Sometimes a horseman, rushing downhill, turned a complete somersault with his horse, but never failed to come off on his feet, his great iron or silver spurs clashing on the ground like fetters. It wanted a good horse, a bold rider, and a strong arm to make a successful ostrich baller. But good horses, strong arms, and bold riders were plentiful on the pampas in those days.

All the gaucho's life, though, was not ostrich-hunting. He had the grim reality of the pampa Indians ever close to him. The wild Indians for three hundred years kept the frontiers in a turmoil. Compounded as the gaucho was of Indian and Spaniard, still the hatred between him and his wilder cousin the Indian was keen, as if they had been both Christians of different but nearly approaching sects. To the gaucho's heaven no Indian went. On the plains around the mythic city of Trapalanda no gaucho rode.

Like the Arabs of to-day, the Indians chiefly came to steal the gauchos' women and horses.

In the mysterious country known as *tierra adentro* quite a colony of so-called Christians lived. These Christians, chiefly unattached to any especial form of Christianity, were as a general rule gauchos who had committed crimes and fled to the Indians for protection. Sometimes, however, after the *pronunciamiento*, which followed usually upon an election for the presidentship, some leader of the opposition had to cross the mysterious shifting line known as the frontier and sojourn for a while amongst the Indians. If so, he generally became a sort of minor chief, a *caciquillo*, as the phrase was, and took to himself a wife or two, or even three, and amongst them generally a Christian captive. About forty years ago an officer called Saá, forced, from some cause or other, to make his habitation with the Indians, rose to such eminence as almost to imperil the republic.

Don José Hernández, the gaucho poet, relates the adventures of one Martín Fierro, who suffered many things with the Pampas and Ranqueles. In the long evenings, seated round the fire, passing the maté round, the adventures of Martín were sure to be discussed. The gauchos seemed to take him as an embodiment of themselves and all their troubles (surely the greatest test a poet has of popularity) and talk of him as if at any moment he might lift the mares' hide which acted as a door and walk into the hut. Those of the company who could read (not the majority) were wont to read aloud to the unlettered from a well-worn greasy book, printed on flimsy paper in thin and broken type, after extracting the precious books from the recesses of their saddle-bags, or from their riding-boots. The others got it by heart and then repeated it as a sort of litany.

Almost all the founders of the Argentine Republic were of the gaucho class. Rosas,[4] the tyrant of Buenos Aires, who died a quiet and respected country gentleman close to Southampton, had passed his youth on the great cattle farms. It is said he could take his saddle into the several pieces of which the *recado* is composed, and place it piece by piece upon the ground whilst galloping, and then replace it without dismounting from his horse. It is certain that in his youth he often performed the well-known gaucho feat of jumping on a bare-backed, unbroken horse, and forcing it to obey him by sheer strength. This feat, which seems so impossible in Europe, I have often seen attempted, and sometimes executed. Urquiza,[5] the great rival of Rosas, also was originally a country man, and so of Quiroga (the Tiger of the Llanos),[6] Artigas,[7] and many others. Take them for all in all, perhaps no other country ever has produced a similar class of men. The Tartars of the Steppes have been since the commencement of history banded in tribes; so of the Arabs, Cossacks, Berbers, and Indians both of the pampas and the prairies

[4] Juan Manuel de Rosas (1793–1877), Argentine dictator, 1829–52, who ended the postindependence anarchy by ruling despotically, exiling, imprisoning, and murdering his opponents.

[5] Justo José de Urquiza (1800–70), another caudillo, who overthrew Rosas. See Graham's sketch "San José" in *Progress* for a vivid and realistic description of Urquiza's murder.

[6] See note 5 of the introduction.

[7] José Gervasio Artigas (1774–1850), caudillo of the Banda Oriental, known as the "Father of Uruguayan Independence."

of the north. The gaucho, on the contrary, has lived a solitary life since he first came into existence as a class. In a thatched hut upon a plain as boundless as the sea without a tree, without a land-mark, used to be his home. There, with his wife and children and his animals, he lived, his nearest neighbour perhaps a league away. He hardly ever had a gun, or, if he had one, seldom ammunition, his arms being the *bolas*, which he jocularly called *las tres Marías*, a sword-blade, broken to convenient length and made a knife of, and the *lazo*. With this equipment he passed his life, living on meat and maté, without a drop of milk in the midst of herds of cattle, without a vegetable, without a luxury except tobacco and an occasional glass of caña. So he became a kind of link between the Indian and the white man, a better rider than the latter, even more savagely careless of his own and other's life than the Indian of the pampa. Not of a jealous temperament, leaving his wife and family for months, sometimes for years, and on returning not objecting to a new child or two about his hearth. Children of course are useful in the pampas, where boys climb up the legs of a horse and ride at five years old.

A patriot too, hating all Europeans (Spaniards especially), and despising them for their poor riding, and, like most patriots, easily befooled by knaves and made to leave his home and scour the country to restore the liberties of the republic which had never been in danger. Though quarrelsome, seldom apparently excited, but when aroused ready to kill a man with as much indifference as a bullock. Azara[8] relates that one of them, having a quarrel with another, got off his horse and said, "I now intend to kill you," and taking out his knife instantly did so, the other not resisting. So it is said a gaucho, seeing his brother groaning with rheumatic fever, unsheathed his knife and took him by the beard and cut his throat to ease his misery. Patient of hardship and starvation the gaucho was, beyond belief. As he would say himself, it is incredible what the male Christian can undergo. The race seems to have begun in the first fifty years after the Conquest; by the middle of this century it had reached its apogee, in the time of Rosas; when I lived amongst them they were still the dominant class in all the immense prairies of the republics of Uruguay and the Argentine Confederation. Then

[8]Félix de Azara, *Apuntamientos para la historia natural de los quadrúpedos del Paraguay y Río de la Plata*. 2 vols. (Madrid, 1802).

you might see them on a Sunday at the *pulpería*, gorgeous with silver trappings on their horses, dressed in ponchos of vicuña wool, loose black merino trousers like a Turk's, and riding-boots of patent leather stitched in patterns with red or yellow thread. Now so great has been the change you scarce can see them, and, horror of horrors, I am told that when you do, they dress in flannel shirts and trousers stuffed into their boots like Texans. Shortly, I take it, the gaucho will wear a morning suit and buttoned boots, and play at whist instead of *truco* and the *taba*. When he gets off his horse he will give it to a boy to hold, instead of sitting on the *cabresto*, with his knife stuck upright in the ground over his social game. It may be he and his *china* will be married in a church, and that the intrusion of a little fair-haired *inglesito* in his family will be a thing not to be tolerated. Polo will take the place of barebacked races on the *cancha*, and when his horse at night falls into a hole the man will fall upon his head instead of on his feet. Before that time I hope in Buenos Aires some sculptor of repute will do a statue of a gaucho and his horse, for since the riders in the Parthenon no horseman has been at once so strong and picturesque upon his horse.

Bolas, *lazo*, gaucho, Indian, all will soon have gone, if to Trapalanda I know not, but I hope so. Men will rob in counting-house and on exchange with pen and book, instead of on the highway with *trabuco* and *facón*. The country is getting settled, I have little doubt; cheap Spanish Bibles will soon be forced on those who cannot read them; the long-horned Spanish cattle will be replaced by Hereford or shorthorn; where the ostrich scudded, the goods train will snort and puff. Happy those who like the change, for they will have their way. Civilisation, which more surely plants its empty sardine tin as a mark on the earth's face than ever Providence placed its cross (on purpose to convert Constantine) in the sky, and the hideous pall of gloom and hypocrisy which generally accompanies it, will have descended on the pampas. Instead of the quaint announcements of strayed horses, signed by the *alcalde* on the *pulpería* door, a smug telegraph clerk at the wooden wayside station will inform the delighted inhabitants of the continued firmness of grey shirtings. ¡*Ay de mí*! [9] ¡Pampa!

[9] Exclamation of grief, "Woe is me!"

THE HORSES OF THE PAMPAS

An Argentine friend of mine (old style) wrote to me the other day from Paris:

I know you will think me a barbarian [I did not], but this Paris, this exhibition, this hurrying to and fro, this Eiffel Tower which I had to go up, have bored me dreadfully.

Strange, too, that on the pampas, as I read Daudet, the Goncourts, and Zola,[1] it seemed so interesting to me. Now, I would give it all for an hour's gallop in my own country.

It was perhaps this letter (on which my friend, to show his contempt of our civilisation, had affixed no stamp) that set me thinking of horses in general and of the horses of the pampas in particular.[2]

Thus thinking, the thoughts of the Eight Hours Bill[3] on which you asked me to write became vaguer and dimmer. Therefore (a Scotchman must have his therefore) I send you these rambling and incoherent reminiscences of a life I have lived, of men I have known, and of horses that have been to me what horses never can

---

[1] All late nineteenth-century French writers. Alphonse Daudet (1840–97) was a novelist and short-story writer, usually associated with the naturalist school, founded by the novelist and critic, Emile Zola (1840–1902). The brothers Edmond Louis Antoine Houat de Goncourt (1822–96) and Jules Alfred (1830–70) were art critics, novelists, and historians. Edmond founded the academy and the literary prize that bear their name.

[2] This theme is treated at more length in *The Horses of the Conquest*.

[3] One of Graham's many radical ideas as an M.P. See introduction.

be to a man who surveys them through the eyes of his stud groom.

Short-tailed, long-tailed, in cart or carriage, ridden by 'Arry or by Lord Henry, the horse of Europe (excepting always the coster's pony) delights me not, or very little. He seems to me a species of property, a sort of investment for capital, precarious sometimes, an unsatisfactory one too often.

Is he ill, his malady must be ministered to in the shape of beer to his groom; does he die, my equine investment is lost; I must try another.

On the pampas it is different. He is part of me, I live on him, and with him; he forms my chiefest subject of conversation, he is my best friend, more constant far than man, and far exceeding woman.

What wonder, therefore, that my friend's letter brought back to me the broad plains, the countless herds of horses, and wild life, the camp fire, the thousand accidents that make life alike so fascinating and so fatiguing in the desert.

Most people know that there are great plains called pampas. Books of travel more or less authentic have informed them that these are roamed over by countless herds of horses.

As to what these horses are like, where they come from, and if there are any special peculiarities that distinguish them from other horses, few have inquired.

It seems to me that there are certain differences between the horses of Spanish America and the horses of any other country.

That they should more or less resemble those of the south of Spain, from whence they came, is nothing to be wondered at. That special conditions of food, climate, and surroundings should have produced a special type, is nothing extraordinary.

What, then, are the general characteristics of these horses?

That which specially attracts the attention of all those who see them for the first time is the great difference to be observed betwixt them when in motion and at rest. Saddled with the *recado*, the American adaptation of the Moorish *enjalma* (the heavy bed on horseback, with its semi-Moorish trappings), standing patiently before the door of some gaucho's house from morn till sunset, they appear the most indolent of the equine race. But let the owner of the house approach with his waving poncho, his ringing spurs, his heavy hide and silver-mounted whip, and his long, flying black hair; let him by that mysterious process, seemingly an action of the will, and known only to the gaucho, transfer himself to their backs, without apparent physical exertion, and all is changed. The dull, blinking animal wakes into life, and in a few minutes his slow gallop, regular as clockwork, has made him and his half-savage rider a mere speck upon the horizon.

In a country where a good horse costs a Spanish ounce, it is not wonderful that all can ride, and all ride well. In a country where if you see a man upon a plain, you are always certain that it will be a man on horseback; in a country where the great stock-owners count their *caballadas* by the thousand (Urquiza, the tyrant of Entre Ríos, had about 180,000 horses), it is to be supposed that much equine lore, "hoss sense" the Texans call it, has grown up. It is to be looked for that a special style of riding has arisen, as that what we in Europe think strange is there regarded as an ordinary occurrence of every-day life.

It would indeed be as impossible to measure the pampas horse by the standard of an English horse as to measure a gaucho by the standard of an ordinary city man. Each man and each animal must be estimated according to the work he is required to do. Putting aside cart horses and those employed in heavy draught, almost every horse in England, except the cab horse, is an object of luxury. He has a man to look after him, is fed regularly, is never called on to endure great fatigue, carry much weight, still less to resist the inclemency of the weather. He is valued for his speed, for his docility, or merely for his pecuniary value in the market. In the pampas none of these things is of prime importance. We do not require great speed from our horses, we care nothing as to their docility, and their pecuniary value is small. What we do look for is endurance, easy paces, sobriety, and power of withstanding hunger and thirst. A horse that will carry a heavy man seventy miles is a good horse, one that can do ninety miles with the same weight is a better horse, and if he can repeat the performance two or three days in succession, he is the best, no matter if he be piebald, skewbald, one-eyed, cow-houghed, oyster-footed, or has as many blemishes as Petruchio's own mustang.[4]

Talking with some gauchos, seated on the gravel, one starlit

---

[4] The nag belonging to Petruchio, husband of Katharine the shrew, in Shakespeare's *The Taming of the Shrew*.

night, before a fire of bones and dried thistles, the conversation fell as usual upon horses. After much of the respective merits of English and Argentine horses, after many of the legends as closely trenching on the supernatural as is befitting the dignity of horsemen in all countries, an ancient, shrivelled gaucho turned to me with, "How often do you feed your horses, Don Roberto, in England? Every day?" Thereupon, on being answered, he said, with the mingled sensitiveness and fatuity of the mixed race of Spanish and Indian, "God knows, the Argentine horse is a good horse, the second day without food or water, and if not He, why then the devil, for he is very old." In all countries the intelligent are aware that you cannot estimate a horse's goodness by his stature. The average stature of the pampas horse is about 14-½ hands—what we should call a pony in England. In his case, however, his length of loin, his lean neck, and relatively immense stride, show that it is no pony we have to deal with, but a horse, of low stature if you will, but one that wants a man to ride him.

Intelligent and fiery eyes, clean legs, round feet, and well-set sloping shoulders, long pasterns, and silky manes and tails, from the best points of the pampas horse. His defects are generally slack loins and heavy head, not the "coarse" head of the underbred horse of Europe, but one curiously developed that may or may not be, as Darwin says it is, the result of having to exert more mental effort than the horse of civilisation.

Of his colour, variable is he—brown, black, bay, chestnut, piebald, and gray—making a kaleidoscopic picture as on the dusky plains or through the green *monte* a herd of them flash past, with waving tails and manes, pursued by gauchos as wild and fiery-eyed as they. As on the steppes of Russia, the plains of Queensland and Arabia, the trot is unknown. To cross a pampa loaded with the necessaries of desert life, without a path to follow, it would be a useless pace. The slow gallop and the jogtrot, the *paso castellano* of the Spaniards, the Rhakran of the Turks, is the usual pace. The pacer of the North American, the ambler of the Middle Ages, is in little esteem upon the pampas. You spur him, he does not bound; he is a bad swimmer. As the gaucho says, "he is useless for the *lazo*, though perhaps he may do for an Englishman to ride." "*Manso como para un inglés*" (tame enough for an Englishman to ride) is a saying in the Argentine Republic.

Where did these horses come from, from whence their special powers of endurance? How did these special paces first characterise them, and how is it that so many of the superstitions connected with them are also to be found amongst the Arabs? My answer is unhesitatingly, from the Arabs. All the characteristics of the Arabs are to be observed in the Argentine horses; the bit used is that of Turkey and Morocco, the saddle is a modification of the Oriental one, and the horses, I think, are in like manner descended from those in Barbary.

It is pretty generally known that the conquest of America was rendered much easier to the Spaniards by the fact that they possessed horses, and the natives had never seen them.

Great, well-watered, grassy plains, a fine climate, and an almost entire absence of wild beasts—what wonder, therefore, that the progeny of the Spanish cavalry horses has extended itself (in the same way as did the horses turned loose at the siege of Azov in the sixteenth century on the steppes of Russia) all over the pampas, from the semi-tropical plains of Tucumán and Rioja right down to the Straits of Magellan? Spanish writers tell us that Córdoba was the place from which the conquerors of America took most of their horses. To ride like a Cordobese was in the Middle Ages a saying in Spain, and such it has remained unto this day. Cervantes makes one of his characters say "he could ride as well as the best Cordobese or Mexican," proving the enormous increase of horses in the New World even in his time, not much more than a hundred years after the Conquest. In the plains of Córdoba, to this day, large quantities of horses are bred, but of a very different stamp from their descendants of the pampas. Whence then did the original stock come from? Córdoba was the richest of the Moorish kingdoms of Spain in the thirteenth century. It was directly in communication with Damascus. Thus there is little doubt that the Cordobese horses were greatly improved by the introduction of the Arab blood. However, Damascus was a long way off, and the journey a difficult and a dangerous one. It therefore seems more probable to me that the most of the Cordobese horses came over from Barbary. A remarkable physical fact would seem to bear out my belief. Most horses, in fact almost all breeds of horses, have six lumbar vertebrae. A most careful observer, the late Edward Losson, a professor in the Agricultural College of Santa Catalina near Buenos Aires, has noted the remarkable fact that the horses of the pampas have only five. Following up his researches, he has found that the only other breed of horses in which a similar peculiarity is to be found is that of Barbary.

Taking into consideration the extreme nearness of the territories of Andalusia and Barbary, and the constant communication that in Mahommedan times must have existed between them, I am of opinion that the horses of the pampas are evidently descended from those of Barbary.

It is not within my knowledge to state whether a similar configuration is to be observed in the Cordobese horses of to-day. But this is a point very easily cleared up.

The genet, too (the progeny of the ass and horse), has the same number of vertebrae. Is it impossible that in former times the union of an African mare and a genet may have produced the race of Berber horses which were taken by the Moors to Spain, and thence to the pampas? The genet and the mule are not characterised by the same infecundity. During the last fifty years, in the south of France, many cases have been observed of the reproductiveness of the former animal.

The following story may serve to show that the idea of a mixed race of horses and asses that were not mules has been considered by the Arabs from the remotest ages as possible.

In the Western Soudan there are three celebrated breeds of horses, according to the Emir Abd-el-Kader—the Hâymour breed, the Bou-ghareb, and the Meizque. Of these, the Hâymour breed is considered the best, and possesses many of the same qualities that are so striking in the horses of the pampas—speed, bottom, and robustness. The Emir says that it is not uncommon for them to perform a journey of 130 kilometres in 24 hours. I myself have frequently ridden horses of the pampas 90 miles, and on one occasion 103 miles, in the same time.

The origin of the Hâymour breed is thus related. An Arab chief was obliged to leave a wounded mare in a small oasis, where there was grass and water, but near which no tribes ever passed. About a year afterwards, happening whilst hunting to pass the oasis, he saw his mare, well, and about to foal. Having taken her to the tents, her foal proved of singular excellence, and became the mother of a famous desert stock. The Arabs, knowing that no horses ever passed there (the wild horse is unknown in these deserts), believed that the foal was the progeny of a wild ass, Hamar-el-omâkheh, and to the foal they gave the name of Hâymour, the foal of the wild ass or onager.

Be this as it may, whether Pegasus or an onager was the progenitor of the horses of the pampas, the fact remains that they are renowned for the rare qualities that made the horse of Barbary famous in the Middle Ages. Nothing more enjoyable on a frosty morning than to career over the plain, hunting ostriches on a good horse; nothing more fascinating (at twenty-two) than to rattle along behind a good *tropilla* of ten or twelve horses, following their mare with tinkling brass bell. Then indeed, with silver-mounted saddle and toes just touching the heavy silver stirrups (the gaucho rides long and never puts his feet home into the stirrups, for fear of sudden fall), you bound along over the grassy seas, and cover perhaps 100 or 120 miles a day.

It is not only necessary in La Plata to ride well; a man must always fall well, that is, on his feet. Standing once watching the always interesting spectacle of a *domador* on horseback, with bare head and red silk handkerchief laid turbanwise round it, struggling with a violent colt, I rashly remarked that he rode well. "Yes, he sits well," was the answer; "let us see how he falls." Fall he did, after one or two more plunges, and his horse, a blue and white colt, on the top of him. The colt, after a struggle or two, regained its feet; the man never stirred again. His epitaph was, "What a pity he did not know how to fall!" "But, after all," remarked a bystander, "he must have died *de puro delicado*" (of very delicateness), so incredible did it seem that a man could have been fool enough to let a horse fall on him. The same superstitions exist amongst the Arabs and the gauchos as to horses and their colours. Thus, the horse with a white fore and white hind foot is sure to be fast. The gauchos say he is crossed, *cruzado*, and that accounts for it. In the same way the Arabs say he is sure to be lucky. Both peoples unite in praising the dark chestnut. "*Alazán tostado, más bien muerto que cansado*," says the proverb.[5] The Arabs have a similar one. Both unite in distrusting a light chestnut with a white tail and mane. "He is for Jews," say the Arabs. The gauchos also assign him to an unlucky caste. "*Caballo ruano para las putas.*"[6] A dun horse, unless he have a black tail and mane and red eyes, can never be good. Only a madman would ride a horse of any colour that had a white ring round its fetlock. It is unlucky. In peace it will stumble, in war fail you. Greys will not stand the sun. The roan is slow. One striking

[5] "Sorrel horse sooner dead than tired."
[6] "The roan horse is only fit for whores."

difference though. The Arab dislikes the piebald. "He is own brother to the cow." The gaucho esteems him highly. The object in life of a rich gaucho is to have a *tropilla* of piebalds. The author of *El Fausto*,[7] a well-known gaucho poem, makes his hero ride a piebald.

Like the Arab, the gaucho uses long reins open at the end, to hold a horse by if he is thrown. Like the Arab, he rides upright in the saddle. Like him, too, he stands at the horse's head to mount, looking towards its tail, and catching the saddle by the pommel, instead of the cantel, like Europeans and Australians, and throws himself at one motion into the saddle without pausing in the stirrup, his horse in the meantime going on, for no one has his horse held in the pampas from one end of the 900 miles of territory from Buenos Aires to the Andes. From the frontier of Bolivia to Patagonia you will never find a man with the heavy hands so common in Europe. This I attribute partly to the severe bit and partly to the fashion of never passing the reins through the fingers, but holding them in the hollow of the hand, which is carried rather high with the elbow turned down, and not at right angles to the body, as with us. The Arab habit of mounting on the off side has been dropped by the gaucho, but it is practised both by the Indians of the pampas and those of the prairies of North America. I had once to mount an Indian's horse. It proved unmanageable till the owner called out in bad Spanish, "Christian frightening horse, he mount quiet on Indian side." In the pampas he who is not an Indian is a Christian.

Any details, even as incomplete and rambling as are these, about the gauchos and their horses will soon be valuable. This race of tender-hearted, hospitable, nomad creatures is passing away. I shall regret them. I shall remember the gaucho sailing over the pampas, his eye fixed apparently on nothing, yet seeing everything. I shall remember him in his quaint costume at the great cattle brandings, see him catch the ostrich with the *bolas*, and never forget him in his most characteristic action, viz. when twenty-eight or thirty of them, proceeding to their respective horses, seem like drops of water to have incorporated themselves with the horses, without noise and without effort, and then, without the clatter that characterises all European equestrian performers, take wing as it were a flight of swallows. Often

[7]See note 26 of the introduction.

during the babble of the House of Commons, when in the hot summer nights we are hard at work substituting the word "and" for the word "but," and leaving out all the words from "whereinsoever" down to "which in so after" in some senseless Bill, I shall think with regret of the seven wild horses and the stubborn mules which I have so frequently seen harnessed to a diligence.

The strange, wild customs, soon to be forgotten; the old-world life, so soon to fade away. Impressed as lines upon a picture in my memory remain the gaucho wakes, in which the company, to light of tallow dips and the music of a cracked guitar, through the long summer nights danced round the body of some child to celebrate his entry into Paradise.[8]

The races at the *pulpería*, the fights with the long-bladed knives for honour and a quart of wine, the long-drawn melancholy songs of the *payadores*, the gaucho improvisatores, ending in a prolonged *Ay*—celebrating the deeds and prowess of some hero of the Independence wars—these things, these ways will disappear. Gaucho and horse, Indian with feathered lance, will go, and hideous civilisation will replace them both. In their place will rise the frightful wooden house, the drinking-house, the chapel, the manufactory. Those who are pleased with ugliness will be contented. Those who, like myself, see all too much of it already, may regret that light and colour, freedom and picturesqueness, are so rapidly being extirpated from every corner of the world.

At least we may be allowed to express the hope that in the heaven the gaucho goes to, his horse may not be separated from him.

[8] Described in detail in "Un angelito."

EL RODEO

The vast, brown, open space, sometimes a quarter of a mile across, called *el rodeo*, which bears the same relation to the ocean of tall grass that a shoal bears to the surface of the sea, was the centre of the life of the great cattle estancias of the plains. To it on almost every morning of the year the cattle were collected and taught to stand there till the dew was off the grass. To *parar rodeo* was the phrase the gauchos used, equivalent to the cowboys' "round up" on the northern plains.

An hour before the dawn, when the moon was down, but the sun not up, just at the time when the first streaks of red begin to fleck the sky, the gauchos had got up from their *recaos*. In those days it was a point of honour to sleep on the *recao*, the *carona* spread out on the ground, the *jergas* on it, the *cojinillo* underneath the hips for softness, the head pillowed upon *los bastos*, and under them your pistol, knife, your *tirador*, and boots, yourself wrapped up in your poncho and with your head tied up in a handkerchief. The gauchos had looked out in the frost or dew, according to the season of the year, to see the horse they had tied up over-night had not got twisted in his stake-rope, and then returned to sit before the fire to take a *matecito cimarrón* and smoke. Every now and then a man had left the fire, and, lifting the dried mare's-hide that served for door, had come back silently, and, sitting down again, taken a bit of burning wood, ladling it from the fire upon his knife's edge, and lit his cigarette. At last, when the coming dawn had lit the sky like an Aurora Borealis lights a northern winter's night, they had risen silently, and shouldering their saddles, had gone out silently to saddle up.

Outside the horses stood and shivered on their ropes, their backs arched up like cats about to fight. Frequently when their intending rider had drawn the pin to which they were attached, and, after coiling up the rope, approached them warily, they sat back snorting like a steam-engine, when it breasts a hill. If it was possible, the gaucho saddled his horse after first hobbling his front feet, although he was sure to throw the saddle-cloths and the *carona* several times upon the ground. When they were put firmly upon his back, the rider, cautiously stretching his naked foot under the horse's belly, caught up the cinch between his toes. Passing the *látigo* between the strong iron rings both of the *encimera* and the cinch, he put his foot against the horse's side and pulled till it was like an hour-glass, which operation not infrequently set the horse bucking, hobbled as he was.

If, on the other hand, the horse was but half-tamed, a *redomón* as the phrase was, his owner led him up to the *palenque*, tied him up firmly to it, and after hobbling and perhaps blindfolding him, saddled him after a fierce struggle and an accompaniment of snorts. When all was ready, and the first light was just about to break, showing the pampa silvery with mist and dew, and in the winter morning often presenting curious mirages of woods hung in the sky, the trees suspended upside down, the *capataz* would give the signal to set off. Going up gently to their horses, the gauchos carefully untied them, taking good care no coil of the *maneador* should get caught in their feet, and then after tightening the broad hide girth, often eight or nine inches broad, led them a little forward to let them get their backs down, or buck if they so felt inclined. Then they all mounted, some of the horses whirling round at a gallop, their riders holding their heads towards them by the *bozal* in the left hand, and with the reins and pommel of the saddle in the right. They mounted in a way peculiar to themselves, bending the knee and passing it over the middle of the saddle, but never dwelling on the stirrup, after the European way, so that the action seemed one motion, and they were on their horses as easily as a drop of water runs down a window-pane, and quite as noiselessly.

Calling the dogs, generally a troop of mongrels of all sorts, with perhaps a thin black greyhound or two amongst the pack, the gauchos used to ride off silently, their horses leaving a trail of footsteps in the dew. Some bucked and plunged, their riders shouting as their long hair and ponchos flapped up and down at every bound the horses made. They left the estancia always at the *trotecito*, the horses putting up their backs, arching their necks and playing with the bit, whose inside rollers, known as *coscojo*, jingled on their teeth.

Then after a hundred yards or so one would look at the others and say *"Vamos,"* the rest would answer *"Vámonos"* and set off galloping, until the *capataz* would order them to separate, telling them such and such a "point" of cattle should be about the hill which is above the river of the sarandís, there is a bald-faced cow in it, curly all over; you cannot miss her if you try. Other "points" would have a bullock with a broken horn in them, or some other animal, impossible to miss—to eyes trained to the plains.

In a moment all the horsemen disappeared into the "camp" just as the first rays of the sun came out to melt the dew upon the grass. This was called *campeando*, and the owner or the *capataz* usually made his aim some "point" of cattle which was the tamest and fed closest to the house, and probably contained all the tame oxen and a milk cow or two. When he had found them he drove them slowly to the rodeo, which they approached all bellowing, the younger animals striking into a run before they reached it, and all of them halting when they felt their feet on the bare ground. Once there, the *capataz*, lighting a cigarette, walked his horse slowly to and fro, occasionally turning back any animal that tried to separate and go back to the grass.

Most likely he would wait an hour, or perhaps two, during which time the sun ascending gathered strength and brought out a keen acrid smell from the hard-trodden earth of the rodeo, on which for years thousands of cattle had been driven up each day. The "point" of cattle already there would soon begin to hang their heads and stand quite motionless, the *capataz'* horse either become impatient or go off into a contemplative state, resting alternately on each hind leg.

Such of the dogs who had remained with him would stretch themselves at full length on the grass. At last faint shouts and sounds of galloping and baying dogs would be heard in the distance, gradually drawing near.

Then a dull thundering of countless feet, and by degrees, from north, south, east, and west, would come great "points" of cattle, galloping. Behind, waving their ponchos, brandishing their short *rebenques* round their heads, raced the vaqueros, followed by the dogs. As each "point" reached the rodeo, the galloping men would check their foaming horses so that the cattle might arrive at a slow pace and not cause a stampede amongst the animals that were already on the spot.

At last all the "points" had arrived. Three, four, five, or ten thousand cattle were assembled, and the men who had brought them from the thick cane-brakes and from the *montes* of the deltas of the streams, after having loosed their girths and lit cigarettes, proceeded slowly to ride round the herd to keep them on the spot. The dogs lay panting with their tongues lolling out of their mouths, the sun began to bite a little, and now and then a wild bullock or light-footed young cow, or even a small "point" of cattle, would break away, to try to get back to its *querencia*, or merely out of fright.

Then with a shout a horseman, starting with a bound, his horse all fire, his own long hair streaming out in the wind, would dart out after them, to try to head them back. "*Vuelta, ternero,*" "*vuelta, vaquilla,*"[1] they would cry, riding a little wide of the escaping beast. After a hundred yards or so, for the first rush of the wild native cattle was swift as lightning, the rider would close in. Riding in front of the escaping truant, he would try to turn it back, pressing his horse against its side.

If it turned, as was generally the case, towards the herd, after three or four hundred yards of chase, the gaucho checked his horse and let the animal return at a slow gallop by itself till it had joined the rest.

If it was a fierce bullock or a fleet-footed cow, and even after he had bored it to one side, it started out again, or stopped and charged, he rode beside it beating it with the handle of his *arreador*. When all these means had failed, as a last resource he sometimes ran his horse's chest against its flank, and gave it thus a heavy fall. This was called giving a *pechada*, and if repeated a few times usually cowed the wildest of the herd, though now and then an escaping animal had to be lassoed and dragged back, and then if it broke out again the gauchos used to rope it, and after throwing it, dissect a bit of skin between the eyes, so that it fell and blinded the poor beast and stopped him running off. These were the humours of the scene, till after half an hour or so of gently riding round and round, the rodeo, from having been at

[1] Back, calf! Back, little cow!

first a bellowing, kaleidoscopic mass of horns and hoofs, of flashing eyes and tails lashing about, like snakes, a mere confusion of all colours, black, white and brown, dun, cream and red, in an inextricable maze, became distinguishable, and you perceived the various "points," each recognizable by some outstanding beast, either in colour or in shape. The *capataz* and all the gauchos knew them, just as a sailor knows all kinds of ships, and in an instant, with a quick look, could tell if such and such a beast was fat, or only in the state known to the adept as *carne blanca*, or if the general condition of the herd was good, and this with a rodeo of five thousand animals.

Their searching eyes detected at a glance if a beast had received a wound of any kind, if maggots had got into the sore, and sometimes on the spot the cow or bullock thus affected would be lassoed, cast, its wound washed out with salt and water, and then allowed to rise. Needless to say, this operation did not improve its temper, and as occasionally, in order to save trouble, the gauchos did not rope it by the neck and put another rope on the hind legs, both horses straining on the ropes to keep them taut, but merely roped and cast and then put a fore leg above the horn, and let a man hold down the beast by pulling on its tail passed under the hind leg, the man who stood, holding the cow's horn full of the "remedy," was left in a tight place.

If he had not an easy horse to mount, the infuriated beast sometimes pursued him with such quickness that he had to dive beneath the belly and mount from the offside. If by an evil chance his horse broke away from him to avoid the charge, two gauchos rushing like the wind, their iron-handled whips raised in the air like flails, ready to fall upon the bullock's back, closed in upon the beast and fenced him in between their horses, at full speed, and as they passed, thundering upon the plain, men, horses, and the flying animal all touching one another and straining every nerve, the man in peril, seizing the instant that they passed, sprang lightly up behind the near-side rider, just as a head of thistledown stops for a moment on the edge of a tall bank, tops it, and disappears.

When the rodeo had stood an hour or so, if nothing else was in the wind, the vaqueros galloped home slowly, smoking and talking of the price of cattle in the *saladeros*, the races to be held next Sunday at some *pulpería* or other, *La flor de mayo*, *La rosa del sur*, or *La esquina de los pobres diablos*, and the rodeo, when it felt itself alone, slowly disintegrated just as a crowd breaks up after a meeting in Hyde Park,[2] and all the various "points" sought out their grazing grounds.

On days when they required fresh meat at the estancia, when it was necessary in gaucho phrase to *carnear*, then the *capataz* and two peones, coiling their *lazos* as they went, rode into the rodeo, the cattle parting into lanes before them, and after much deliberation and pointing here and there, with sage remarks on the condition of the herd, he would point his finger at a beast. Then, cautiously, the two vaqueros, with the loop of their *lazo* trailing on the ground, taking good care to hold it in their right hands, high and wide, so that their horses did not tread in it, would close upon their prey. Watching him carefully, the horses turning almost before the men gave them the signal with the hand or heel, the cattle edging away from them, they would conduct the animal towards the edge of the rodeo with his head to the "camp."

When he was clear, with a shrill cry they spurred their horses and the doomed beast began to gallop, unless perchance he doubled back towards the herd, in which contingency the operation had to be gone through again. Once galloping, the efforts of the riders were directed to keep him on the move, which in proportion to his wildness was harder or more easy to achieve, for a wild cow or bullock generally "parts" more easily than a tame animal. Perhaps the distance was a mile, and this they traversed at full gallop, hair, poncho, mane, and tail all flying in the wind, with a thin cloud of dust marking their passage as they went. When they got near the house one rider looked up at the other and said, "Now is the time to throw." In an instant, round his head revolved the thin hide-plaited rope, the ring (the last six feet in double plait) shining and glistening in the sun. The wrist turned like a well-oiled machine, the horse sprang forward with a bound, and the rope, winding like a snake, whistled and hurtled through the air.

It fixed as if by magic round the horns, the rider generally keeping in his hand some coils of slack for any casualty that might occur. The instant that it settled round the horns the rider spurred his horse away to the left side, for it was death to get

[2] Well known gathering place in London for political, religious, and other such meetings.

entangled in the rope. In fact, in every cattle district maimed hands and feet showed plainly how dangerous was the game. The check, called the *tirón*, came when the animal had galloped twenty yards or so. It brought him to a stop, his hind legs sliding to one side. The horse leaned over, straining on the rope, the victim bellowed and rolled its eyes, lashing its tail against its flanks and pawing up the turf.

If the position of the animal was near enough, so as to save the carriage of the meat, the last act straight began. If not, after avoiding dexterously a charge or two, keeping the rope taut, and free from his horse's legs or even sides or croup, unless he was a well-trained cattle horse, the other peon riding up behind, twisting his *lazo* round his head, urging his horse against the lassoed animal, rode up and drove him nearer in. Once within handy distance from the house, the man who had been driving threw his rope and caught the bullock by the heels. Sometimes they threw him down and butchered him; at other times, the man who had him by the horns, keeping his *lazo* taut, he and his horse throwing their weight upon the rope, called to his fellow to dismount and *carnear*.

If he was an expert, throwing his reins upon the ground, he slipped off quickly, and crouching like a jaguar about to spring, ran cautiously to the offside of the enlassoed beast, drawing his long *facón*. Avoiding any desperate horn-thrust, like a cat avoids a stone, and taking care not to get mixed up with the rope, he plunged his knife deep down into the throat. The gushing stream of blood sprang like the water from a fire-plug, and the doomed creature sank upon its knees, then rocked a little to and fro, and with a bellow of distress, fell and expired.

If, on the other hand, the animal was fierce, or the man did not care to run the risk, he advanced, and, drawing his *facón* across its hocks, hamstrung it, and brought it to the ground, and then came up and killed it, when it was rendered helpless. On such occasions it was terrible, and quite enough to set a man against all beef for ever (had there been any other food upon the plains), to see the bullock jumping upon its mutilated legs and hear it bellow in its agony.

Last scene of all, the horses either unsaddled or attached to the *palenque*, or else to a stout post of the corral, the slayers, taking off their ponchos or their coats, skinned and cut up the beast. So rapidly was this achieved, that sometimes hardly an hour had elapsed from the "death bellow" to the time when the raw joints of meat were hung in the *galpón*. the hide was stretched out in the sun, and the *chimangos* and the dogs feasted upon the entrails, whilst the wild riders, dusty and bloodstained, took a maté in the shade.

There was another and a wilder aspect of the rodeo, which, like a *pampero*, burst on the beholders so suddenly that when it passed and all had settled down again, they gazed, half stunned, out on the tranquil plain. It might be that a *tropero* was parting cattle for a *saladero*, his men cutting out cattle, riding them towards a "point" of working bullocks, held back by men about a quarter of a mile from the main body of the herd. All might be going well, the rodeo kept back by men riding round slowly. The parties might be working quietly, without much shouting; the day serene, the sun unclouded, when suddenly an uneasy movement would run through the cattle, making them sway and move about, after the fashion of the water in a whirlpool, without apparent cause.

If the *tropero* and the overseer or the owner of the place himself were men who knew the "camp," and few of them were ignorant of all its lore, they did not lose a moment, but calling as gently as possible to the peones, they made them ride as close to one another as they could, in a great circle round about the beasts. It might be that their efforts would pacify the animals, but in all cases the "cutting out" was over for the day.

A little thing, a hat blown off, a poncho waving, a horse suddenly starting or falling in a hole, would render all their efforts useless and as vain as those of him who seeks to keep a flight of locusts from lighting on a field. In an instant the cattle would go mad, their eyes flash fire, their tails and heads go up, and, with a surge, the whole rodeo, perhaps five or six thousand beasts, would, with a universal bellow, and a noise as of a mighty river in full flood, break into a stampede. Nothing could stay their passage—over hills, down steep *quebradas*, and through streams they dashed, just as a prairie fire flies through the grass. Then was the time to see the gaucho at his best; his hat blown back, held by a broad black ribbon underneath his chin, and as he flew along, slipping his poncho off, the *capataz* galloped to head the torrent of mad beasts.

The peones, spreading out like the sticks of a fan, urged on their horses with their great iron spurs, and with resounding blows of their *rebenques* as they strove hard to close and get in front. Those who were caught amongst the raging mass held their lives only by their horses' feet, pushed here and there against the animals, but still unmoved, upright and watchful in their saddles, and quick to seize the slightest opportunity of making their way out. If by mischance their horses fell, their fate was sealed; and the tornado past, their bodies lay upon the plain, like those of sailors washed ashore after a shipwreck—distorted, horrible.

The men who at the first had spread out on the sides, now closing in, had got in front, and galloped at the head of the mad torrent, waving their ponchos and brandishing their whips. They, too, were in great peril of their lives, if the herd crossed a *vizcachera* or a *cangrejal*. That was the time for prodigies of horsemanship. If I but close my eyes, I see, at a stampede on an estancia called *El Calá*, a semi-Indian rushing down a slope to head the cattle off. His horse was a dark dun, with eyes of fire, a black stripe down the middle of his back, and curious black markings on the hocks. His tail floated out in the wind, and helped him in his turnings, just as a steering oar deflects a whaleboat's prow. The brand was a small "s" inside a shield. I saw it as they passed. Down the steep slope they thundered, the Indian's hair rising and falling at each spring that the black dun made in his course. His great iron spurs hung off his heels, and all his silver gear, the reins, the *pasadores* of the stirrups, the *chapeado* and *fiador*, and the great spurs themselves, jingled and clinked as he tore on to head the living maelstrom of the stampeding beasts. Suddenly his horse, although sure-footed, keen, and practised at the work, stepped in a hole and turned a somesault.

He fell, just as a stone from the nippers of a crane, and his wild rider, opening his legs, lit on his feet so truly, that his great iron spurs clanked on the ground like fetters, as he stood holding the halter in his hand. As his horse bounded to his feet, his rider, throwing down his head and tucking his left elbow well into his side, sprang at a bound upon his back and galloped on, so rapidly that it appeared I had been dreaming, and only have woke up, thirty years after, to make sure of my dream. Sometimes the efforts of the peones were successful, and the first panic stayed, the cattle let themselves be broken into "points," and by degrees and with great management were driven back to the rodeo and kept there for an hour or two till they had quieted down. If, on the other hand, they kept on running, they ran for leagues, till they encountered a river or a lake, and plunging into it, many were drowned, and in all cases many were sure to stray and mix with other herds, or, wandering away, never returned again.

The whole impression of the scene was unforgettable, and through the dust, both of the prairie and the thicker dust of years, I can see still the surging of the living lava stream and hear its thunder on the plain.

LA PULPERÍA

It may have been the *Flor de mayo, Rosa del sur*, or *Tres de junio*, or again but have been known as the *pulpería* upon the *Huesos*, or the *esquina* on the Naposta. But let its name have been what chance or the imagination of some Neapolitan or Basque had given it, I see it, and seeing it, dismounting, fastening my *redo-món* to the *palenque*, enter, loosen my *facón*, feel if my pistol is in its place, and calling out "Carlón," receive my measure of strong, heady red Spanish wine in a tin cup. Passing it round to the company, who touch it with their lips to show their breeding, I seem to feel the ceaseless little wind which always blows upon the southern plains, stirring the dust upon the pile of fleeces in the court, and whistling through the wooden *reja* where the *pulpero* stands behind his counter with his pile of bottles close beside him, ready for what may chance. For outward visible signs, a low, squat, mud-built house, surrounded by a shallow ditch on which grew stunted cactuses, and with *paja brava* stick-ing out of the abode of the overhanging eaves. Brown, sun-baked, dusty-looking, it stands up, an island in the sea of waving hard-stemmed grasses which the improving settler passes all his life in a vain fight to improve away; and make his own particular estancia an Anglo-Saxon Eden of trim sheep-cropped turf, set here and there with "agricultural implements," broken and thrown aside, and though imported at great trouble and expense, destined to be replaced by ponderous native ploughs hewn from the solid ñandubay, and which, of course, inevitably prove the superiority of the so-called unfit. For inward graces, the *reja* before which runs a wooden counter at which the flower of the *gauchaje* of the district lounge, or sit with their toes sticking through their potro boots, swinging their legs and keeping time to the cielito of the *payador* upon his cracked guitar, the strings eked out with fine-cut thongs of mare's hide, by jingling their spurs.

Behind the wooden grating, sign in the pampa of the eternal hatred betwixt those who buy and those who sell, some shelves of yellow pine, on which are piled ponchos from Leeds, ready-made *calzoncillos*, *alpargatas*, figs, sardines, raisins, bread—for bread upon the pampa used to be eaten only at *pulperías*—saddle-cloths, and in a corner the *botillería*, where vermuth, absinthe, squarefaced gin, Carlón, and *vino seco* stand in a row, with the barrel of Brazilian caña, on the top of which the *pulpero* ostentatiously parades his pistol and his knife. Outside, the tracks led through the *vizcacheras*, all converging after the fashion of the rails at a junction; at the *palenque* before the door stood horses tied by strong rawhide *cabrestos*, hanging their heads in the fierce sun, shifting from leg to leg, whilst their companions, hobbled, plunged about, rearing themselves on their hind legs to jump like kangaroos.

Now and then gauchos rode up occasionally, their iron spurs hanging off their naked feet, held by a rawhide thong; some dressed in black bombachas and vicuña ponchos, their horses weighted down with silver, and prancing sideways as their riders sat immovable, but swaying from the waist upwards like willows in a wind. Others, again, on lean young colts, riding upon a saddle covered with sheepskin, gripping the small hide stirrup with their toes and forcing them up to the posts with shouts of "*Ah, bagual!*" "*Ah, Pehuelche!*" "*Ahijuna!*"[1] and with resounding blows of their short, flat-lashed whips, which they held by a thong between their fingers or slipped upon their wrists, then grasping their frightened horses by the ears, got off as gingerly as a cat jumps from a wall. From the rush-thatched, mud-walled ranchería at the back, the women, who always haunt the outskirts of a *pulpería* in the districts known as *tierra adentro*, Indians, and semi-whites, mulatresses, and now and then a stray Basque or Italian girl, turned out, to share the quantity they considered love with all mankind.

[1] "Ah, bronco!" "Ah, Injun!" "Ah, son of a bitch!"

But gin and politics, with horses' marks, accounts of fights, and recollections of the last revolution, kept men for the present occupied with serious things, so that the women were constrained to sit and smoke, drink maté, plait each other's hair searching it diligently the while), and wait until Carlón with *vino seco*, square-faced rum, *cachaza*, and the medicated log-wood broth, which on the pampa passes for *vino francés*, had made men sensible to their softer charms. That which in Europe we call love, and think by inventing it that we have cheated God, who clearly planted nothing but an instinct of self-continuation in mankind, as in the other animals, seems either to be in embryo, waiting for economic advancement to develop it; or is perhaps not even dormant in countries such as those in whose vast plains the *pulpería* stands for club, exchange, for meeting-place, and represents all that in other lands men think they find in Paris or in London, and choose to dignify under the style of intellectual life. Be it far from me to think that we have bettered the Creator's scheme; or by the substitution of our polyandry for polygamy, bettered the position of women, or in fact done anything but changed and made more complex that which at first was clear to understand.

But, be that as it may and without dogmatism, our love, our vices, our rendering wicked things natural in themselves, our secrecy, our pruriency, adultery, and all the myriad ramifications of things sexual, without which no novelist could earn his bread, fall into nothing, except there is a press-directed public opinion, laws, bye-laws, leaded type, and headlines, so to speak, to keep them up. True, nothing of all this entered our heads, as we sat drinking, listening to a contest of minstrelsy *por contrapunto* betwixt a gaucho *payador* and a *matrero negro* of great fame, who each in turn taking the cracked *changango* in their *lazo*-hardened hands, plucked at its strings in such a style as to well illustrate the saying that to play on the guitar is not a thing of science, but requires but perseverance, hard finger-tips, and an unusual development of strength in the right wrist. Negro and *payador* each sang alternately; firstly old Spanish love songs handed down from before the independence, quavering and high, in which Frasquita rhymed to *chiquita*, and one Cupido, whom I never saw in pampa, *loma, rincón, bolsón,* or *médano,* in the chañares, amongst the woods of ñandubay, the *pajonales,* sierras, *cuchillas,* or in all the land, figured and did nothing very special;

flourished, and then departed in a high falsetto shake, a rough sweep of the hard brown fingers over the jarring strings forming his fitting epitaph.

The story of *El Fausto*, and how the gaucho, Aniceto, went to Buenos Aires, saw the opera of *Faust*, lost his *puñal* in the crush to take his seat, sat through the fearsome play, saw face to face the enemy of man, described as being dressed in long stockings to the stifle-joint, eyebrows like arches for tilting at the wing, and eyes like water-holes in a dry river bed, succeeded [the Spanish songs], and the negro took up the challenge and rejoined. He told how, after leaving town, Aniceto mounted on his *overo rosao*, fell in with his *compadre*, told all his wondrous tale, and how they finished off their bottle and left it floating in the river like a buoy.[2]

The *payador*, not to be left behind, and after having tuned his guitar and put the *cejilla* on the strings, launched into the strange life of Martín Fierro, type of the gauchos on the frontier, related his multifarious fights, his escapades, and love affairs, and how at last he, his friend, Don Cruz, saw on an evening the last houses as, with a stolen *tropilla* of good horses, they passed the frontier to seek the Indians' tents. The death of Cruz, the combat of Martín with the Indian chief—he with his knife, the Indian with the *bolas*—and how Martín slew him and rescued the captive woman, who prayed to heaven to aid the Christian, with the body of her dead child, its hands secured in a string made out of one of its own entrails, lying before her as she watched the varying fortunes of the fight, he duly told. *La vuelta de Martín* and the strange maxims of Tío Viscacha, that pampa cynic whose maxim was never to ride up to a house where dogs were thin, and who set forth that arms are necessary, but no man can tell when, were duly recorded by the combatants, listened to and received as new and authentic by the audience, till at last the singing and the frequent glasses of Carlón made *payador* and negro feel that the time had come to leave off *contrapunto* and decide which was most talented in music with their *facóns*. A personal allusion to the colour of the negro's skin, a retort calling in question the nice conduct of the sister of the *payador*, and then two savages foaming at the mouth, their ponchos wrapped round their arms, their

---

[2]In two footnotes Graham added quotations in Spanish from the original *Fausto* which I have omitted, as Graham has paraphrased them in the paragraph above.

bodies bent so as to protect their vitals, and their knives quivering like snakes, stood in the middle of the room. The company withdrew themselves into the smallest space, stood on the tops of casks, and at the door the faces of the women looked in delight, whilst the *pulpero*, with a pistol and a bottle in his hands, closed down his grating and was ready for whatever might befall. *"Negro," "ahijuna," "miente," "carajo,"* [3] and the knives flash and send out sparks as the returns *du tac au tac* [4] jar the fighters' arms up to the shoulder-joints. In a moment all is over, and from the *payador's* right arm the blood drops in a stream on the mud floor, and all the company step out and say the negro is a *valiente, muy guapetón,* and the two adversaries swear friendship over a tin mug of gin. But all the time during the fight, and whilst outside the younger men had ridden races barebacked, making false starts to tire each other's horses out, practising all the tricks they knew, as kicking their adversary's horse in the chest, riding beside their opponent and trying to lift him from his seat by placing their foot underneath his and pushing upwards, an aged gaucho had gradually become the centre figure of the scene.

Seated alone he muttered to himself, occasionally broke into a falsetto song, and now and then half drawing out his knife, glared like a tiger-cat, and shouted *"Viva Rosas,"* though he knew that chieftain had been dead for twenty years.

Tall and with straggling iron-grey locks hanging down his back, a broad-brimmed plush hat kept in its place by a black ribbon with two tassels under his chin, a red silk Chinese handkerchief tied loosely round his neck and hanging with a point over each shoulder-blade, he stood dressed in his *chiripá* and poncho, like a mad prophet amongst the motley crew. Upon his feet were potro boots, that is the skin taken off the hind leg of a horse, the hock-joint forming the heel and the hide softened by pounding with a mallet, the whole tied with a garter of a strange pattern woven by the Indians, leaving the toes protruding to catch the stirrups, which as a *domador* he used, made of a knot of

---

[3] Insults that may be rendered thus: "Nigger!" "Son of a bitch!" "Liar!" "Carajo" is an obscene exclamation with sexual connotations. See glossary.

[4] A fencing term meaning "to parry with the riposte"; also "to retort quickly." One remembers that Graham was an expert fencer, both in Paris, where he figured prominently in international competitions in the mid-1870's, and in Mexico, where he directed a fencing academy. See Sir William Rothenstein's portrait of him—"The Fencer."

hide. Bound round his waist he had a set of ostrich balls covered in lizard skin, and his broad belt made of carpincho leather was kept in place by five Brazilian dollars, and through it stuck a long *facón* with silver handle shaped like a half-moon, and silver sheath fitted with a catch to grasp his sash. Whilst others talked of women or of horses, alluding to their physical perfections, tricks or predilections, their hair, hocks, eyes, brands, or peculiarities, discussing them alternately with the appreciation of men whose tastes are simple but yet know all the chief points of interest in both subjects, he sat and drank. Tío Cabrera (said the others) is in the past, he thinks of times gone by; of the Italian girl whom he forced and left with her throat cut and her tongue protruding, at the pass of the Puán; of how he stole the Indian's horses, and of the days when Rosas ruled the land. *Pucha, compadre,* those were times, eh? Before the "nations," English, Italian and Neapolitan, with French and all the rest, came here to learn the taste of meat, and ride, the *maturrangos,* in their own countries having never seen a horse. But though they talked at, yet they refrained from speaking to him, for he was old, and even the devil knows more because of years than because he is the devil, and they knew also that to kill a man was to Tío Cabrera as pleasant an exercise as for them to kill a sheep. But at last I, with the accumulated wisdom of my twenty years, holding a glass of caña in my hand, approached him, and inviting him to drink, said, not exactly knowing why, *"Viva Urquiza,"* and then the storm broke out. His eyes flashed fire, and drawing his *facón* he shouted *"Muera!—Viva Rosas,"* and drove his knife into the mud walls, struck on the counter with the flat of the blade, foamed at the mouth, broke into snatches of obscene and long-forgotten songs, as *"Viva Rosas! Muera Urquiza; dale guasca en la petiza,"*[5] whilst the rest, not heeding that I had a pistol in my belt, tried to restrain him by all means in their power. But he was maddened, yelled, "Yes, I, Tío Cabrera, known also as *el Cordero,* tell you I know how to play the violin (a euphemism on the south pampa for cutting throats). In Rosas' time, *Viva el general,* I was his right-hand man, and have dispatched many a Unitario[6] dog either to Trapalanda or to hell. Caña, blood, *Viva Rosas, Muera!"* then tottering and shaking, his

[5] Isolated line of a song that could be translated: "Long live Rosas! Death to Urquiza; whip his podgy little nag."

[6] The Unitarians, who favored centralized government, were the opponents of Rosas' "federalists."

knife slipped from his hands and he fell on a pile of sheepskins with white foam exuding from his lips. Even the gauchos, who took a life as other men take a cigar, and from their earliest childhood are brought up to kill, were dominated by his brute fury, and shrank to their horses in dismay. The *pulpero* murmured *"salvaje"* from behind his bars, the women trembled and ran to their *toldería* holding each other by the hands, and the guitar-players sat dumb, fearing their instruments might come to harm. I, on the contrary, either impelled by the strange savagery inherent in men's blood or by some reason I cannot explain, caught the infection, and getting on my horse, a half-wild *redomón*, spurred him and set him plunging, and at each bound struck him with the flat edge of my *facón*, then shouting *"Viva Rosas,"* galloped out furiously upon the plain.

LOS INDIOS

No one, who has not lived upon the southern pampa in the days when a staunch horse was of more value in time of trouble than all the prayers of all the good men of the world, can know how constantly the fear of Indians was ever present in men's minds.

The *indiada* of the old Chief Catriel was permanently camped outside Bahía Blanca. They lived in peace with all their neighbours; but on the sly maintained relations with *los indios bravos*, such as the Pampas, Ranqueles, Pehuelches, and the rest who, though they had their *toldos* out on the Salinas Grandes, and dotted all the way along the foothills of the Andes right up to the lake of Nahuel-Huapi and down to Cholechel, occasionally burst like a thunder-cloud upon the inside camps, as suddenly as a *pampero* blew up from the south.

All their incursions, known to the gauchos as *malones*, were made by the same trails. They either entered the province near the town of Tapalqué by the great waste between the Romero Grande and the Cabeza de Buey, or through the pass, right at the top of the Sierra de la Ventana, the curious hill with the strange opening in it, from which it takes its name.

The terror and romance of the south frontier were centred in the Indian tribes. When they broke in amongst the great estancias of the south, all but the chiefs riding upon a sheep-skin, or without even that, carrying a lance made of a bamboo, fifteen to twenty feet in length, the point a sheep-shear, fastened to the shaft by a piece of a cow's tail, or other bit of hide wrapped round it green, then left to dry till it became as hard as iron, and with a tuft of horse-hair underneath the blade, looking like a human scalp, the deer and ostriches all fled in front of them, just as the spindrift flies before a wave.

Each warrior led a spare horse, taught to run easily beside him and leave his hand free for the spear. They rode like demons of the night, their horses all excited by the fury of their charge, leaping the small *arroyos*, changing their feet like goats upon a stony place, and brushing through the high grasses with a noise as of a boat crashing through reeds. Now and again they struck their hands upon their mouths to make their yells a loud prolonged "Ah, Ah, Ah-a-a," more wild and terrifying.

Each warrior carried round his waist two or three pair of *bolas*; the two large balls hanging on the left side, and the small handball, on the right, just resting on the hip. All had long knives or swords, which as a rule they shortened for convenience of carriage to about the length of a sword-bayonet, wearing them stuck between the girth and the skirt of the saddle, if they should chance to have a saddle, and if they had none, stuck through a narrow woollen sash made by their women in the *tolderías*, worked in strange, stiff, concentric patterns, bound round their naked waists. All were smeared over with a coat of ostrich grease, though never painted, and their fierce cries and smell were terrifying to the gauchos' horses, making them mad with fear. Some twenty paces in advance rode the cacique, sometimes upon a silver-mounted saddle, choosing if possible a black horse to set it off well, and with his silver reins, seven feet in length, held high in his left hand as, spurring furiously, he turned occasionally to yell out to his men, grasping his spear about the middle as he careered along.

To meet them thus, alone upon the plains, say when alone upon a lazy horse, out looking up strayed cattle, was an experience not easily forgotten—and one which he who had it remembered vividly, if he escaped their lynx-eyed scouting, up to his dying day.

Your only chance, unless, as was unlikely, you had a *pingo* fit for God's saddle, as the gauchos said, was to alight, and having led your horse into a hollow, to muffle up his head in the folds of your poncho, to stop him neighing, and keep as still as death. Then, if you had not been perceived, and little on the plains escaped an Indian's eye, you almost held your breath, until the thunder of the Indians' horses' feet had died away, and mounting with your heart thumping against your sides, cautiously stole up the hollow, and getting off again, holding your horse by a long rope, peeped stealthily over the brow to see if all was clear. If out upon the plains you saw the ostriches, the deer, or cattle running, or dust arise without a cause, you had to get back to the hollow and wait a little. Lastly when you were certain all had passed, you drew the *látigo* of the hide-cinch, placing your foot against the horse's side to get more purchase, till he was like an hour-glass with the strain. Then mounting, you touched him with the spur, and galloped for dear life, till you got to a house, shouting as you rode up, *"los indios,"* a cry which brought every male Christian running to the door.

Quickly the tame horses would be driven up and shut in the corral; all the old arms loaded and furbished up; for, strange as it may sound, the gauchos of the south, although they were exposed to constant inroads of the Indians, never had anything but an old blunderbuss or so, or a pair of flintlock pistols, and those out of repair.

The Indians themselves, having no arms but spears and *bolas*, were seldom formidable except out on the plain. A little ditch, not five feet deep and eight or ten across, kept a house safe from them, for as they never left their horses, they could not cross it, and as they came to plunder, not especially to kill, they wasted little time upon such places, unless they knew that there were young and handsome women shut up in the house. "Christian girl, she more big, more white than Indian," they would say, and woe betide the unlucky girl who fell into their hands.

Hurried off to the *toldos*, often a hundred leagues away, they fell, if young and pretty, to the chiefs. If not, they had to do the hardest kind of work; but in all cases, unless they gained the affections of their captor, their lives were made a burden by the Indian women, who beat and otherwise ill-used them on the sly.

Such were the Indians on the warpath, from San Luis de la Punta, right down to Cholechel. Stretches of "camp" now under corn were then deserted or, at the best, roamed over by *manadas* of wild mares.

A chain of forts, starting upon the Río Quinto and running north and south, was supposed to hold the Indians in check; but in reality did little, as they a slipped through to plunder, quite at their own sweet will. The mysterious territory known by the name of *tierra adentro*, began at Las Salinas Grandes, and stretched right to the Andes, through whose passes the Indians, by the help of their first cousins, the Araucanians, conveyed such of the cattle and the mares they did not want, to sell or to exchange for silver horse-gear, known to the gauchos by the name of Chafalonia Pampa, and highly coveted as having no alloy.

In type and habits there was little difference between *la indiada mansa* of the Chief Catriel and their wild brethren of the plains. Both were a yellow coppery colour, not tall, but well proportioned, all but their legs, which were invariably bowed by their lives passed on horseback from their youth. Both sexes wore the hair long, cut square across the forehead and hanging down the back, and both had rather flat and brutal faces, and all the men had restless eyes, perpetually fixed on the horizon as if they lived in fear.

Their beards were sparse, their constitutions hardy, and men and women both went down to the stream and bathed before the sun rose, taking care to be prepared to pour a calabash of water on the ground when the first rays appeared.

I see them now, coming back in a long string from the water, and hear their salutation *"Mari-Mari"* as they passed dripping on their way, their long black hair, lustrous and heavy, hanging loose down their backs.

Tierra adentro served the wilder gauchos for a sure refuge in their times of trouble, to which to fly after some "trouble" or another, in which some man had lost his life, or to escape from serving in some revolutionary force or any other cause.

José Hernández, in his celebrated *Martín Fierro*, has described how Cruz and his friend took refuge with the Indians, and well do I remember, for we all knew the whole book by heart, taking my turn for a hundred lines or so, round the camp fire, out on the Napostá. The wood engraving, primitive and cheap, in which Cruz and Martín were shown jogging on at the *trotecito* wrapped in their ponchos, driving the *tropilla*; and with the foal, looking like a young camel, bringing up the rear, is quite as well fixed in my memory as is the picture of the Conde Duque, the Emperor Charles the Fifth at Mulhouse, *"Las Hilanderas,"* [1] or any other work of art.

The line beneath it always impressed us, and we all tried to get the last verses to recite, so as to round up with the epic, *"Al fin, por una madrugada clara, vieron las últimas poblaciones,"* [2] the *pob-*

laciones being, if I remember rightly, some low and straw-thatched ranchos, surrounded by a ditch.

Their subsequent adventures are they not set down with some prolixity in *La vuelta de Martín?*[3]

The serious side of *tierra adentro* was in the refuge it afforded to revolutionary chiefs. The brothers Saá and Colonel Baigoiria held a sort of sub-command for years, under the great cacique Painé, and to them came all the discontented and broken men, whom they formed into a kind of flying squadron, ranging the frontiers with the Indians, as fierce and wild as they.

All kinds of Christian women, from the poor *china* girl, carried off like a mare from an estancia, to educated women from the towns, and once even a prima donna, journeying from Córdoba to Mendoza, were to be found in that mysterious "Inside Land." On one occasion a lady carried off from San Luis found herself about to be the prey of several chiefs, who were preparing to settle matters by a fight.

Throwing herself about Baigoiria's neck, who happened to be there, she cried, "Save me, *compadre*," and he, after some trouble, took her to his house. There he had several other wives; but white women, prisoners amongst the Indians, were said never to quarrel, so that they lived with a white man. Their fate with Indians was not much to be envied, except as in the case of the great chief Painé, who for ten years at least was ruled by a white girl he took at the sack of an estancia, somewhere near Tapalqué.

In the Arcadia of the *tolderías*, especially in those close by the apple forests of the Andes, the life of those who dwelt in them must have been a survival of another age, without a parallel in all the world.

[1]Graham is referring here to the portrait of El Conde Duque de Olivares and "The Spinners," both painted by the Spanish master Velázquez (1599–1660), and to the portrait of Charles V at Mühlberg, by the Italian master, Titian (c. 1487–1576).

[2]"At last, on a clear morning, they saw the last houses." In fact, in spite of Graham's claim to know *Martín Fierro* by heart, he quotes slightly inaccurately here. The verses should read:

Y cuando la habían pasado,
una madrugada clara
le dijo Cruz que mirara
las últimas poblaciones

[3]*La vuelta de Martín Fierro* (1879) is the conclusion to the poem in which the hero is reintegrated into modern society.

In North America the Indian tribes all had traditions of their own, a polity and a religion, often complicated.

Amongst the *toldos* of the pampas, except a perfunctory sun-worship and a most real faith in the Gualichú,[4] that evil spirit to which mankind in every age has paid at least as much attention as to the principle of good, nothing of old traditions had been left. They lived almost exactly like the gauchos, with the exception that they grew a little maize, and fed on mare's flesh, instead of beef. The Indian's *toldo* was but little inferior to the gaucho's hut. Most of the Indians spoke a little Spanish. Both Indian and gaucho wore the same clothes (the Indians when they could get them) in time of peace. In time of war, they went about almost stark naked, save for a breech-clout, and generally the hat was, as it is to Arabs, the stumbling-block, the Indians preferring to have their long black locks well dressed with mare's grease, or with ostrich oil, as a protection from the sun. Their carelessness of life and their contempt of death exceeded that even of their first cousins and deadly enemies, the gauchos, of whom it is said that one of them coming to see his friend, found him in the agonies of rheumatic fever, and after having looked at him compassionately, said, "Poor fellow, how he suffers," and drawing out his knife took the sufferer by the beard and cut his throat. Cutting of throats was a subject of much joking both amongst gauchos and the Indians. Amongst the former it was called to "do the holy office," and a coward was said to be mean about his throat, if at the last he showed the slightest fear. The agonies and struggles of a dying man were summed up briefly, "he put out his tongue when I began to play the violin" (i.e., with the knife), phrases and actions which had their counterpart or origin amongst the Indians.

I who write this have seen the Indian children playing carnival, with hearts of sheep and calves for scent bottles, squirting out blood on one another in the most natural way.

At the rejoicings in the *tolderías*, after a successful *malón* or raid in some estancia, the amount of mare's flesh that the Indians used to eat was quite phenomenal. Some of them hardly stopped to cook it, or at the best but scorched it at the fire. Some ate it raw, drinking the blood like milk, and when half drunk—for caña was never wanting in the *toldos*—and well daubed over with the

4See Graham's sketch "The Gualichú Tree."

blood, it made one wonder whether the chain connecting man with the orang-outang had any link with them.

Their choicest delicacy was the fat piece along a young colt's neck; this they ate always raw, and I remember·once having to taste it in response to a compliment addressed me by a young warrior, who yelling "There's a good Christian," thrust the fat dripping meat into my unwilling hand. The effect was lasting, and to this day I cannot look on a piece of green turtle fat floating in the soup without remembering the Indian delicacy.

Well, well, the *toldos*, those on the edge of the great apple forests of the Andes, and those between Las Salinas Grandes and the Lago Argentino, all are gone. All the wild riders now ride in Trapalanda, the mysterious city in which no Christian ever breathes his horse. Over the treacherous *guadal*, the *vizcachera*, or through the middle of a *cangrejal*, no more wild horsemen gallop, certain to fall upon their feet, if their horse step into a hole; or if they chanced to fail to land upon their feet, rise and leap on from the off-side leaning upon their spear.

No longer, on a journey, will they, as it appeared without a cause, suddenly strike their hands upon their mouths and yell, and then when asked the reason, answer, "Huincá, he foolish; Auca do that because first see the sierra," as in the days of yore.

Round the Gualichú tree, no longer hands from north and south will meet, and whilst within its influence forbear to fight; even refrain from stealing a fine horse during the time they celebrate their medicine dance. In separating, no Indian now will tear a piece from off his poncho and stick it on a thorn; the tree was a chañar, if I remember right.

Men looking for strayed horses, sleeping beside some lonely river, no longer have to shiver half the night on guard and burn their feet against the fire, placed in a hollow, dug with their knives in the green turf, so as to show no light, till it was time to saddle up and march.

No one will travel, as I did with a friend, now riding as I hope in some mysterious Trapalanda of his own (fit for men of no faith, but in good works), from Tapalqué down to the Sauce Grande, passing no house that was not burned and sacked, except a chance estancia surrounded by a ditch and full of women and of wounded men. We started with an alarm of Indians at Tapalqué, the plaza full of men all arming, and with wild-eyed and yelling countrymen galloping in on foaming horses, calling out "*los indios,"* what time the comandante, seated in a cane-chair, sat taking maté as he passed his rough recruits in an extemporaneous review.

We camped on the Arroyo de los Huesos, swam the Quequén Salado, buried a man we found dead at Las Tres Horquetas, and after a week's riding, through camps swept clear of cattle and of mares, came to the Sauce Grande just in time to take a hand in a brief skirmish and see the Indians drive off the few remaining horses in the place.

Those times are gone, and now the plough breaks up the turf that had remained intact and virgin since the creation of the world.

THE CAPTIVE

Somehow or other none of the camp could sleep that night. It may have been that they were hungry, for they were just returning from a bootless attempt to overtake a band of Indians who had carried off the horses from an estancia on the Napostá. Night had fallen on them just by the crossing of a river, where a small grove of willows had given them sufficient wood to make a fire, for nothing is more cheerless than the fierce transient flame ("like a nun's love") that cow-dung and dry thistle-stems afford. Although they had not eaten since the morning, when they had finished their last strips of *charqui* they had a little *yerba*, and so sat by the fire passing the maté round and smoking black Brazilian cigarettes.

The stream, either a fork of the Mostazas or the head waters of the Napostá itself, ran sluggishly between its banks of rich alluvial soil. Just at the crossing it was poached into thick mud by half-wild cattle and by herds of mares, for no one rode where they were camped in those days but the Indians, and only they when they came in to burn the settlements. A cow or two which had gone in to drink and remained in the mud to die, their eyes picked out by the caranchos, lay swelled to an enormous size, and with their legs sticking out grotesquely, just as a soldier's dead legs stick out upon a battlefield.

From the still, starry night the mysterious noises of the desert rose, cattle coughed dryly as they stood on rising ground, and now and then a stallion whinnied as he rounded up his mares. Vizcachas uttered their sharp bark and tucotucos sounded their

metallic chirp deep underneath the ground. The flowers of the
chañar gave out their spicy scent in the night air, and out beyond
the clumps of piquillín and molle, the pampa grass upon the
river-bank looked like a troop of ostriches in the moon's dazzling
rays.

The Southern Cross was hung above their heads, Capella was
just rising, and from a planet a yellow beam of light seemed to fall
into the rolling waves of grass, which the light wind just stirred,
sending a ghostly murmur through it, as if the sound of surf upon
some sea, which had evaporated thousands of years ago, was
echoing in the breeze.

A line of sand-hills ran beside the stream. Below their white
and silvery sides the horses, herded by a man who now and then
rode slowly to the fire to light a cigarette, grazed on the wiry
grass. The tinkling bells of the *madrinas* had been muffled, as
there was still a chance the Indians might have cut the trail, and
now and then the horse guard cautiously crawled up the yielding
bank and gazed out on the plain, which in the moonlight looked
like a frozen lake.

Grouped round the fire were most of the chief settlers on the
Sauce Grande, Mostazas, and the Naposta.

The brothers Milburn, who had been merchant sailors,
dressed in cord breeches and brown riding-boots, but keeping,
as it were, a link with ships in their serge coats, were there,
sitting up squarely, smoking and spitting in the fire.

Next to them sat Martín Villalba, a wealthy cattle-farmer and
major in the militia of Bahía Blanca. No one had ever seen him in
his uniform, although he always wore a sword stuck underneath
the girth of his *recao*. The light shone on his Indian features and
was reflected back from his long hair, which hung upon his
shoulders as black and glossy as the feathers of a crow. As he sat
glaring at the blaze he now and then put up his hand and
listened, and as he did so, all the rest of those assembled listened
as well, the man who had the maté in his hand holding it in
suspense until Villalba silently shook his head, or, murmuring,
"It is nothing," began to talk again. Spaniards and Frenchmen sat
side by side with an Italian, one Enrique Clerici, who had served
with Garibaldi[1] in his youth, but now was owner of a *pulpería*

---

[1]Giuseppe Garibaldi (1807–82), one of the fathers of Italian independence.

that he had named "The Rose of the South," and in it hung a picture of his quondam leader, which he referred to as "my saint."

Claraz, the tall, black-bearded Swiss, was there. He had lost one finger by a tiger's bite in Paraguay, and was a quiet, meditative man who had roamed all the continent, from Acapulco down to Punta Arenas, and hoped some day to publish an exhaustive work upon the flora of the pampa, when, as he said, he found a philanthropic publisher to undertake the loss.

The German, Friedrich Vögel, was bookkeeper at an estancia called *La casa de Fierro*, but being young and a good horseman had joined the others, making a contrast to them as he sat beside the fire in his town clothes, which, though they were all dusty and his trouser-legs coated thick with mud, yet gave him the appearance of being on a picnic, which a small telescope that dangled from a strap greatly accentuated. Since he had started on the trail eight or nine days ago, he had hispaniolised his name to Pancho Pájaro, which form, as fortune willed it, stuck to him for the remainder of his life in South America.[2] Two cattle-farmers, English by nationality, known as "*El Facón Grande*" and "*El Facón Chico*"[3] from the respective size of the knives they carried, talked quietly, just as they would have talked in the bow-window of a club, whilst a tall, grey-haired Belgian, handsome and taciturn, was drawing horses' brands with a charred mutton-bone as he sat gazing in the fire. Of all the company he alone kept himself apart, speaking but seldom, and though he had passed a lifetime on the plains, he never adventured his opinion except men asked for it, when it was taken usually as final, for everybody knew that he had served upon the frontier under old General Mansilla in the Indian wars.[4]

A tall, fair, English boy, whose hair, as curly as the wool of a merino sheep, hung round his face and on his neck after the fashion of a Charles II wig, was nodding sleepily.

Exaltación Medina, tall, thin, and wiry, tapped with his whip

[2] Here and throughout the sketches Vögel is known as Pancho Pájaro, not Pájaros, as the German plural form might indicate. It is difficult to determine whether this error is due to Graham's shaky knowledge of German, or to the bookkeeper's ignorance of the subtleties of the Spanish language.

[3] Graham devotes the sketch "Facón Grande" to these settlers.

[4] General Mansilla (1831–1913) wrote his famous *Excursión a los indios Ranqueles* in 1870.

upon his boot-leg, on which an eagle was embroidered in red silk.

He and his friend, Florencio Freites, who sat and picked his teeth abstractedly with his long silver-handled knife, were gauchos of the kind who always rode good horses and wore good clothes, though no one ever saw them work except occasionally at cattle-markings. They both were *badilleros*, that is, men from Bahía Blanca, and both spoke Araucano, having been prisoners amongst the infidel, for their misfortunes, as they said, although there were not wanting people who averred that their connection with the Indians had been in the capacity of renegades by reason of their crimes.

Some squatted cross-legged like a Turk, and some lay resting on their elbows, whilst others, propped against their saddles, sat with their eyes closed, but opened them if the wind stirred the trees, just as a sleeping cat peers through its eyelids at an unusual noise.

When the last maté had been drunk and the last cigarette end flung into the blazing brands, and yet a universal sleeplessness seemed to hang in the air, which came in fierce, hot gusts out of the north, carrying with it a thousand cottony filaments which clung upon the hair and beards of the assembled band, Claraz suggested that it might be as well if someone would tell a story, for it was plain that, situated as they were, no one could sing a song. Silence fell on the group, for most of those assembled there had stories that they did not care to tell. Then the mysterious impulse that invariably directs men's gaze towards the object of their thoughts turned every eye upon the Belgian, who still was drawing brands on the white ashes of the fire with the burnt mutton-bone. Raising his head he said: "I see I am the man you wish to tell the story, and as I cannot sleep an atom better than the rest, and as the story I will tell you lies on my heart like lead, but in the telling may perhaps grow lighter, I will begin at once."

He paused, and taking off his hat, ran his hands through his thick, dark hair, flecked here and there with grey, hitched round his pistol so that it should not stick into his side as he leaned on his elbow, and turning to the fire, which shone upon his face, set in a close-cut, dark-brown beard, slowly began to speak.

"Fifteen—no, wasn't it almost sixteen years ago—just at the time of the great Indian *malón*—invasion, eh? the time they got as far as Tapalqué and burned the *chacras* just outside Tandil, I was living on the Sauce Chico, quite on the frontier—I used to drive my horses into the corral at night and sleep with a Winchester on either side of me. My nearest neighbour was a countryman of mine, young—yes, I think you would have called him a young man then. An educated man, quiet and well-mannered, yes, I think that was so—his manners were not bad.

"It is his story I shall tell you, not mine, you know. Somehow or other I think it was upon an expedition after the Indians, such as ours to-day, he came upon an Indian woman driving some horses. She had got separated from her husband after some fight or other and was returning to the tents. She might have got away, as she was riding a good horse—piebald it was with both its ears slit, and the cartilage between the nose divided to give it better wind. Curious the superstitions that they have." Florencio Freites looked at the speaker, nodded and interjected, "If you had lived with them as long as I have, you would say so, my friend. I would give something to slit the cartilage of some of their Indian snouts." No one taking up what he had said, he settled down to listen, and the narrator once again began.

"Yes, a fine horse that piebald, I knew him well, a little quick to mount, but then that woman rode like a gaucho—as well as any man. As I was saying, she might have got away—so said my friend—only the mare of her *tropilla* had not long foaled, and either she was hard to drive or the maternal instinct in the woman was too strong for her to leave the foal behind—or she had lost her head or something—you can never tell. When my friend took her prisoner, she did not fight or try to get away, but looked at him and said in halting Spanish '*Bueno*, I am taken prisoner, do what you like.' My friend looked at her and saw that she was young and pretty, and that her hair was brown and curly, and fell down to her waist. Perhaps he thought—God knows what he did think. For one thing, he had no woman in his house, for the last, an Italian girl from Buenos Aires, had run off with a countryman of her own, who came round selling saints—a *santero*, eh? As he looked at her, her eyes fell, and he could have sworn he saw the colour rise under the paint daubed on her face, but he said nothing as they rode back towards his rancho, apart from all the rest. They camped upon the head waters of the Quequén Salado, and to my friend's astonishment, when he had staked out his horse and hers and put the hobbles on her mare, so that her *tropilla* might not stray, she had lit the fire and put a little kettle on to boil. When they had eaten some tough *charqui*, moistened in warm water, she handed him a maté and stood submissively filling it for him till he had had enough. Two or three times he looked at her, but mastered his desire to ask her how it was that she spoke Spanish, and why her hair was brown.

"As they sat looking at the fire, it seemed somehow as if he had known her all his life, and when a voice came from another fire, 'You had better put the hobbles on that Indian mare, or she'll be back to the *querencia* before the moon is down,' it jarred on him, for somehow he vaguely knew his captive would not try to run away.

"So with a shout of 'All right, I'll look out,' to the other fires, he took his saddle and his ponchos, and saying to the Indian woman, 'Sleep well, we start at daybreak,' left her wrapped up in saddle-cloths, with her feet towards the fire. An hour before the dawn the camp was all astir, but my friend, though an early riser, found his captive ready, and waiting with a maté for him, as soon as he got up and shook the dew out of his hair, and buckled on his spurs.

"All that day they rode homewards, companions leaving them at intervals, as when they struck the Saucecito, crossed the Mostazas, just as it rises at the foot of the Sierra de la Ventana, or at the ruined rancho at the head waters of the Naposta. Generally, as the various neighbours drove their *tropillas* off, they turned and shouted farewell to the Indian woman and my friend, wishing them a happy honeymoon or something of the kind. He answered shortly, and she never appeared to hear, although he saw that she had understood. Before they reached his rancho he had learned a little of the history of the woman riding by his side. She told him, as Spanish slowly seemed to make its way back to her brain, that she was eight-and-twenty, and her father had been an estanciero in the province of San Luis; who with her mother and her brothers had been killed in an invasion of the Indians eight years ago, and from that time she had lived with them, and had been taken by a chief whose name was Huinchan by whom she had three sons. All this she told my friend mechanically, as if she had been speaking of another, adding, 'The Christian women pass through hell amongst the infidel.'" The narrator paused to take a maté, and Anastasio sententiously remarked, "Hell, yes, double-heated hell: do you remember, *che*, that Chilian girl you bought from that Araucan whose eye one of the Indian girls gouged out?" His friend Florencio showed his teeth like a wolf and answered, "Caspita, yes; do you remember how I got even with her? Eye for an eye, tooth for a tooth, as I once heard a priest say was God's law!" The maté finished, the Belgian once again took up his tale.

"When my friend reached his home he helped his captive off her horse, hobbled her mare, and taking her hand led her into the house and told her it was hers.

"She was the least embarrassed of the two, and from the first took up her duties as if she had never known another life.

"Little by little she laid aside her Indian dress and ways, although she folded carefully and laid by her *chamal*, with the great silver pin shaped like a sun that holds it tight across the breast. Her ear-rings, shaped like an inverted pyramid, she put aside with the scarlet fichú that had bound her hair, which, when she was first taken, hung down her back in a thick mass of curls that had resisted all the efforts of the Indian women, aided by copious dressings of melted ostrich fat, to make straight like their own. Timidly she had asked for Christian clothes, and by degrees became again a Spanish woman, careful about her hair, which she wore high upon her head, careful about her shoes, and by degrees her walk became again the walk she had practised in her youth, when with her mother she had sauntered in the evening through the plaza of her native town, with a light swinging of her hips.

"Her Indian name of Lincomilla gave place once more to Nieves, and in a week or two some of the sunburn vanished from her cheeks.

"All the time of her transformation my friend watched the process as a man may watch the hour-hand on a clock, knowing it moves, but yet unable to discern the movement with his eyes.

"Just as it seems a miracle when on a fine spring morning one wakes and sees a tree which overnight was bare, now crowned with green, so did it seem a miracle to him that the half-naked Indian whom he had captured, swinging her whip about her head and shouting to her horses, had turned into the señorita Nieves, whilst he had barely seen the change. Something intangible seemed to have grown up between them, invisible, but quite impossible to pass, and now and then he caught himself regretting vaguely that he had let his captive slip out of his hands. Little by little their positions were reversed, and he who had been waited on by Lincomilla found himself treating the señorita Nieves with all the—how you say—*égards* that a man uses to a lady in ordinary life.

"When his hand accidentally touched hers he shivered, and then cursed himself for a fool for not having taken advantage of the right of conquest the first day that he led the Indian girl into his home. All would have then seemed natural, and he would have only had another girl to serve his maté, a link in the long line of women who had succeeded one another since he first drove his cattle into the south camps and built his rancho on the creek. Then came a time when something seemed to blot out all the world, and nothing mattered but the señorita Nieves, whom he desired so fiercely that his heart stood still when she brushed past him in her household duties; yet he refrained from speaking, kept back by pride, for he knew that, after all, she was in his power in that lone rancho on the plains. Sleeping and waking she was always there. If he rode out upon the *boleada* she seemed to go with him; on his return there she was standing, waiting for him with her enigmatic smile when he came home at night.

"She on her side was quite aware of all he suffered, suffering herself just as acutely, but being able better to conceal her feelings, he never noticed it, or saw the shadowy look that long-suppressed desire brings in a woman's eyes. Their neighbours, ordinary men and women, had no idea things were on such an exalted footing, and openly congratulated him on his good luck in having caught an Indian who had turned to a white girl. When he had heard these rough congratulations on his luck, he used to answer shortly, and catching his horse by the head, would gallop out upon the plain and come home tired, but with the same pain gnawing at his heart. How long they might have gone on in that way is hard to say, had not the woman—for it is generally they who take the first step in such things—suddenly put an end to it. Seeing him sitting by the fire one evening, and having watched him follow her with his eyes as she came in and out, she walked up to him and laid her hand upon his shoulder, and as he started and a thrill ran through his veins, bent down her face and pressing her dry lips to his, said, 'Take me,' and slid into his arms.

"That was their courtship. From that time, all up and down the Sauce Chico, the settlers, who looked on love as a thing men wrote about in books, or as the accomplishment of a necessary function without which no society could possibly endure, took a proprietary interest in the lovers, whom they called *los de Teruel*, after the lovers in the old Spanish play, who loved so constantly.[5]

"Most certainly they loved as if they had invented love and meant to keep it to themselves. Foolish, of course they were, and primitive, he liking to rush off into Bahía Blanca to buy up all the jewellery that he could find to give her, and she, forgetting all the horrors of her life amongst the Indians, gave herself up to happiness as unrestrained as that of our first mother, when the whole world contained no other man but the one she adored.

"As in a day out on the southern plains, when all is still and the wild horses play, and from the lakes long lines of pink flamingoes rise into the air and seem translucent in the sun, when the whole sky becomes intensest purple, throwing a shadow on the grass that looks as if the very essence of the clouds was falling like a dew, the Indians say that a *pampero* must be brewing and will soon burst with devastating force upon the happy world, so did their love presage misfortune by its intensity."

"A strong north wind is sure to bring a *pampero*," interpolated one of the listeners round the fire.

"Yes, that is so, and the *pampero* came accordingly," rejoined the story-teller.

"Months passed and still the neighbours talked of them with amazement, being used to see the force of passion burn itself out, just as a fire burns out in straw, and never having heard of any other kind of love except the sort they and their animals enjoyed.

"Then by degrees Nieves became a little melancholy, and used to sit for hours looking out on the pampa, and then come in and hide her head beneath her black Manila shawl, that shawl my friend had galloped to Bahía Blanca to procure, and had returned within two days, doing the forty leagues at a round gallop all the way.

"Little by little he became alarmed, and feared, having been a man whose own affections in the past had often strayed, that she was tired of him. To all his questions she invariably replied that she had been supremely happy, and for the first time had known love, which she had always thought was but a myth invented by the poets to pass the time away. Then she would cry and say that

[5]Graham refers here to the nineteenth-century Spanish romantic drama, *Los amantes de Teruel* (1837), of Juan Eugenio Hartzenbusch (1806–80).

he was idiotic to doubt her for a moment, then catching him to her, crush him against her heart. For days together she was cheerful, but he, after the fashion of a man who thinks he has detected a slight lameness in his horse, but is not certain where, was always on the watch to try and find out what it was that ailed her, till gradually a sort of armed neutrality took the place of their love. Neither would speak, although both suffered almost as much as they had loved, until one evening as they stood looking out upon the pampa yearning for one another, but kept apart by something that they felt, rather than knew, was there, the woman with a cry threw herself into her lover's arms. Then with an effort she withdrew herself, and choking down her tears, said, 'I have been happy, dearest, happier by far than you can understand, happier than I think it is ever possible to be for any man. Think of my life, my father and my mother killed before my eyes, myself thrown to an Indian whom my soul loathed, then made by force the mother of his children—his and mine. Think what my life has been there in the *tolderías*, exposed to the jealousy of all the Indian women, always in danger till my sons were born, and even then obliged to live for years amongst those savages and become as themselves.

" 'Then you came, and it seemed to me as if God had tired of persecuting me; but now I find that He or nature has something worse in store. I am happy here, but then there is no happiness on earth, I think. My children—his and mine—never cease calling. I must return to them—and see, my horses all are fat, the foal can travel, and—you must think it has been all a dream, and let me go back to my master—husband—bear him more children, and at last be left to die when I am old, beside some river, like other Indian wives.' She dried her eyes, and gently touching him upon the shoulder, looked at him sadly, saying, 'Now you know, dearest, why it is I have been so sad and made you suffer, though you have loaded me with love. Now that you know I love you more a hundred times than the first day, when, as you used to say, I took you for my own, you can let me go back to my duties and my misery, and perhaps understand.'

"Her lover saw her mind was fixed, and with an effort stammered, '*Bueno*, you were my prisoner, but ever since I took you captive I have been your slave.—When will you go?'

"Let it be to-morrow, *sangre mía*, and at daybreak, for you must take me to the place where you first saw me; it has become to me as it were a birthplace, seeing that there I first began to live.' Once more he answered, '*Bueno,*' like a man in a dream, and led her sadly back into their house.

"Just as the first red streaks of the false dawn had tinged the sky they saddled up without a word.

"Weary and miserable, with great black circles round their eyes, they stood a moment, holding their horses by their *cabrestos*, till the rising sun just fell upon the doorway of the poor rancho where they had been so happy in their love.

"Without a word they mounted, the captive once more turned to Lincomilla, dressed in her Indian clothes, swinging herself as lightly to the saddle as a man. Then gathering the horses all together, with the foal, now strong and fat, running behind its mother, they struck into the plains.

"Three or four hours of steady galloping brought them close to the place where Lincomilla had been taken captive by him who now rode silently beside her, with his eyes fixed on the horizon, like a man in a dream.

" 'It should be here,' she said, 'close to that tuft of sarandís— yes, there it is, for I remember it was there you took my horse by the bridle, as if you thought that I was sure to run away, back to the Indians.' "Dismounting, they talked long and sadly, till Lincomilla tore herself from her lover's arms and once more swung herself upon her horse. The piebald *pingo* with the split ears neighed shrilly to the other horses feeding a little distance off upon the plain, then, just as she raised her hand to touch his mouth, the man she was about to leave for ever stooped down and kissed her foot, which rested naked on the stirrup, after the Indian style. 'May the God of the Araucans, to whom you go, bless and encompass you,' he cried; 'my God has failed me,' and as he spoke she touched her horse lightly with the long Indian reins. The piebald plunged and wheeled round, and then struck into a measured gallop, as his rider, gathering her horses up before her, set her face westward, without once looking back.

"I—that is, my friend stood gazing at her, watching the driven horses first sink below the horizon into the waves of grass, the foal last disappearing as it brought up the rear, and then the horse that Lincomilla rode, inch by inch fade from sight, just as a ship slips down the round edge of the world. Her feet went first, then the *caronas* of her saddle, and by degrees her body, wrapped in the brown *chamal*.

"Lastly, the glory of her floating hair hung for a moment in his sight upon the sky, then vanished, just as a piece of seaweed is sucked into the tide by a receding wave.

"That's all," the story-teller said, and once again began to paint his horses' brands in the wood ashes with his mutton-bone, as he sat gazing at the fire.

Silence fell on the camp, and in the still, clear night the sound of the staked-out horses cropping the grass was almost a relief. None spoke, for nearly all had lost some kind of captive, in some way or other, till Claraz, rising, walked round and laid his hand upon the story-teller's shoulder. "I fear," he said, "the telling of the tale has not done anything to make the weight upon the heart any the lighter.

"All down the coast, as I remember, from Mazatlán to Acapulco, pearl-fishers used to say unless a man made up his mind to stay below the water till his ears burst, that he would never be a first-rate pearl-diver.

"Some men could never summon up the courage, and remained indifferent pearl-divers, suffering great pain, and able to remain only a short time down in the depths, as their ears never burst. It seems to me that you are one of those—but, I know I am a fool, I like you better as you are."

He ceased, and the grey light of dawn fell on the sleepless camp on the north fork of the Mostazas (or perhaps the Napostá); it fell upon the smouldering fire, with Lincomilla's lover still drawing horses' marks in the damp ashes, and on the group of men wrapped in their ponchos shivering and restless with the first breath of day.

Out on the plain, some of the horses were lying down beside their bell-mares. Others stood hanging their heads low between their feet, with their coats ruffled by the dew.

THE GUALICHÚ TREE

Just where the Sierra de la Ventana fades out of sight, a mere blue haze on the horizon, close to the second well in the long desert *travesía* between El Carmen and Bahía Blanca, upon a stony ridge from which to the north the brown interminable pampa waves a sea of grass, and to the south the wind-swept Patagonian stone-strewed steppes stretch to the Río Negro, all alone it stands. No other tree for leagues around rises above the sun-browned, frost-nipped grass, and the low scrub of thorny carmamoel and elicui. An altar, as some think, to the Gualichú, the evil spirit, which in the theogony of the wandering Indian tribes has so far hitherto prevailed over the other demon who rules over good, that all the sacrifices which they make fall to his lot. An espinillo, some have it; a tala, or a chañar, as others say; low, gnarled, and bent to the north-east by the continual swirl of the *pampero* which rages on the southern plains, the tree, by its position and its growth, is formed to have appealed at once to the imagination of the Indian tribes. Certain it is that in the days before the modern rifle slew them so cowardly (the slayers, safe from the weak assaults of lance and *bolas* by the distance of their weapons' range, and rendered as maleficent as Gods by the toil of men in Liège or Birmingham, who at the same time forged their own fetters, and helped unknowingly to slay men they had never seen), no Araucanian, Pampa, Pehuelche, or Ranquele passed the Gualichú Tree, without his offering. Thus did they testify by works to their belief both in its power, its majesty, and might.

The gauchos used to say the tree was the Gualichú incarnated.

They being Christians by the grace of God, and by the virtue of some drops of Spanish blood, spoke of the Indians as idolators. The Indians had no idols, and the gauchos now and then a picture of a saint hung on the walls of their low reed-thatched huts, to which a mare's hide used to serve as door. So of the two, the gauchos really were greater idolators than their wild cousins, whom they thus contemned, as Catholics and Protestants condemn each other, secure in the possession of their church and book, and both convinced the other must be damned.

So all the gauchos firmly held that the Indians thought the tree a God, not knowing that they worshipped two great spirits, one ruling over good, and the more powerful over evil, as is natural to all those who manufacture creeds.

Before a gaucho passed below the mountains of Tandil, the Jesuits knew the tribes, and Father Falkner has written of the faiths of the Pehuelches and the other tribes who roamed from Cholechel to Santa Cruz, round the Salinas Grandes, about the lake of Nahuel-Huapi, and in the apple forests which fringe the Andes on their Southern spurs.[1]

Of all the mountains which faith can, but hitherto has not attempted to, remove, the monstrous cordillera of misconception of other men's beliefs is still the highest upon earth. So, to the gauchos, and the runagates (forged absolutely on their own anvils), who used to constitute the civilising scum which floats before the flood of progress in the waste spaces of the world, the Gualichú Tree was held an object half of terror, half of veneration, not to be lightly spoken of except when drunk, or when ten or a dozen of them being together it was not worthy of a man to show his fear.

Among the Indians, and in the estimation of all those who knew them well, the tree was but an altar on which they placed their free-will offerings of things which, useless to themselves, might, taking into account the difference of his nature from their own, find acceptation and be treasured by a God.

So fluttering in the breeze it stood, a sort of everlasting Christmas tree, decked out with broken bridles, stirrups, old tin cans, pieces of worn-out ponchos, *bolas*, lance-heads, and skins of animals, by worshippers to whom the name of Christian meant

[1] Thomas Falkner, *A Description of Patagonia, and the adjoining parts of South America* (London, 1774).

robber, murderer, and intruder on their lands. No Indian ever
passed it without suspending something to its thorny boughs,
for the Gualichú, by reason of his omnipotent malevolence, was
worth propitiating, although he did not seem to show any particular discernment as to the quality of the offerings which his
faithful tied upon his shrine. Around the lone and wind-swept
tree, with its quaint fruit, has many a band of Indians camped,
their lances, twenty feet in length, stuck in the ground, their
horses hobbled and jumping stiffly as they strayed about to eat,
what time their masters slew a mare, and ate the half-raw flesh,
pouring the blood as a libation on the ground, their wizards (as
Father Falkner relates) dancing and beating a hide-drum until
they fell into the trance in which the Gualichú visited them, and
put into their minds that which the Indians wished that he
should say.

The earliest travellers in the southern plains describe the tree
as it still stood but twenty years ago; it seemed to strike them but
as an evidence of the lowness of the Indians in the human scale.
Whether it was so, or if a tree which rears its head alone in a vast
stony plain, the only upright object in the horizon for leagues on
every side, is not a fitting thing to worship, or to imagine that a
powerful spirit has his habitation in it, I leave to missionaries, to
"scientists," and to all those who, knowing little, are sure that
savages know nothing, and view their faith as of a different
nature from their own. But, after all, faith is not absolutely the
sole quality which goes to make belief. No doubt the Indians saw
in the tree the incarnation of the spirit of their race, in all its
loneliness and isolation from any other type of man. Into the tree
there must have entered in some mysterious way the spirit of
their own long fight with nature, the sadness of the pampa, with
its wild noises of the night; its silent animals, as the guanaco,
ostrich, mataco, the quirquincho, and the Patagonian hare; its
flights of red flamingoes; the horses wild as antelopes and shyer
than any animal on earth; the rustle of the pampas grass upon the
watercourses, in which the pumas and the jaguars lurk; the birth
of spring covering the ground with red verbena and the dark
leaden-looking grass which grows on the *guadal*; the giant bones
of long-extinct strange animals which in some places strew the
ground; all the lone magic of the summer's days, when the light
trembles, and from every stem of grass the fleecy particles, which
the north wind blows, tremble and quake, whilst over all the sun

beats down, the universal god worshipped from California to Punta Arenas by every section of their race.

To Christians too the tree had memories, but chiefly as a landmark, though few of them, half in derision, half in the kindliness which comes of long communication (even with enemies) who would pass without an offering of an empty match-box, a dirty pocket-handkerchief, a brimless hat, or empty sardine tin—something, in short, to bring the beauty of our culture and our arts home to the Indians' minds. One Christian at least had offered up his life beneath its boughs—an ostrich hunter, who, finding ostriches grow scarce, the price of ostrich feather fall, or being possessed with a strange wish for regular, dull work, had hired himself to carry mail bags from Bahía Blanca to Carmen de Patagones, the furthest settlement in those days, towards the south. As all the country which he travelled was exposed to Indian raids, and as he generally, when chased, had to throw off his saddle and escape barebacked (*en pelo*, as the gauchos say), by degrees he found it too expensive to make good the saddles he had lost. So all the eighty leagues he used to ride *en pelo*, use having made him part and parcel of his horse. An ostrich hunter from his youth up, aware one day that he would die the ostrich hunter's death, by hunger, thirst, or by an Indian's lance, well did he know the great green inland sea of grass in which men used to sleep with their faces set towards the way they had to go, knowing that he who lost the trail had forfeited his life, unless by a hard, lucky chance he reached an Indian *toldería*, there to become a slave. Well did the ex-ostrich hunter know the desert lore, to take in everything instinctively as he galloped on the plain, to mark the flight of birds, heed distant smoke, whether the deer or other animals were shy or tame, to keep the wind ever ablowing on the same side of his face, at night to ride towards some star; but yet it fell upon a day, between the first well and the Río Colorado, his horse tired with him, and as his trail showed afterwards, he had to lead it to the second well, which he found dry. Then after long hours of thirst, he must have sighted the Gualichú Tree, and made for it, hoping to find some travellers with water skins; reached it, and having hung his mail bags on it to keep them safe, wandered about and waited for relief. Then, his last cigarette smoked and thrown aside (where the belated rescuers found it on the grass), he had sat down stoically to meet the ostrich hunter's fate. A league or two along the trail his horse had struggled on, making for the water which he knew must be in the river Colorado, and like his master, having done his best, died in the circle of brown withered grass which the last dying struggle of an animal upon the pampa makes.

Landmark to wandering gauchos, altar or God to all the Indian tribes, a curiosity of nature to "scientists," who, like Darwin, may camp beneath its boughs, and to the humourist looking half sadly through his humour at the world, a thorny Christmas tree, but scarce redeemed from being quite grotesque, when, amongst its heterogeneous fruit, it chanced to bear a human hand, a foot, or a long tress or two of blue-black hair, torn from some captive Christian woman's head, long may it stand.

You in the future, who, starting from Bahía Blanca, pass the Romero Grande, leave the Cabeza del Buey on the right hand, and at the Río Colorado exchange the grassy pampa for the stony southern plains, may you find water in both wells, and coming to the tree neither cut branches from it to light your fire, or fasten horses to its trunk to rub the bark. Remember that it has been cathedral, church, town-hall, and centre of a religion and the lives of men now passed away; and, in remembering, reflect that from Bahía Blanca to El Carmen, it was once the solitary living thing which reared its head above the grass and the low thorny scrub. So let it stand upon its stony ridge, just where the Sierra de la Ventana fades out of sight, hard by the second well, right in the middle of the *travesía*—a solitary natural landmark if naught else, which once bore fruit ripened in the imaginations of a wild race of men, who at the least had for their virtue constancy of faith, not shaken by unanswered prayer; a tombstone, set up by accident or nature, to mark the passing of light riding bands upon their journey towards Trapalanda—passing or passed— but all so silently, that their unshod horses' feet have scarcely left a trail upon the grass.

LOS SEGUIDORES

Only the intimate life of man with the domestic animals which takes place upon the pampas of the River Plate could have produced *los seguidores*.

Brothers, or trained to be as brothers by being tied together by the neck till they had conquered the repugnance which every animal, including man, has for his fellow, this was the name the gauchos gave two horses which to their owner were as one. The followers (*los seguidores*) on the darkest night trotted along, the loose horse following the mounted brother, as it had been a shadow on the grass. At night, when one was picketed to feed, the other pastured round about him like a satellite, and in the morning sometimes the two were found either asleep or resting with their heads upon each others' necks. When saddled for a march, the owner mounting never even turned his head to look, so sure he was that the loose horse would follow on his trail. Even in crossing rivers, after the first deep plunge which takes the rider to his neck, one swam behind the other, spurting out water like a whale, or biting at the quarters of the ridden horse, and on emerging, both of them shook themselves like water dogs, and the unmounted follower patiently waited for the start, and then after a plunge or two, to shake the water from his coat, trotting along contentedly behind his brother on the plain.

Such a pair I knew, the property of one Cruz Cabrera, a gaucho living close to the little river Mocoretá which separates the province of Entre Ríos from that of Corrientes to the north. Both horses were *picazos*, that is, black with white noses, and so like

94

each other that it was a saying in the district where he lived, "Like, yes, as like as are the two *picazos* which Cruz Cabrera rides." In a mud rancho, bare of furniture save for a horse's head or two to sit upon, an iron spit stuck in the floor, a kettle, a bed, made scissorswise of some hard wood with a lacing of rawhide thongs, an ox's horn in which he kept his salt, and a few pegs on which he hung his silver reins and patent leather boots with an eagle worked in red thread upon the legs, the owner of the *seguidores* lived. A mare's hide formed the door, and in a corner a saddle and a poncho lay, a pair or two of *bolas*, and some *lazos*; rawhide bridles hung from the rafters, whilst in the thatch was stuck a knife or two, some pairs of sheep shears and a spare iron spit. Outside his rancho fed a flock of long-haired, long-legged sheep resembling goats, two or three hundred head of cattle, and some fifty mares, from which the celebrated *seguidores* had been bred.

His brother Froilán lived with him, and though only a year separated them in age, oceans and continents were set between them in all the essential qualities which go to make a man.

The elder brother was a quiet man; hard working too, when he had horses on which to work, and peaceable when no one came across his path, and when at the neighbouring *pulpería* he had not too incautiously indulged in square-faced gin (Albert Von Hoytema, the Palm Tree brand), on which occasions he was wont to forget his ordinary prudence, and become as the profane. But, in the main, an honourable, hard-riding man enough, not much addicted to brand his neighbours' cows, to steal their horses, or to meddle with their wives, even when military service or the exigencies of ordinary gaucho life called men out on the frontier, or made them seek the shelter of the woods.

Froilán never in all his life had done what is called honest work. No cow, no horse, no sheep, still less a *china* girl, ever escaped him; withal, a well-built long-haired knave before the Lord, riding a half-wild horse as if the two had issued from the womb together as one flesh. A great guitar player, and what is called a *payador*—that is, a rhymester—for, as the gauchos say, "The townsman sings, and is a poet, but when the gaucho sings he is a *payador*." A lovable and quite irresponsible case for an immortal soul, about the possession or the future state of which he never troubled himself, saying, after the fashion of his kind, "God cannot possibly be a bad man," and thus having made, as it

were, a full profession of his faith, esteeming it unworthy of a
believing man to trouble further in so manifest a thing.

In fact, a pagan of the type of those who lived their lives in
peace, content with nature as they found her, in the blithe days
before Mohammedanism and Christianity, and their mad
myriad sects, loomed on the world and made men miserable,
forcing them back upon themselves, making them introspective,
and causing them to lose their time in thinking upon things
which neither they nor anyone in the ridiculous revolving world
can ever solve, and losing thus the enjoyment of the sun, the
silent satisfaction of listening to the storm, and all the joys which
stir the natural man, when the light breeze blows on his cheek as
his horse gallops on the plain.

But still the neighbours (for even on the pampa man cannot live
alone, although he does his best to separate his dwelling from
that of his loved fellow human beings) preferred Froilán before his elder brother, Cruz. Their respect, as is most natural, for
respect is near akin to fear, and fear is always uppermost in the
mind towards those who have a severer code of life than we
ourselves (and hatred ever steps upon its heels), was given to
Don Cruz. He was a serious man and formal, complying outwardly with all the forms that they themselves were disregardful
of, and so religious that it was said once in Concordia he had
even gone to mass after a drinking bout. But as the flesh is
weak—as is but just when one reflects upon the providential
scheme, for without its weakness where would the due amount
of credit be apportioned to the Creator of mankind—Cruz
would, when all was safe, fall into some of the weaknesses his
brother suffered from, but in so carefully concealed and hidden
fashion that the said weaknesses in him seemed strength. Still
the two brothers loved one another after the fashion of men who,
living amongst unconquered nature, think first of their daily
battle with a superior force and have but little leisure for domestic ties. Love, hate, attachment to the animals amongst whom
they lived, and perhaps a vague unreasoned feeling of the beauty
of the lonely plains and exultation in the free life they led, were
the chief springs which moved the brothers' lives.

The elementary passions, which moved the other animals, and
which, though we so strenuously deny their strength, move all of
us, despite of our attempts to bury them beneath the pseudo
duties and the unnecessary necessities of modern life, acted there

directly, making them relatively honest in their worst actions, in a way we cannot understand at all in our more complicated life. With the two brothers all went well, as it so often does with those who, neither honest nor dishonest, yet keep a foot in either camp, and are esteemed as estimable citizens by those in office, and are respected by dishonest men as having just enough intelligence to guard their own. Their flocks and herds multiplied steadily, and when the locusts did not come in too great quantities, or the green paroquets refrained from eating the green corn, the patch of maize which Cruz grew, partly for an occasional dish of *mazamorra*, and more especially to keep the *seguidores* in condition during winter, was duly reaped by the aid of a Basque or a Canary Islander, and stored in bunches hanging from the roof of a long straw-thatched shed. Before their house upon most days of every year stood a half-starved and much tucked-up young horse, enduring the rough process known as "being tamed," which consisted in being forcibly thrown down and saddled on the ground, then mounted and let loose, when it indulged in antics which, as the gauchos used to say, made it more fit for a perch for a wild bird than for the saddle of a Christian man.

The *seguidores*, the greatest objects of the brothers' love, were black as jet, with their off-fore and the off-hind feet white, so that the rider, riding on a cross, was safe from the assaults of evil fiends by night, and from ill luck which makes its presence felt at every moment when the Christian thinks himself secure. Both of the horses were so round you could have counted money on their backs; their tails just touched their pasterns, and were cut off square; their noses both were blazed with white, and in addition one had a faint white star upon his forehead, and the other one or two girth marks which had left white hairs upon his flank. Both had their manes well hogged, save for a mounting lock, and on the top of the smooth arch made by the cut-off hair, castles and crosses were ingeniously cut, giving them both the appearance of having been designed after the pattern of the knight at chess. Both horses were rather quick to mount, not liking to be kept a moment when the foot was in the stirrup iron, and both of them, well trained to *lazo* work, could keep a strain upon the rope when once a bull was caught, so that their master could get off and, creeping up behind, despatch the animal, thus lassoed, with a knife. Rather straight on the pasterns, and a little heavy in the shoulder, they could turn, when galloping, in their own length, their unshod feet cutting the turf as a sharp skate cuts ice when a swift skater turns at topmost speed. Full-eyed, flat-jointed, their nostrils red and open, their coats as soft as satin, and their gallop easy as an iceboat's rush before the wind, the two *picazos* were as good specimens of their race as any of the breed between Los Ballesteros and the Gualeguay, or from San Fructuoso to the mountains of Tandil.

In the mud-reed-thatched hut, or to be accurate, in another hut beside it, dwelt the mother of the two brothers and their half-sister Luz. The mother, dried by the sun and cured by the smoke of sixty years (which blackened all the thatch, polishing it as it had been japanned), loved her two sons in the submissive fashion in which a mare may love her colts when they are grown to their full strength. Seated upon a horse's head, she watched the meat roast on a spit, boiled water for the perpetual maté, and seldom went outside the house. A Christian, if simple faith, convinced of all things hard to believe and quite impossible to understand, can make one such, she was. Although the nearest church was twenty leagues away, and in her life she had been but a few times there, she knew the dogmas of her faith to the full, as well as if communion with the church and the free use of books had placed hell fire always in her view. Octaves, novenas, and the rest she never missed, and on the rare occasions when some neighbouring women rode over to take maté and eat *mazamorra* with her, she acted as a sort of fuglewoman, leading the hymns and prayers out of a tattered book, which, in times past, she had partly learned to read. Outside religion, she was as strict in her materialism as the other women of her race, making herself no spiced conscience about any subject upon earth. From her youth upwards she had seen blood shed as easily as water; had seen the uncomplaining agony of the animals under the knife, observing *"pobrecito"* when a lamb's throat was slowly cut, and then (being a Christian, and thus of a different flesh to that of beasts) hurrying up quickly to assist in taking off its skin. Like most of us, of her own impulse she was pitiful, but yet not strong enough to stand against the universal cruelty which habit has rendered second nature to the most tender-hearted and the kindest of mankind. Spanish and Indian blood had made her look at things without the veil, which northern melancholy has cast over them, and thus she clearly looked at all, without hypocrisy, just as she saw the locusts moving in a cloud, the dust storms whirling in the air, and all the other wild phenomena of life upon the plains. She saw the human beast in all his animalism, and thought it no disgrace to admit that in essentials all his actions sprang from the motives which influenced all the other links in the same chain of which she formed a part. Seeing so clearly, she saw that Luz, although their sister, was an object of desire to both her brothers, and the old woman knew that fire and tow are safe to make a blaze if they are brought too close. Much did she muse upon the problem, muttering to herself proverbs which spoke of the necessity of a stone wall between a male and female saint, and she resolved to keep Luz from her brothers, as far as it was possible within the narrow limits of the hut. The girl herself, like many *chinas* when just grown up, was pretty, and attractive as a young deer or colt may be attractive, by its inexperience and youth. In colour, something like a ripe bamboo, with a faint flush of pink showing through upon the cheeks and palms; round-faced and dark-eyed, dressed in a gay print gown made loose, and round her neck a coloured handkerchief, Luz was as pretty as a girl upon the pampas ever is, for, being semi-civilised and Christian, she lacked the graces of a half-clothed Indian maid, and yet had not resources which in a town make many a girl, designed by nature to scrub floors and suckle fools, a goddess in the eyes of those who think a stick well dressed is more desirable than Venus rising naked from the foam.

She, too, having seen from youth the tragedy of animal birth, love, and death displayed before her eyes, was not exactly innocent; but yet, having no standard of false shame to measure by, was at the same time outspoken upon things which in Europe old women of both sexes feign to be reticent about, and still was timid by the very virtue of the knowledge which she had. The life of women on the pampa, or, for that matter, in all wild countries, is of necessity much more circumscribed than that of those their sisters, who, in other lands, approach more nearly to their more godlike brothers, by the fact of wearing stiffly starched collars and most of the insignia of man's estate. Philosophers have set it down that what is known as sexual morality is a sealed book to women, and that, whilst outwardly conforming, most of them rage inwardly at the restrictions which men, to guard their property, have set upon their lives. This may be so, for who can read what passes in the heart of any other man, even if he has felt

its closest beat for years? And it may well be that the most Puritan
of happy England's wives chafe at the liberty their husbands all
enjoy, and from which they, bound in their petticoats, stays,
flounces, furbelows, veils, bonnets, garters, and their Paisley
shawls, are impiously debarred.

But speculations upon sex problems did not greatly trouble
Luz, who, when she thought, thought chiefly of the chance of
going into town, buying new clothes, attending mass, and meeting her few friends, and so it never came into her head but that
her two half-brothers, both of them far older than herself, regarded her but as their sister and a child. Some say the heart of
man is wicked from his birth, and so it may be to those men who,
reading in their own, see naught but mud. But if it is so, then
either the framer of man's heart worked on a faulty plan, or those
who furbish for us codes of morality, have missed his meaning
and misunderstood his scheme. As the brothers never thought,
most likely never had heard in all their lives about morality,
which in despite of theorists seems not to be a thing implanted in
mankind but supergrafted mainly with an eye to the consecration
of our property, they found themselves attracted towards Luz
after a fashion which, had it happened in regard to any other girl,
they could have understood. Certain it is that both of them felt
vaguely that she was near to them in blood, and neither of them
perhaps had formulated in his mind exactly what he felt. They
watched each other narrowly, and neither cared to see the other
alone with Luz, but neither Cruz or Froilán spoke to their half-
sister or to each other, but by degrees they grew morose and
quarrelsome, making their mother miserable and their half-sister
sad at their changed temper both to each other and to her. Their
mother, with the experience of her sixty years, saw how the
matter lay, and recognized that on the pampa strange things did
take place, for, as she said, "*el cristiano macho* is the hardest to
restrain of all God's beasts," having had no doubt experience of
his ways with her two husbands in the days gone by. So, whilst
the petty tragedy was brewing, so to speak, nature, serene,
inimitable, and pitilessly sad, but all unconscious of the puny
passions of mankind, unrolled the panorama of the seasons as
quietly as if no human souls hung trembling in the scales. Night
followed day, the scanty twilight scarcely intervening, the hot
sun sinking red upon the low horizon as at sea, and in an instant
the whole world changed from a yellow sun-burnt waste to a cool

shadow, from the depths of which the cries of animals ascended to the unhearing sky which overhung them like a deep blue inverted bowl flecked with a thousand stars. The frogs croaked with a harsh metallic note, and from the thorny trees great drops of moisture hung, or dripped upon the roofs. Again night yielded up its mysteries to the dawn, advancing, conquering, and flushed with power. So by degrees the summer melted insensibly to autumn, and the vast beds of giant thistles, with stems all frosted over with their silver down, began to vanish, and the thin animals wandered about or perished in the sand, as the *pampero* whistled across the plains. But winter too faded before the inexorable, unfelt turning of the world; the red verbenas spread like carpets, covering the earth as with a blanket, the shoots of pampas grass shot up green spikes almost between the dusk and dawn, and on their little meeting places outside their towns, vizcachas sat and looked out on the world and found it good, whilst the small owls which keep them company nodded their stupid-looking, wise, little heads and gave assent.

The horses played upon the edges of the woods rearing and striking at each other with their fore-feet, and some, who in the autumn had been left thin and tired out, suddenly thought upon their homes, and, throwing up their heads, snorted, and, trotting round a little, struck the home trail as surely as a sea-gull finds its way across the sea.

But all the magic of the perpetual, kaleidoscopic change of season, which ought to interest any man a million times more keenly than his own never-changing round of sordid cares, brought no distraction to the brothers, who had grown to look upon each other partly as rivals, and partly with astonishment that the same thoughts which tortured each one were present in the other's mind. But the mere fact of feeling the identity of thought confirmed them in their purpose, and in a measure served to confirm them in their course, for men catch thoughts from one another as they take diseases, by contagion with the worst particles of the sick man they touch.

Upon the pampa, where the passions have full play, quite unrestrained by the complexity of life which in more favoured lands imprisons them in bands of broadcloth and of starch, it was impossible that in the compass of a little hut the situation could endure for long. No doubt it might have been more admirable had one or both the brothers seen the error of their ways, repented, and in chivalry and ashes gone their respective ways to do their duty in the counting-house of life. No doubt in many of the neighbouring farms girls lived as pretty as their half-sister Luz—girls whom they might have loved without a qualm, and made the mothers of their dusky, thievish children, with or without the blessing of a priest. They might have told their guilty love, and been stricken to the earth by the outraged majesty of their sister's womanhood, or felled to the ground with a bullock's head swung by the nervous hand of her who gave them birth. But chance, that orders everything quite in a different way from that we think should be the case, had ordered otherwise, and the simple tragedy upon the Mocoretá was solved more quickly and as effectually as if justice or outraged public feeling had seen fit to intervene.

How it occurred, up to his dying day Froilán was never sure, but, seated in the semi-darkness, cutting some strips of mare's hide to mend a broken girth, their mother and their sister sitting by, high words broke out between the brothers without apparent cause. Cruz, passing, in gaucho fashion, in an instant from a grave, silent man to a foaming maniac, rushed on his brother, a long thin-bladed knife clutched in his hand. Almost before Froilán had had time to draw his knife, or stand on guard, his brother tripped and fell, and the knife piercing his stomach, he lay on the mud floor with but a short half hour of agonizing life. Pressing the knife into the wound, he beckoned to his brother with the other hand, asked his forgiveness, made him swear to see their sister married to some honourable man, and promise that his own body should be laid in consecrated ground. Then, turning to his mother, he asked her blessing, and, summoning his last strength, drew the knife from the wound, and in an instant bled to death. His mother closed his eyes and then with Luz broke out into a death wail, whilst Froilán stood by half stupidly, as if he had not comprehended what had taken place.

The simple preparations over, the short but necessary lie arranged, the *alcalde* duly notified, and the depositions of the chief actor and the witnesses painfully put on record in a greasy pocket-book, nothing remained but to carry out the wish of the dead man, to lie in consecrated earth. At daybreak Froilán had the two *seguidores* duly tied before the door, saddled and ready for the road. The neighbours helped to tie the dead man upon his saddle, propping him up with sticks. When all was ready, Froilán mounted his own horse, and took the road to Villaguay, the dead man's horse cantering beside his fellow, as if the rider that he bore had been alive.

Their mother and their sister watched them till they sank into the plain, their hats last vanishing as a ship's top sails sink last into the sea. Then, as she drew her withered hand across her eyes, she turned to Luz, and saying gravely, "The male Christian is the wildest thing which God has made," lifted the mare's hide hung before the door and went into the hut.

A SILHOUETTE

The great brown plains of Entre Ríos wore an unfamiliar air. Herds of tame mares had run half wild. They snorted and made off a thousand yards away, their tangled manes and tails all knotted up with burs, streaming out in the wind. The cattle had become as fierce as buffaloes, and anyone who lost his horse had to make long detours, for to approach them was as dangerous as to come near a tiger or a lion. Only about the flat-roofed, whitewashed houses, set in their frames of peach groves, did a few animals remain domestic, and even those, at the approach of man, often made off and joined their fellows on the plains.

Sheep were close-herded, not by mere boys who climbed up to their saddles by placing a small, brown, prehensile toe upon their horse's knees, but by armed men.

The deer and ostriches ran if they saw a man a mile away, and disappeared down the brown grassy swells, just as a flying-fish shoots down the watery hills raised by the North-East Trades.

Men, *campeando* horses that had strayed, if they were forced to ascend a little hill, got off, and creeping on all fours, surveyed the country cautiously, and then, having made sure that all was quiet on the plain beyond, remained as short a time as possible standing against the sky. If at the crossing of a river, where the thick belts of hard-wood trees obscured the view, two travellers came unexpectedly upon each other face to face, their hands at once sought pistol or *facón*, and as they crossed at a sufficient distance to escape a sudden shot or lasso cast, cautiously passed the time of day, and not infrequently, seized with a panic, spurred their

104

horses, and galloped for a mile or so before they drew their reins.

The sight, on the horizon, of a band of men made the few dwellers in the scattered mud-built ranchos flee to the woods, driving their horses, carrying their wives and children, at full speed, leaving their scanty household goods to the protection of their dogs.

For months the revolution had been going on, the rival bands roaming about and stealing horses, slaughtering the cattle, and now and then, if they could catch a man or two alone, cutting their throats just as they cut a sheep's, driving the knife in at the point with the edge outwards, and bending back the head.

The death of General Justo de Urquiza had broken up the province into two hostile camps, and Reds and Whites maddened and raved about the land,[1] avoiding one another for the most part, but fighting furiously when circumstances brought them to striking distance and there was no escape. Prisoners had little chance, and those who fell alive into the enemies' hands were foolish not to have kept a cartridge, as now and then they were sewn up in hides fresh stripped from off an ox, then left to die, exposed to sun and rain, and eaten by the flies. Others were killed in various ingenious ways, and the best anyone could hope for was to be shot, or have his throat cut out of hand. No hypocritical pretence of treating fallen enemies as friends had ever crossed the minds of anybody, and war was carried on just as it might have been between wild beasts, quite naturally, and with the full amount of cruelty with which our nature had endowed us, free and unrestrained. Still, on the whole, things were no worse than they are in European wars, except that every man who fought knew that he did so with a halter round his neck.

As all the rank and file on either side were pressed, occasionally fathers and sons or brothers found themselves opposed to one another, and, strange to say, the claims of party as a general rule proved stronger than the call of blood, and not infrequently it chanced that friends were called upon to kill each other, and did so, as it appeared, without a qualm of conscience, so strong is discipline, and so amenable mankind to every influence, whether of custom or of use.

It chanced upon a day, near Villaguay, two brothers owned a

[1] The traditional enemies, Blancos and Colorados, in the confused civil wars of nineteenth-century Argentina and Uruguay.

small estancia, known as *Las Arias*, close to a strip of *monte* near a river in which carpinchos swam and tortoises abounded, and where green parakeets flew shrieking through the maize field, and built their hanging nests in the old espinillo trees which here and there stood up amongst the corn. The thick green grass fed mares and cattle, and kept them fat and sleek, when on the outside "camps" animals starved from the lack of pasture, and trailed themselves laboriously for miles to drink at water-holes, upon the face of which carcasses bloated in the sun, floated like bladders, and in whose mud, cows and thin mares got stuck like flies in treacle, and slowly starved, surrounded by a troop of vultures, who sat and waited patiently, just as the faithful followers of some great politician sit faithfully expecting the glad moment when his death shall free them and unchain their tongues, which have got stiff for want of exercise during their leader's life.

The brothers lived the ordinary life of men in those days, on the plains. From their youth upwards they had scanned the pampa as sailors scan the sea, reading it like a book, and knowing almost instinctively all the lore men learn when born to look at nature as an enemy, between whom and themselves a temporary truce exists, but which at any moment may be broken in the twinkling of an eye. Men were, of course, all hostile to them, and their philosophy, short, pithy, and extracted from the simples of their lives, bade them beware, and as they said themselves, "Never facilitate," that is, never to sit down on the left of anyone, for by so doing he had you at a disadvantage when high words ensued, and you essayed to draw your knife. So, at the passing of a river, if you could well avoid it, you did not ride into the water first, especially if you were wearing silver spurs or reins, or any of the massive trappings with which on feast days men adorned their horses, for it might chance that you received a knife-thrust in the back from a too much admiring friend, or perhaps merely because the sudden lust to kill, so frequent amongst dwellers on the plains, rose in the heart of the man following you, just as in islands far out at sea a roller suddenly sets in during a calm and sweeps away boats anchored off the shore.

To these two brothers, with their quiet, but occasionally bloody, pastoral life, whose only care was to acquire some silver horse gear, to keep their cattle fat, and their *tropilla* sleek and tame, and in whose minds a vague but stimulating idea that they were free, with no one daring to constrain them in their lives, the fear of revolution hung like a black cloud, which somehow it had always seemed impossible should burst. Not that they cared about the matter in the abstract, knowing that when a government went out a revolution followed, just as inevitably as blood pours out after you plunge a knife into a sheep. It seemed to them quite natural, for, judging by themselves, they knew no one gave up a woman or a horse without a fight, and what so natural as that a man who had enjoyed the sweets of being "government" should struggle to retain his place at the knife's point, and to the utmost of his might?

So, as they lived their lives, religiously catching a horse at night, to stake out ready to stand all day and blink and hang his head, if not required for work, and sitting hours in the kitchen drinking their maté, and illustrating all their points by diagrams drawn with the point of a *facón* on the mud floor, upon them came one morning, as a *pampero* comes up on a summer's day, the news that General Fulano had "pronounced." [2] Soon came the usual rumours, in a revolution, of men impressed to serve, of horses taken, of cattle killed, and now and then mysterious parties of armed men passed, almost, as it were, hull down on the horizon of the pampean ocean, a gleam of sun falling occasionally on a lance head or rifle barrel, before they sank beneath the grassy waves which roll towards the south.

Much did the brothers and their mother deliberate on what was best to do to avoid the ruin which they foresaw would fall upon them. The mother, an old *china* woman, wrinkled and brown, was urgent that her two sons should get together all their best horses and "emigrate," that is, cross either into Santa Fe or Uruguay, and, as she said, "Play armadillo." But they, used to the district, and knowing the recesses of the *montes* by the rivers as well as if they had been tigers or carpinchos, thought it was best to stay at home and wait.

They held their council, after the gaucho fashion, in the kitchen, sitting upon hard blocks of ñandubay or horses' heads, passing the maté round, and now and then holding it in their hands and listening, as a horse snorted, or a stallion, gathering up his mares, galloped past in the dark. Occasionally the tame chajá gave its shrill cry, causing the mother to look up and say

[2] That is, General So-and-so had issued a *pronunciamiento*, announcing a military uprising, a popular way of changing governments in Latin America, even today.

that either it would rain, because, as all men knew, when the chajá cried, that it had to rain, even against God's will, or that there was a thief afoot after the horses staked out near the house.

They sat and talked, watching the negro *capataz* Gregorio come in and out, the firelight falling on his silver-handled knife as he walked to and fro as noiselessly as if he were a ghost, in his white potro boots. His "*santas tardes*" broke the silence, and, sitting down, he took the maté from the attendant negro girl who stood by, with a small kettle ready on the fire to fill the gourd, and suck at the *bombilla* to see it was not choked before she handed it about. The others looked at him in silence till he had drunk his maté, for it would be bad manners to speak first to anyone who comes into a room. Unsheathing his long knife, after apology for drawing it before a lady, he laid it by his side, and, taking out a lump of black tobacco, dexterously cut enough, and tearing from a sheet of paper, about as large as a good sheet of foolscap, a piece of the right size, and holding it between his toes which stuck out from his potro boots, made toeless so as to catch the stirrup, he rubbed the cut tobacco fine and made a cigarette. Lighting it with a cinder held upon his knife, he blew a thin blue cloud from his thick nostrils, and began slowly.

"Sí, sí, señor, they say that parties of the Reds have been about the Gualeguay, not twenty leagues away. López Jordán[3] is moving southward with a horde of Correntinos, infidels who all speak Guaraní. From Villaguay down to Calá, and right through Montiel, scarcely a horse is left, and all the beasts they kill they roast with the hide on, so that there is a double loss, both of the meat and hide."

A "Sí, señor," half whispered, was his answer, and through the door, glistening amongst the leaves of the peach *monte*, the giant fireflies, known as tulipanes, flitted like humming-birds that had been rubbed with phosphorus, and from the plain, stretching out white in the bright moonlight, the acrid scent of sheep floated upon the air, their bleating in the fold seeming like distant bells. Occasionally dogs barked, and now and then the shrill chajá repeated his wild note and flapped his horny wings with a strange hollow sound.

[3] A provincial caudillo who rebelled against the government of President Sarmiento, before being finally silenced in 1876. This is the uprising in which Graham was embroiled. See the introduction.

Gregorio, suddenly starting to his feet, went out, and after listening anxiously, lay down, and, with his ear close to the ground, remained a little motionless, then getting up said, "Just at the pass, you know, where the tall seibo grows, I hear the noise of a large body of armed men."

"Why armed?" one of the maté drinkers said.

"Firstly, because no body so considerable as this is likely to be out at night except in arms, and secondly, because I hear steel scabbards ring, which probably are those worn by the officers, for the men wear them sticking through their girths."

In the twinkling of an eye the quiet kitchen was in confusion, and the two brothers hurriedly kissed their mother and, rushing out to where their horses fed attached to stake ropes, mounted in haste, barebacked, and quickly gathering up the horses feeding round their mare, whom they released as if by magic, one brother slipping off his horse as lightly as a leaf falls from a tree, to take the bell from off her neck, like shadows disappeared into the night, all the loose horses galloping in front.

A dropping shot or two and a wild galloping of unseen horses showed that the brothers had been seen by the advanced guard of the marauding party, but soon the unfamiliar noises died away, and left the plain silent and peaceful and as if nothing more was passing than the quiet setting of the stars.

Inside the kitchen the night wore on, with now and then a prayer, and with the maté going round from hand to hand, and now and then the negro *capataz* went out, lay down and listened, and coming back, sat gravely down, saying that he heard nothing, but that the Three Marías were getting low on the horizon, and then it was time for sleep, seeing that even they, the blessed three, set in the heavens by God Himself to keep the holy Trinity before men's eyes, would soon retire to rest.

The mother of the boys, escorted by her negro maidservant, carrying a kettle in her hand so that her mistress might take a maté before she went to bed, went out, and passed into the grey light of the coming dawn; passing beneath the stunted China trees, skirting the well round which a pack of yellow dogs as lean as wolves were sleeping, who blinked at them and then dozed off again.

The women stopped before the entrance to the low white house, listened intently for a moment just as wild horses listen, even before they are alarmed, and then quietly closed the door, almost mechanically, as if they had been walking in their sleep.

The *capataz*, left all alone, smoked silently for a few minutes, then rising, he extinguished the *candil* which burned in an inverted mare's bell, stuck between the mouldings of a broken cattle brand driven into the earthen floor. Then, taking off his *chiripá*, he placed his knife close to his hand, just underneath his saddle, and stretching himself out, his feet towards the fire, wrapped himself in his poncho, and fell asleep. Towards daylight he was roused by the dogs barking, and, looking out in the first light of the false dawn, saw a man riding a tired horse, hatless and wet, advancing to the house. Taking his long silver-handled *facón* in his left hand, concealed beneath the poncho which had covered him asleep, he cautiously advanced to the *palenque*, and waited till the man came up. At twenty yards away he knew him, and called out, "Ah! *patroncito*, what has happened? Where are your brother and the horses?" But a glance at the exhausted rider showed him that something untoward had occurred. Sliding off, all in one motion, so quickly that his right foot almost seemed to touch the ground before the left, and yet so quietly that he scarce moved the dew upon the grass, the young man slipped the bridle from his horse, which stood a moment hanging its head, with flanks tucked up and the wet dew clinging upon its quarters; and then, shaking like a retriever dog, lay down and rolled, then shook itself again, and quietly began to feed.

Lifting the dried mare's hide, that hanging from two pegs served as a door, they passed into the kitchen, and then the *capataz* had blown the ashes of the banked-up fire into a glow, and thrown a bundle of dried thistle stalks upon it, he heated water, and, handing the young man a maté, said, "Drink, *patroncito*, and tell me what it is. Where is your brother? Is he alive, or riding in the plains of Trapalanda, as the Indians say?"

Sucking the hot and bitter liquid to the dregs, Panchito then began: "No, ño Gregorio, my brother is not dead, and luckily only rides with a party of the Colorados who came upon us with our horses swimming the river, and waited for us to come out, just as a man sent forward in an ostrich hunt waits for the driven birds. My brother turned his horse to cross again, but as he did so, a party lined the bank we just had left, and took him prisoner at once. I let my hat drop in the stream to draw their fire, and threw myself beside my horse, and when we touched the shore, darted at once full speed into the woods. They fired, but missed me, and the trees prevented them from throwing *bolas* at my horse. So here I am safe, tired, and wet, with all our horses gone, and my poor brother Cruz obliged to serve amongst the Colorados as long as General López keeps the field."

As they sat talking, little by little the sun rose through the mist, which hung on every blade of grass and fell in drops off the low eaves of the estancia buildings, and clung about the coats of animals. Vizcachas peeped out timidly from their holes, and tucotucos sounded their last note from underneath the ground, before retiring for the day. Sheep bleated in the fold, and cattle, sleeping on the highest ground that they could find, stretched out their heads, but did not rise to eat, knowing the wet, white dew upon the grass would be injurious to them, whilst from the *monte* by the riverside the noise of myriads of birds just waking filled the air with sound.

"Let us go out and meet the sun as do the accursed Indians in the far south of Buenos Aires, where I once was a soldier," Gregorio said.

Rising, they went out to the door, and as they stood and scanned the plain, a noise of galloping fell on their ears.

"What have we done," Panchito said, "to irritate the Lord that he allows another band of these accursed Reds to visit us? Providence surely cannot remember that our father was a White?"

Suddenly over a low hill a man appeared racing upon a barebacked horse, his knife between his teeth. After him swept a band of ragged soldiers, some getting out their *bolas* for a throw. Both onlookers recognized at once the rider and his horse.

"My brother Cruz." "Yes, on his blue roan horse," the *capataz* replied. Even as they spoke, the foremost soldier, with a long cast of the *bolas*, caught the blue roan round the hind legs, and with a plunge or two he fell, and the pursuers gathered round their prey. Leading upon their horses, the agonized onlookers scoured to the place, and just arrived to hear a sergeant say, "We must make an example; the young man has been once within our ranks, besides, his father was a cursed White—you negro there, dismount and cut his throat."

Pale and disordered with his fall, Cruz stood, disarmed and helpless, looking mechanically at the rising sun, knowing he saw it for the last time upon earth. Its light fell on his face, flushing his cheeks and bathing all the group of gauchos and their horses in its life-giving rays. Facing about, the sergeant cried, "Keep those men back till I have finished with this dog," and then signing the negro forward, who advanced, drawing his knife and scenting blood, just as a wolf lays bare its fangs before he pounces on a lamb, with a quick movement threw the prisoner on his face, wrenched back his head, and plunged his dagger in his throat. With a convulsive movement and a whistling sound, as when the air is suddenly let out of a pricked bladder, the blood gushed out, staining the grass, and feet of the impassive gauchos who stood round. The victim's eyes glazed slowly, then turned back horribly, exposing all the white, and a convulsive grin deformed his features, whilst the negro pressed his body with his foot, just as a butcher presses the body of a sheep, to cause the blood to flow. A few convulsive movements of the legs showed life was passing, and then the body lay extended on the grass, helpless and limp, and looking like a bundle of old clothes.

The sergeant spoke the funeral oration, as the negro wiped his knife, saying, "The young man might have made a soldier, for he was brave, and was no miser of his throat."

Then they all mounted, lightly as a flock of birds, and struck across the plain, their horses leaving a dark trail as they brushed through the dew-bespangled grass.

Panchito, slipping off, cast himself on his brother's body with a groan, mechanically throwing the reins over his horse's head upon the ground to stop him moving off. The horse snorted a little at the fresh-spilt blood, and then stood like a statue, outlined and motionless against the sky, in the full glare of the new-risen sun.

LA TAPERA

Men, as they loped across the pampa on their horses, greeting each other from afar, as sailing ships speak at a distance, running down the trades, used to avoid the place. Round the remains of the deserted house, and all about the grass-grown mounds, which once had been adobes, but which the winter rains had melted back to mud, straggled remains of a deserted peach grove. Cattle and horses had rubbed the trees till they shone bright as a malacca cane, and sheep had left their wool in the rough fibres near the roots. A squat ombú, shaped like an umbrella, grew near the fallen-in well, and cast its shade at midday on a stray horse or cow, for people shunned the spot, knowing *las ánimas* at night made it their trysting-place. Thus, reasoning men, though not afraid, being aware their baptism would shield them from the attacks of ghosts or evil spirits, yet did not care to take the risk of riding through the peach *monte* of the *tapera*, as the deserted house was called. For "squares" on every side of it stretched a gigantic warren of land-crabs, in which a horse sank to the shoulder without warning, and wags, when heated at the *pulpería* with square-faced gin or caña, used to say that the real reason of the ill fame which the place enjoyed was from the danger of its *cangrejal*. But the same men, the fumes of caña or of gin evaporated, were no more anxious than the rest to ride up to the place, or give their horses water at the well, although no land-crab's hole had any terrors for them. No matter how or when their horses fell, they were all certain to come off upon their feet, holding their reins or halter in their hands.

Even at noonday, when the shade of the ombú spread grate-fully over the cracked and gaping earth, and lizards flattening themselves against the stones drank in the sunbeams, reflecting gems of light from their prismatic backs, and when in the still air a hum of insects made the deserted ranchería appear to be in-habited with midday ghosts, no one off-saddled by the well. At evening as the sun sank out of sight, dipping at once below the flat horizon, as it had been at sea, vizcachas sat and chattered on their mounds, and teru-teros, flying low, uttered their wailing cry, men passing by settled their hats upon their heads, and whirling their *rebenques* in the air, passed like the Walkyrie,[1] their ponchos fluttering in the wind. At night the armadillos emerging from their holes trotted about, looking as if they had survived from some old world in which they knew the pterodac-tyl and iguanodon. Then terror glued the hair of those who, passing in the offing of the grassy sea, imagined that the fireflies flitting in the trees were spirits, whilst the harsh cry of the chajá re-echoed through the night as if some soul, which had departed confessionless and lost, bemoaned its fate. Yet, of itself, nothing in the *tapera* spoke of anything but natural decay, and nothing made it different from any other house, deserted on the plains, either from natural causes or from Indians' attack.

By the slow, yellow, deep-sunk stream below it, pampa-grass and sarandí grew thickly, and from the muddy banks small landslips fell as the water lapped against them in the floods, and tortoises now and again put up their heads, and when alarmed sank out of sight, as if a stone had fallen into the pools. One pictured in one's mind the house peopled and cheerful, with its corral for horses and for cows, all made of ñandubay secured by thongs, each post seeming a knee from some wrecked vessel, and honeycombed by ants, which yet could not destroy its iron heart. The smell of folded sheep bleating at daybreak in the enclosure made of prickly bush entered the nostrils of the mind instinc-tively, and in the wiry grass tame horses fed, grouped round their bell-mare, whilst ostriches mingled familiarly with cows and stalked about close up to the corrals, as in the still clear air the tucotuco's cry rose up from underneath the ground.

[1] According to the Norse myth, the Valkyrie or Walkyrie were Odin's hand-maidens who selected those destined to be slain in battle. Wagner used the myth as the basis for his opera *The Walkyrie*, first produced in 1870.

Nothing spoke of a tragedy, as happens often when men travel to a spot where some king met his death, and find a tea-garden set up, with the slain despot's effigy used for advertisement. But no advertisement defiled the lonely place, and grasshoppers still twittered in the sun, and paroquets flew chattering through the trees, and over all the sun shone brassily, exaggerating all, till on the plain a distant rider loomed like a windmill, an ostrich seemed a tree, and birds upon the wing low down upon the edge of the horizon bulked large as bullocks, whilst the pale pampa deer at every spring covered a league of sight. Sometimes a traveller in the heated atmosphere discerned a lake, and, riding to it, found himself standing dryshod on the spot which he had seen with water lapping to the reedy edges of the pool. Cities arose and hung roof downwards in the air, and castles (those of Trapalanda) formed in the sky, and trees upon the farther side of hills were visible, their roots growing in the sky, whilst their boughs floated like the arms of some great jelly-fish in a backwater on a beach. Now and again, and looking carefully on this side and on that, two gauchos, either looking for strayed horses or going to the neighbouring *esquina*, would meet upon the plain, and after greetings spoken from afar (for it is not a prudent thing to come up quickly to a man you do not know), rode up, and after asking with minuteness as to each other's health, got off their horses quietly, as cats get off a wall, and fastening them to the long tufts of grass, sat down to ask the news and pass the time of day. Then, if they had no cards, and when a cigarette had been laboriously made by chopping up tobacco with a knife long as a sword, and paper cut from a sheet as large as the announcement of a bull-fight, and fire procured with care and oaths from flint and steel, the talk would surely turn on the deserted house.

"Strange how it should be so, but so it is, that God the Father has divided all men into Whites and Reds, whereas the animals are of one party, eh, Tío Chinche?"

"Well, ño Carancho," the other would reply, "the animals are animals, but why is it that you say this?"

"Ah yes—yes, sí, señor, I recollect it well. López Jordán was then our chief, and we had galloped all the province, from the Ibicuy right to the frontier by the Yucari, close to the Mocoretá, and into Corrientes, where men all speak the Guaraní, a heathen speech scarce fitter for a Christian than is Neapolitan or English, or any of the idioms which the gringos jabber in their beards. Jordán, as you remember, was a Red, and so was I—why—ah, yes, why—because my father was one, and because a party of the Reds had taken me, and, as you know, once in the files, there is no pardon if a man deserts.

"Well, as I said, for months we wandered up and down, fighting and killing all the Whites we met—the good times, eh?"

"Me pango, dijo el chimango." [2]

"Good times, yes, times for men. The cattle that we killed, and ate their beef cooked in its hide, the houses that we burned— Women—yes—but I have had my absolution—from a priest in Gualeguay, and did my penitence, walking on foot a month, beside the infantry, Canario—women—why, brother, were you never in the wars?

"So, one day, after months of the work, months without ever drinking broth or taking maté, and with the vice quite contraband, for black tobacco was not to be had, we came up to this place. I rode a half-tamed horse, a black with a white nose and feet, son of a mother who could never have said no; fitter, indeed, to be a perch for a wild bird than for the saddle of a Christian man. We came, I say, to where the walls of the *tapera* stand. It was not a *tapera* then, do you see; not a *tapera* but an estancia, well stocked, fit for the Anchorenas,[3] with sheep in the corrals and a *manada* of fat mares, all piebald, with colts fit for the saddle of a president.

"One we called Pancho Pájaro was in our ranks, a youth well favoured, and a rider fit to get on a wild colt and take it, to finish taming, to the moon. He galloped up, and said, "This is my father's house," and we who had hoped to plunder all the cattle and the sheep, for the estanciero was a White, were not best pleased, but still, as was our custom, were about to pass the house, as it was that belonging to the father of a comrade, and so was sacred; and besides the night was falling, and in war it is not prudent that you should camp close to a house, unless, of course, that it is burned. But as ill-luck, or good, would have it, for the thing turned out to our advantage, as we were wheeling into

[2] Obscure saying referring to the booty they took, and their way of taking it. See *pangar* in the glossary.

[3] An Argentine family, descended from the Spanish aristocracy, proverbially wealthy.

column, from the trees, a party of the accursed Whites broke cover, and charged upon us with a shout.

"I had no cartridges, and was obliged to rely upon 'white arms' entirely; and my horse without a mouth, and hot as if he had been nurtured on red pepper and dry wine of Spain, gave me but little chance. Crack went the guns, and *lazos* whistled, *bolas* hurtled through the air, and as God willed it, or His Blessed Mother chose, we routed them, and they fled through the trees, just as the night was coming on.

"Pancho, who rode on a cat-coloured horse, fat and well bitted, spurred out from the ranks, twisting the *bolas* round his hand, and launching them, threw and entangled the hind legs of the last White, just as his horse emerged from the peach grove out upon the plain."

"Ah, ño Carancho, that is the way—the *bolas*, eh!—the *bolas* do not deny the shot as pistols do."

"That is so, Tío Chinche, and, as I said, the horse, being caught round its hind legs, soon faltered, and Pancho, riding like the wind, ranged up and drove his sword through the man's back, before that he had time to leave his saddle and seek the shelter of the trees. He fell without a groan, the blood staining a fine vicuña poncho, which I had hoped to buy from Pancho when the fight was done.

"He, getting off his horse, advanced and turned the body over with his foot."

"To cut his throat, eh, ño Carancho?"

"Yes, and to cut out your tongue, thief of the sacrament, who stops a man upon his tale, as he who draws off his attention just as he swings his *lazo* in the air.—There was no need, for the man fell dead as Namuncurá,[4] and the moon falling on his face showed Pancho that he had killed his brother, and from that time would be accursed of God.

"That is the story, gossip, and the reason that the house became deserted; for Pancho, wandering away, turned infidel, and lived with the wild Indians till his death, and his old father dying without sons, the rancho fell into decay. God in His mercy made all kinds of men, the Whites and Reds alike; He sets them up and down, as we do ninepins, and all life is a fandango."

[4]Manuel Namuncurá, an Argentine caudillo, who for a spell ruled the pampa, before submitting to Colonel Belisle in 1886.

"Yes, ño Carancho, but all do not dance, eh?"

Then, slowly saddling up, they used to mount, and strike into a little trot until they came to a slow-running stream, where, after watering their horses, and exchanging salutations, they would separate and sink into the plain, as birds sink out of sight into the sky.

UN ANGELITO

All day we had been riding over the south campo of the prairie of Buenos Aires, between the mountains of Tandil and where the trail which led to Bahía Blanca crosses the Tres Arroyos.

It seemed that never had our *tropilla* given so much trouble to drive; still it was well selected, both as to colour and general undesirability to ride. The mare was brown and white, the foal which followed her lemon and white with four black feet, the horses black and white, all with their manes well hogged after the gaucho fashion, leaving a lock upon the withers by which to mount; and all in such condition that one could have counted money on their backs—two of them were neither tame nor wild; two neither wild nor tame; two but half broken, one difficult to mount, another almost impossible to catch, and when caught, worth nothing but to fasten to a stake at night to drive the others up on in the morning; and one but fitted, as the gauchos say, to make a perch for a wild bird.

The suffocating north wind blew hot and fatiguing as the Hamsin. On every side a sea of grass, grass and more grass; "*paja y cielo*" (grass and sky), as the natives of the country style their favourite landscape.

Nothing to break the brown eternity of the pampa but here and there a green ombú, shaped like an umbrella, or an occasional straggling line of pampa grass, which marked the edges of some watercourse, and by comparison seemed as tall as does a poplar in the plains of Lombardy.

An ostrich now and then scudded across our path, with wings

119

spread out to catch the wind, like a ship running down the North-East Trades.

Sometimes a Patagonian hare sprang from the grass and lurched, apparently quite slowly, out of sight.

In the district we were crossing, all the rivers salt, and, though as clear as crystal, bitter as gall. The rare travellers, seen from afar, almost hull down like ships upon the sea, grew by degrees larger as they approached, and hat, and poncho, and then saddle and horse came into sight.

When they drew near, they drove their horses all together, and coming forward, riding from side to side, holding their pistol or *facón*, advanced, halted a stone-throw off, shouting their salutations. If all seemed right, they then advanced and asked for news about the Indians; for all the country had been laid waste, the houses burnt, men killed, and women and cattle carried off, about a week before.

It usually appeared that the next house—that is, the one the traveller had left three leagues behind—was smouldering, the body of the owner lying before the door, swollen to the dimensions of an ox and festering in the sun.

We in our turn related how at the *puesto* five leagues away, close to the pass of the Quequén Salado, we had seen a woman's body hanging naked to a post, and decorated with leaves torn from a Bible skewered artistically about it where decency required.

With mutual recommendations to have prudence, to beware of smokes, to ride with care, to get off at the little hills which break the pampa into inequalities, and crawling up to scan the horizon well before descending, we separated with a fallacious "Go with God," knowing full well our only trust was in our spurs.

Not quite the sort of time that any one would choose to sleep out on the open "camp."

Towards evening we reached what in those countries is called, by courtesy, a fort—that is, it had been once a fort, and therefore had a shallow ditch all round it, and a flat roof, on which reposed a rusty cannon, choking the embrasure.

Around the fort a grove of peaches, known as the *monte*, straggled and furnished a fruit, hard as a turnip, but esteemed a delicacy upon the plains.

A strong corral of posts of ñandubay, all bound together with strips of hide, and a *palenque*—that is, a post to fasten horses to—formed the outworks to the place.

The *palenque* marks the boundary to which the wayfaring man, if not a fool, may safely venture on his horse.

To pass beyond it uninvited, especially at night, exposes one to the chance of a casual shot, or at the least to the assaults of a pack of dogs which seize your horse's tail.

Your caballero leaves his horses some way off, and rides up slowly, and still sitting on his horse, calls *"Ave María!"* in a loud voice, to which the owner answers, *"Sin pecado concebida,"* [1] and invites him to get off.

Religion and politeness being thus satisfied, the traveller dismounts, ties up his horse, enters the kitchen, and sits down on a horse's head beside the fire.

The quantity of saddled horses standing outside the house portended something of an unusual kind.

To the *palenque*, to the wheels of bullock-carts, to posts in corral, to tufts of grass, to bones half-buried in the ground, stood horses tied.

Every variety of the piebald race was there—*overo negro, alazán overo, entrepelado, overo porcelano, azulejo*, with *tuviano* and *yaguané*— they all were there, looking as bright and variegated as is a bed of tulips in the setting sun.

Some of them merely hobbled by the forefeet, and weighted down with silver bridles, with heavy "cups" on either side of the mouth, with silver reins seven feet in length tied back upon the saddles, making them arch their necks like rocking-horses; the saddles silver-mounted, silver their *fiadores* and *pretales*, silvered so to speak, like clippers, to the bends; the very rings which formed the buckles of their broad hide girths being of heavy plate. Others, again, were saddled with an old *recado*, not worth a dollar (even of Bolivia); a sheepskin on the top, the stirrups merely knots of hide made to be caught between the naked toes. These last sat back on their *cabrestos* and snorted as you passed them, causing their owners to rush hurriedly from out the house to see if there was danger of their saddles disappearing, and then to mutter, when the horse was quieted, that he was *medio redomón* (that is, but mounted a few times), "for the accursed infidel

---

[1] "Hail, Mary! Conceived without sin."

had taken all the tame horses and left the *pago* upon foot." It puzzled me to think why after an invasion of the Indians so many people had come to visit my acquaintance, Eustaquio Medina, known also as Eustaquio el Tejón.

Soon he came out and welcomed me, asking me to dismount, hobble my mare, and carefully tie up a horse, remarking that in the times we lived Christians should take precautions and always live prepared.

The flesh, the devil, and the world were not the things against which Eustaquio thought a true believer should prepare—at least I think so—for, if he ever thought about such matters, he judged most likely it was the business of his priest to shield him from the devil; the world in the pampas is not too distracting to the mind, and for the flesh he made no struggle, thinking that that which God had made must of necessity be good for man.

After most minute inquiries after the health of all my family, of whom he knew no member, he said—

"We have *un angelito* in our poor house—that is, his body; for his soul is with the blest."

The conscious pride of being, as it were, in direct touch with heaven itself had caused him to forget his grief for his son's death. No people upon earth can be more absolutely material than the gauchos of the pampa, yet one is just as safe amongst them, even in a bargain, as amongst those who analyse their motives and find a spiritual explanation for the basest of their deeds.

Amusements, except ostrich-hunting, cattle-marking, with racing, and others of a nature in which it is not easy for women to participate, are scarce. When a child dies it is the signal for a dance to celebrate its entrance into bliss.

If the Christian faith was really held by anybody in its entirety, this custom would not be solely to be observed amongst the gauchos. As it is, humanity in almost every other country rises superior even to faith, that first infirmity of uninstructed minds.

So in a long, low room lit by a score of candles, made in tin-moulds, and smoking blackly, were assembled some fifty people, gauchos, estancieros, a Basque or two, and the ubiquitous Italian with his organ, who in those days used to pervade the pampa from the Arroyo del Pabón to Tapalqué.

The women, known as *chinas*, though none knows why or wherefore, did not err much upon the score of great expenditure in dress—a cotton gown, apparently in many cases their only garment, except their shift—sat, when not dancing, in rows on chairs along the wall, like swallows on a telegraph-wire, waiting as patiently for any man to hire them as the eleventh-hour labourers in Holy Writ.

The *angelito*, dressed in his best clothes, sat in a chair upon a table, greenish in colour, and with his hands and feet hanging down limply—horrible, but at the same time fascinating. Over his head a cheap Italian lithograph of the Madonna hung by a strip of hide from a deer's horn stuck into the wall. On either side a pious and frightful German print, one of the Prodigal amongst his swine, another flanking it setting him forth in better circumstances, seated in pomp between two German ladies, monstrously fair and fat.

Just underneath the *angelito* sat an old gaucho playing the guitar with the fatuous air with which musicians in countries such as South America invest their trade. Two or three men of the richer classes, as their silver-handled knives and spurs made plain, smoked in a knot apart, whilst in a corner sat some old men talking of horses' marks, and illustrating any difficulty by "painting" the mark in question on the table with their finger dipped in gin.

The younger people danced habaneras, el cielito, the gato, manguri, or one of those slow valses with much balancing of hips affected by the South Americans. Evidently they had been drinking to the fair passage of the new angel into the realms of bliss. Above the rasping music the rattle of the dancers' spurs was heard, and now and then the man at the guitar broke into a shrill falsetto song, in which the company took part. Stretched on a *catre* lay a man wrapped in his poncho, with a deep lance-wound in the groin, given by an Indian a few days before. To keep his blood in order and heal his wound he ate great pieces of beef cooked in the hide, and smoked incessantly.

On passing opposite the body the girls occasionally snatched loose their hands from the clutches of their partners and crossed themselves, and then, as if ashamed of thus indulging in a religious exercise in public, broke into laughter.

Why the presence of a child's body, even if its soul is with the blessed, should set on folk to dance passes my comprehension. Yet so it is, and a commercial element has crept into the scheme.

At the country stores, called *pulperías* in Buenos Aires, sometimes the owner will beg or buy the body of a child just dead to use it as an *angelito* to attract the country people to a revel at his store.

The *pulpería* is the pampa club, news, calumny, and scandal take their rise in it, and there resort all the elite of frontier ruffianism.

One says as naturally, "What do they say at the *pulpería*? as in England, "What is the news at such and such a club, or on the Stock Exchange?" An *angelito* stored in a cool, dark room to keep him from the flies, and then brought out at night to grace a sort of Agapemone,[2] shows past and present linked together in a way which argues wonders, when they both make way for that unfathomable future, the fitting paradise for unimaginative men. From where the custom came, whether from Europe or from the Indians, or if in some form or another it is to be observed in every nation, that I cannot tell: one thing I know, that, in the pampa of Buenos Aires, it and all other customs of a like kind are doomed to disappear.

A cultivated prairie cut into squares by barbed wire fences, riddled with railings and with the very sky shaped into patterns by the crossing lines of telegraphs, may be an evidence, for all I know, of progress; but of all that which makes a pampa what the Indians imagined it when they gave the plains the name—for pampa in the Indian tongue signifies the "space"—no traces will be left.

The semi-nomad horsemen will have vanished; the Indians have gone within my memory, leaving, though savages, by their disappearance, a blank in the world more difficult to fill than if the works of all the Greeks had vanished into air.

The gaucho will go next, the ostriches and the huanacos; little by little the plants of Europe, those parasitic prostitutes, the nettle and the thistle, which follow us to every climate, will usurp the place of native and more congenial kinds.

His will will be accomplished who, having made the earth a paradise, gave it to us to turn into a purgatory for ourselves and all the dwellers in it.

[2] Meaning "abode of love," Agapemone was an institution founded by Henry James Prince in 1845 at Charlinch, Somerset, England. Prince and his followers lived on a communist basis, holding certain spiritual beliefs. Agape originally meant a "love-feast" held by the early Christians in connection with the Lord's Supper.

In this monotony of mud and stucco, through the noise of cabs, of railways and the multitudinous sounds which rob the dweller in a city of any power of hearing such as wild people have, I sometimes see my *angelito* seated in his chair, and wonder in what kind of heaven he is. Often I have assisted at a *velorio*, and done my best to honour the return of some small angel to his native land. Yet this first occasion on the Tres Arroyos still remains most firmly printed in my mind. Eustaquio Medina, the wounded man lying smoking on his *catre*, the decomposing *angelito* in his chair, his mother looking at nothing with her eyes wide open, and the wild music of the cracked guitar seem to revisit me.

Lastly, the pampa stretching away like a great inland sea, silent, and bluish under the southern stars; and rising from it the mysterious noises of the desert which, heard and comprehended, appeal to us in the same fashion as the instinct, calling them north or south, stirs migratory birds.

SAN ANDRÉS

Someone or other has said the dead have a being of their own, as we confess by saying such a one is dead, just as we say he is alive.

The author of the saying seems to have felt the dead had feelings and were not merely essences purified, quite separate and unapproachable by us. Few wish to see, even to think about, their dead "crowned with an aureole." We want them just as they were, just as we knew them, in their life. The rest is vanity, vanity of vanities, and all the creeds are impotent to help. At best they are an anaesthetic, such as curare, which holds the suffering animal paralysed, so that the operator may not feel the pain that it endures or get his hands scratched. So we grieve on, watching the trees turn red and yellow in the fall, blossom again in spring, and be alive with bees in summer, in winter swaying and cracking in the wind.

This is because we never feel the dead have a distinct and real being of their own. In olden times, in Scotland, people thought differently, and it was held that too much grieving for the dead vexed them and broke their rest.

I remember once, coming long years ago to an outlying settlement in the province of Buenos Aires, where all the people came, I think, from Inverness-shire; but, anyhow, once on a time they had been Scotch. Their names were Highland, but were pronounced by those who bore them after the Spanish way, as Camerón, and McIntyré, McLeán, Fergusón, and others, which they had altered in the current of their speech, so as to be

126

unrecognisable except to those who spoke the language and knew the names under their proper forms.

None of these Scoto-Argentines spoke English, although some knew a few words of Gaelic, which I imagine they pronounced as badly as their names.

Four generations—for most of them had left their glens after Culloden[1] —had wrought strange changes in the type. They all were dark, tall, sinewy men, riders before the Lord, and celebrated in the district where they lived as being *muy gaucho*—that is, adroit with *bolas* and lasso, just as the Arabs say a man is a right Arab, when they commend his skill in horsemanship. Having left Scotland after the Forty-Five, most of their forebears had been Catholics, and their descendants naturally belonged to the same faith, though as there was no church in all their settlement I fancy most of them believed rather in meat cooked in the hide and a good glass either of caña or Carlón than dogmas of their creed.

Horses stood nodding in the sun before the door of every house.

Packs of gaunt, yellow dogs slumbered, with one eye open, in the shade.

The bones of the last cow killed lay in the little plaza of the settlement, and bullock-carts, with cumbrous, high wheels and thatched-like cottages, were left as islands here and there in the great sea of grass that surged up to the houses, without a garden or a cultivated field to break its billowing.

Two little stores, in which were piled up hides and sacks of wood, supplied the place with the few outside luxuries the people used, as sardines, black cigarettes, figs, raisins, bags of hard biscuits, sugar, red wine from Catalonia, and caña from Brazil.

Climate had proved a stronger force than race, and for the most part the descendants of the Gael were almost indistinguishable in looks from all the other dwellers on the plains. They themselves did not think so, and talked about their neighbours with a fine scorn as "natives," and were paid back in kind by them with the nickname of *"Protestantes,"* a most unjust reproach to the

---

[1] The tragic battle (1746) in which Prince Charles Edward, "Bonnie Prince Charlie," was defeated by the English. This put an end to the Jacobite Rising.

descendants of the men who lost their all for their old kings and faith.

Protestants they certainly were not, nor for that matter very Catholic, for, as a general rule, people who dwell on plains, far from the world, have less religion than those who live in hills. Still, in the settlement of San Andrés—for the first settlers had called it after the patron saint of their old home—some of their racial traits still lingered fitfully. Born in a country where neither sweet religion nor her twin sister superstition ever had much influence upon the people (who ever saw a gaucho either religious or the least superstitious?),[2] in San Andrés a belief in fairies and the second sight still lingered in men's minds, with many a superstition more consonant with mountains and with mists than the keen atmosphere and the material life of the wild southern plains.

Unlike the gauchos and the Arabs, who bury, as it seems in the most open place that they can find, leaving the dead, as it were, always with the living, as if they thought the pressure of a passing foot somehow brought consolation to those lying beneath the ground, these Protestants railed off their little cemetery with a high fence of ñandubay. The untrimmed posts stuck up knotty and gnarled just as they do in a corral, but all the graves had head- and foot-stones, mostly of hard and undecaying wood, giving an air as of a graveyard in Lochaber by some deserted strath.

There, "Anastasio McIntyré, killed by the Indians," rested in peace. "May God have mercy on him."

A little further on, "Cruz Camerón, assassinated by his friends," expected glory through the intermediation of the saints. "Passers-by, pray for him."

Amparo, widow of Rodrigo Chisholm, lost at sea, had reared a monument in stone, brought from the capital, on which was cut a schooner foundering, with a man praying on the poop. Her pious faith in his salvation and a due sense of local colour showed themselves in a few lines of verse in which the poet, whilst deploring the sad fate of Roderick, cut off so far away from wife

[2]One cannot agree with Graham completely in his interpretation of the gaucho mind. See *Martín Fierro* and some of Graham's own sketches for examples of gaucho superstition. Richard Haymaker makes the same criticism in *Prince Errant and Evocator of Horizons*, p. 168.

and family, was confident that heaven was just as close at sea as on *la tierra firme*, and that the Lord High Admiral Christ watched over seafarers.

Such was the village, or, as the gauchos used to say, the *pago*, for, for a league or two on every side, these Scoto-Argentines were the chief settlers upon the land. Indians occasionally harried their flocks and herds and burned outlying ranches, but nowhere found stouter resistance than from the dwellers in San Andrés, so that, as a general rule, they used to leave the settlement alone.

The patriarchal manners which their forefathers had brought from the Highlands, joined to the curious old-fashioned customs common in those days in Buenos Aires, had formed a race apart, in which Latin materialism strove with the Celtic fervour, and neither gained the day.

A grave sententiousness marked all the older men, whose speech was an amalgam of strange proverbs, drawn from their daily lives. They used to pass their evenings playing the guitar and improvising couplets, whilst the square bottle of trade gin went round, each sipping from the same glass and passing it along. "Never go to a house to ask for a fresh horse when you see that the dogs are thin," one tall, red-bearded man would say, to which his fellow answered, "Arms are necessary, but no one can tell when." "A scabby calf lives all the winter and dies when spring comes in," and "When a poor man has a spree something is sure to turn out wrong with him" were specimens of their wit and humour, not much inferior after all to those recorded of much greater men than them in serious histories.

Sheep-shearings and cattle-markings were their festivities, and now and then, on their best horses, loaded down with plate, they tilted at the ring. The grassy pampa, stretching like the sea on every side of them, but broken as with islands here and there by white estancia houses set in their ring of peach groves, limited their horizon, just as a sailor's view is limited on board a ship to a scant league or two.

In that horizon all of them were born, and most of them had never passed outside of it, except some few who upon rare occasions had gone to Buenos Aires with a troop of cattle, and had returned to talk about its wonders for the remainder of their lives.

Still, none of them were boors, but had the natural good

manners both of the gaucho and the Highlander. The forms of courtesy were long and ceremonious, and when friends met upon the plain, reining their horses in to show how sharply they were bitted, they used to ask minutely after each other's health and of the state in which each member of the family found himself, and then, with an inquiry after a strayed colt, touching their stiff-brimmed hats with a brown, weather-beaten finger, just slack their reins a little and separate, each going at a slow canter through the grass, the wind blowing their ponchos out like sails, and making their long hair wave about like a great bunch of water-weeds moved by the current of a stream.

This was the settlement which no doubt not long ago has turned into a town, with modern improvements, electric lights and drains, beggars and churches; and the few settlers of the older type most probably have all retired into the wilder districts or become millionaires by the increasing value of their lands.

There, though, the older spirit ruled, and the men who spoke Gaelic, or even those whose fathers once had spoken what they called *el gaélico*, were looked upon as the interpreters of the spirit of the race. Of these Don Alejandro Chisholm was the chief.

Tall and grey-bearded, he had that look of shagginess which marks the Highlander. Though he knew but a few words himself, his father used to croon old Gaelic songs, and all his childhood had been passed listening to the traditions which his people treasured in their minds. Somehow they looked upon them as their chief distinction, and seemed to feel by their possession that they were in some way or another superior to the rest of those with whom they lived, the men who passed their lives caring for nothing but the present, whilst they lived in the past.

Don Alejandro used to say: "A native has very little soul. When a friend dies he never thinks of him again, and still less sees him. We, on the other hand, have glimpses now and then of those who leave us, but whose spirits hover about the places that they love."

His daughter, Saturnina, a tall, dark girl, willowy and slight, had married Anacleto, her first cousin, and thus, as her father, with true Highland pride in lineage, used to observe, had never changed her name. Her husband, Anacleto, was an amalgam of the Scot and Argentine. Speaking no word of English or of Gaelic, he yet esteemed himself as half a foreigner, although he was a gaucho to the core. He and his wife were married in a church, a circumstance which marked them out, and people speaking of them used to say they were the couple "married in Latin," which gave them much consideration and a sort of rank. Whether because of the unusual sanctity that blessed their union, from accident or natural causes, their marriage was so happy that throughout the settlement people spoke of a happy couple as being as well mated as *el matrimonio Chisholm*, and looked on them with pride, as being somehow on a different plane from those who perhaps were married by some ambulatory priest after their children had been born.

They had no children, and perhaps on that account were more attached to one another than are those couples whose love is, as it were, dispersed, having more objects on which to spend itself.

There seemed to grow between them that curious identity of mind which comes to all women and all men who have lived long together, but in their case was so much marked that they divined beforehand each other's thoughts, and acted on them almost without words. On the long journeys which the husband took with cattle, his wife used to declare she always knew all he was thinking of, and he, on his return, either to please her, or because she really had guessed right, always confirmed her words. The idea of death sometimes must have presented itself before their minds, but, like most happy people, probably only as a calamity, which might befall humanity in general, but could not touch themselves.

Don Alejandro, who in his long life had seen misfortunes, and was the last of all his race except his daughter, used to look sadly on them, and shaking his grey head, say with a sigh: "God grant I may not live to see the death of either of them. The children, though it is a bad comparison, Lord pardon me for likening Christians to brute beasts, remind me of two horses that I had that followed one another. One broke its neck out ostrich-hunting, and the other never seemed right, and pined in misery after its friend had died."

The inevitable came, when Anacleto was away, far on the southern frontier, out on the *boleada*, beyond the Napostá.

Never before had he been so long separated from his wife. Three months had passed, and now, as he drew close to San Andrés, riding a tired horse, brown, dirty, and with the oppression that the north wind often brings in Buenos Aires weighing upon his mind, the well-known objects seemed to rise out of the plain, just as an island seems to rise out of the sea, although the men on board the ship know it is there, and have been laying off their course to make it, since the beginning of their voyage. He saw the peach *montes* which he had known from childhood circling his neighbours' farms. He crossed the sluggish, muddy stream, bordered with dark green sarandís, hitting the pass with the unerring accuracy of the man born upon the plains. Feeling his horse's mouth, he touched him with the spur, and struck into a lope. Passing the little inequalities of ground, the swells and billows which the dwellers on the pampa know as *lomas* or *cuchillas*, and recollect as well as Scotchmen recollect their hills, though they are almost imperceptible to strangers, he saw the well-remembered old ombú tree of the settlement. Eyes just as keen as were his own had seen him too, and to his great surprise a horseman galloped out to meet him, and as he came a little nearer he recognized the well-known piebald that Don Alejandro cherished as the apple of his eye. Sitting upright in the saddle, and swaying lightly, as if he had been five-and-twenty, to every movement of his horse, Don Alejandro rapidly drew near. Just about twenty yards from where his son-in-law was labouring along on his tired horse he checked the piebald, and stopped as if turned instantly to stone. "Welcome, my son," he said. "Your horse looks tired, but he will take you home quite soon enough."

The words froze upon Anacleto's lips when he looked at the old man's countenance and saw how white and drawn he had become.

"Tell me at once!" he cried; "I see the tidings in your face of evil augury."

When they had drawn a little nearer Don Alejandro grasped his hand, and after looking at the horse his son-in-law bestrode, pointed towards the little cemetery, and said: "Let us go there, my son.—If we go slowly your horse can carry you."

Dismounting at the gate, they tied their horses to a post, and entering, the old man led the traveller up to a little mound.

"Underneath this our treasure lies," he murmured gravely, and with the air of one who has got done with tears after long weeks of grief.

They stood and gazed, holding each other's hands, until Don Alejandro said: "Weep, son, for God has given tears for the soul's health.—Laughter and tears are the two things that lift us higher than the beasts."

His son-in-law threw himself on the grave, driving his fingers into the black soil, and lay there, tired, dirty, and unkempt, like a great wounded bird.

At last he felt a hand upon his shoulder, and heard a voice, which seemed to come from a great distance, saying: "Come, let us go now, and let our horses loose. In half an hour it will be night."

When they had reached their home they both unsaddled. The piebald, with a neigh, bounded away into the night, but Anacleto's horse stood for a moment, and then lay down and rolled, and rising, shook the dust out of his coat, just as a water-dog shakes himself after a long swim.

"He will do well," Don Alejandro said. "When a horse rolls like that after a journey it is a sign that he is strong."

Over the maté, seated round the fire, on the low, solid, wooden benches men used to use out on the pampa, the wanderer heard of how his wife had died.

Next day he passed seated upon her grave, silent and stupified with grief.

Then for a day or two he lounged about, going down to the cemetery at intervals and looking through the posts, like some wild animal.

Weeks passed, and he still roamed about, speaking to no one, but riding off across the plains, returning always just at sundown, to tie his horse up close to the cemetery gate and stand with his head pressed against the bars looking towards the grave. At last Don Alejandro, fearing that he was going mad, as they sat at the end of a hot day, began to speak to him, saying: "It is not well to grieve too long. It is, as we may say, a selfishness. My father, who knew the older generation, those who lost everything for their religion and their king, had listened in his youth to all the lore that they brought with them from that far region where, as they say, the mist blurs everything, My father spoke *gaélico*"—he said the word almost with reverence—" and those who spoke it always were versed in the traditions of our race. He used to tell me that to grieve for the dead beyond due measure disturbed them in their graves, and brought their spirits weeping back again. So I have dried my tears." As he said this he drew his hand across his eyes, and, looking at it, saw that it was dry.

"Grieve no more, Anacleto. We cannot call her back to us alive. To pain the spirit by our selfishness, that would be cowardly."

They sat till it was almost sunset, and then Don Alejandro went down to the corral to see the animals shut in, just in the way that he had gone each evening for the last forty years.

The sun set in a glare, the hot, north wind blowing as from a furnace, making the cattle droop their heads, and bringing troops of horses, with a noise like thunder, down to the water-holes.

The teru-teros, flying low, like gulls upon the sea, almost unseen in the fast-coming darkness, called uncannily. The tame chajá screamed harshly behind the cattle-pens.

A boy, riding upon a sheepskin, drove the tame horses into the corral.

The sheep were folded, and in the dark leaves of the old ombú beside the door, the fireflies glistened, and from the pampa rose the acrid smell that the first freshness of the evening draws from the heated ground. Coming out of the rancho Anacleto looked across the plain.

His eyes were full of tears, but with a gulp he choked them, and muttering to himself, "No, it would be cowardly to break her rest, Don Alejandro says so; he had it from his father, who spoke gaélico," he slowly lit a cigarette, and in the last rays of the light, watched the smoke curl up in the air, blue and impalpable.

FACÓN GRANDE

All the south-western frontier of the province of Buenos Aires, in the far-off days of which I write, was as wild and almost as dangerous as the *apachería* in Arizona. The pampa Indians who owed little to the Apaches in fierceness, cruelty, skill in horsemanship and general devilry, were the scourge of the whole frontier, from Tapalqué to the Gualichú Tree.

The rare estancias were like islands in the great sea of grass that flowed around them, just as waves surround atolls in the South Seas. Most of the estancia houses and the *pulperías* were fortified with a deep ditch, and some of them had a small brass cannon that was chiefly used to signal to the sparse neighbours, for naturally its range was short, and the Indians took care not to advance too near and separated when it was fired, so that it did but little execution on the open plain.

The life, wild, dangerous, and lonely, threw off strange characters, for only men of resolution, who held life cheaply, or outcasts from society, cared to settle in a district where the government could give scant protection and a man was ruined in a night by raiding Indians, who drove his cattle off and left him destitute.

Still there were some who, neither desperate nor outcasts, resolutely took up land and settled down. Of such the most remarkable was a tall Englishman whose name, I think, was Hawker, but better known as *"Facón Grande,"* [1] from the sword

[1]Graham's prodigious memory seems to have failed him here. My research indicates that "Facón Grande" was in fact Enrique J. Edwards. "Facón Chico"

bayonet that he wore stuck through his belt and sticking out
upon both sides after the fashion of the lateen yard of fishing-
boats in the Levant. Tall, dark, and wiry, his hair, that he wore
long, and ragged beard gave him the look of a stage desperado,
but in reality he was a brave and prudent man who knew quite
well the danger that he lived in, but was determined to hang on,
for he had faith in the country's future where he had made his
home.

As he had lived for many years upon the frontier, he dressed in
gaucho fashion, with loose black merino trousers tucked into
high boots. A white pleated shirt always left open at the neck, a
short alpaca jacket, with a broad belt fastened by what was called
a *rastra*, composed of silver coins that served as buttons, and an
Indian poncho, woven in red and black, completed what he
called his "indumentary."

He spoke a strange phonetic Spanish, blameless of grammar
and full of local words, as easily as English. A short half-league
away, his cousin lived, one Ferguson, known to the gauchos as
"*Facón Chico*," from the smaller size of the yet formidable knife
he carried. No greater contrast could be found than that between
the cousins. "*Facón Chico*" was about middle height with sandy
hair and a short well-cropped beard. His face was freckled and
his hands, mottled like a trout, had once been white, of that
unhealthy-looking hue that exposure to the sun often imparts to
red-headed or to sandy-coloured men. For all his quiet appearance and meek ways till roused, he was perhaps the bolder and
more daring of the two. The gauchos said, although he looked
like an archangel who had lost his wings, that in an Indian
skirmish his porcelain-coloured eyes shot fire and he became a
perfect devil, the highest compliment in their vocabulary.

Though he had lived for twenty years in the republic, he hardly
knew more than a few coherent sentences in Spanish, and those
so infamously pronounced that few could understand them.

Curiously enough he spoke Pehuelche fairly fluently, for he
had lived some years with an Indian woman, who, when she
went back to the *tolderia*, had left him as a pledge of their love, or
what you call it, a boy the gaucho humorists had christened

---

was not Hawker either, but Walker, John G.—an excusable *factual* slip, when
one considers this sketch was written more than sixty years after the events
described, but which in no way detracts from the *aesthetic* quality of the work.

"*Cortaplumas*," to the delight, not only of his father, but the whole neighbourhood.

The boy grew up amongst the peons neither exactly tame nor wild. Like other boys born in that outside "camp" upon the frontiers he ran about barefooted, lassoed the dogs and cats, and brought down birds with little *bolas* that he manufactured by himself out of old strips of hide and knuckle-bones. By the age of six or seven he, like all the other boys, was a good rider, climbing up on the saddle, using the horse's knees as a step-ladder for his bare little toes.

Once mounted, he had come into his kingdom, whirling his whip round his head and drumming ceaselessly with his bare heels upon the horse's side, he would set off at the slow machine-like gallop of the plains, either to help round up the horses for the day's work or to snare partridges with a noose at the end of a long cane.

He naturally, perhaps to prove his lineage, carried a knife large enough for a grown man to use, stuck in the pampa Indian wasteband, that kept up his ragged *chiripá*. His wiry jet-black hair stuck out below his hat, and fell upon his shoulders like a mane.

In everything he was a perfect type of the half-bred urchin in the outside "camps."

Had his Pehuelche mother not gone back to her own people, or his father had not married a douce Scottish Argentine, most likely "*Cortaplumas*" would have grown up a gaucho without education, and perhaps have disappeared one day to join his mother in the *toldos*, taking some of his father's best horses with him.

Some years of school in Buenos Aires certainly altered him from the teeth outwards (*de los dientes afuera*), as runs the Spanish saw, and he returned to the estancia a well-mannered silent youth but really little altered, if it is true that character and features go with us to the grave.

It looked as if he would have had as well known a name upon the frontier as his father and uncle, for the lad had remained as good a rider and as clever with the *lazo* as when he left his home. Fate had decreed it otherwise, and before he grew to man's estate the medium with which he might have earned his way to fame had disappeared. Little by little the Indians were forced back into the recesses of the valleys of the Andes. A railway was slowly pushed on right to Bahía Blanca. Lands that had but little value rose in price, and *"Cortaplumas"* had no field where he could have displayed the talents that I, his only chronicler, am certain, if there is anything in the doctrine of heredity, he must surely have possessed. So was a person born as it were with a silver-handled knife already in his belt, fated to leave behind him only the recollection of his delightful name. In those days when there was an Indian raid it always was announced by the arrival from what was known as the "inside country" of flocks of ostriches and bands of deer fleeing before the Indians' advance.

Luckily for the dwellers in their isolated estancias, the Indians never came by night, either from some superstition that they had, or because, even they, skilled as they were in desert travelling, could not find their way, unless there was a moon. Be that as it may, I never once remember a *malón* at night.

Unlike the Indians on the borderlands of Texas and Mexico, the pampa Indians seldom came in isolated bands of twenty or of thirty, but always raided in full force. Both of them always used to attack, if possible, just as the sun was rising, and though we had no *"Facón Grande"* in the north, we did as well as we were able with Wild Bill Hitchcock,[2] and other worthies, heroes who wanted but a Homer to have preserved their names and placed them on a level with Achilles and with Diomed.

Many and various were the types our frontier in the Argentine threw off.

Martín Villalba, at one time *alcalde* of Bahía Blanca, rises before me out of Trapalanda as I write, that Trapalanda, the mysterious country where good gauchos and their horses rode, their horses never tiring, sustained by never-failing grass and water, the nectar and ambrosia of the equine race, their riders never ageing and I suppose their saddlery never wearing out.

In that fair land of the imagination Martín Villalba will have by this time become the *compadre* of Don Segundo Sombra, Martín Fierro, and the immortal rider of *El Fausto*, on his roan and white skewbald, known to all Argentines as *"Lindo el overo rosao!"*[3]

The said Martín was a short, rather stocky man, dressed always

[2] James Butler Hickok (1837–76), a well-known figure of the West, known as "Wild Bill" Hickok.

[3] From the opening lines of the poem *Fausto*, meaning "What a fine dappled roan."

in the style of a better class gaucho, in loose black merino trousers, tucked into high boots with the feet made of calfskin and the legs of patent leather embroidered with an eagle, worked in scarlet thread. His spurs were silver with the rowels, almost as big as a small saucer, and worn dangling off his heels, kept in their place by silver chains, clasped on his instep with a lion's head.

Around the waist he wore a red silk netting sash, such as was used by officers in the army when Queen Victoria ruled, covered by a broad belt of carpincho leather, full of pockets, and fastened by silver coins.

Under the belt the tassels and a foot or so of the sash dangled down on the leg and gave a note of colour on the merino "slacks."

Don Martín, for no one ever called him plain Martín without the Don, always wore a white frilled and pleated shirt, with a high collar, turned down and open at the neck. His short black jacket was of fine alpaca, and over it, spread out into tails, he wore a red silk handkerchief. His hat, known from the Fortín Machado right down to Patagones, was a fine Panama, the only one upon the frontier. He used to say with pride that he acquired it in Buenos Aires, a city that he had visited but once in his career. It had cost him ten sterling pounds of England and he held the money well laid out.

Strange but unconvincing tales of his experiences in that "Babilonia" he would unpack upon occasion, especially after a glass or two of Brazilian caña or *vino seco*, a thick yellow Catalonian wine, that with sardines and biscuits was our banquet at the "camp" *pulperías*. Our chief dessert was either "raisins of the sun," or the dried peaches, known as *orejones*, looking exactly like human ears, that came from Chile and the upper provinces. Over this more or less Gargantuan feast would Don Martín take up his parable.

Though wedlocked, married in Latin, that is, in a church, as he would say, as far as I know the husband but of a single wife, it would appear in Buenos Aires, in his brief sojourn of a fortnight, he had spent the time in a continual orgy of costly but intensely satisfying love. The names and the appearance of the damsels who had accompanied him in his various pilgrimages to Cytherea,[4] he still remembered, as well, he used to say, as the

[4] Another name for Venus, the goddess of love, from the island of Cythera.

brands of the various estancias round about Bahía Blanca in the days of his magistrature.

Certainly Don Martín was one of our best leaders against the Indians, and I can see him still, mounted on his skewbald, his rifle hanging from his saddle and his celebrated Panama, the brim blown back by the wind, as he rode from house to house along the Sauce Grande, the Sauce Corto and the Napostá, warning the neighbours to be ready to resist a raid.

Naturally, "*Facón Grande*" was our general, silent and watchful, his eyes fixed always on the horizon, marking the movements of the cattle, the flight of birds, dust rising on the horizon, reading the pampa like a book in Braille by little indications invisible to those whose mental sense of touch life in a city had left dormant.

Mounted on a tall *pangaré* with a fawn coloured nose, his rifle carried always in his hand, across the saddle-bow, his long black hair gave him a look almost of an Indian, and his great height and perfect seat upon his horse made an ideal picture of a frontiersman.

"*Facón Chico*," always the first to rally to the call, looked in his tweed coat and riding breeches as if he had strayed by accident from some meet of harriers into that wild company.

As talkative as "*Facón Grande*" was silent, his usual greeting was: "Have you heard this one?" Then he would retail some Rabelaisian story interspersed with Spanish words, wrongly pronounced, or a new limerick, of his own mintage.

He, like his cousin, carried his rifle in his hand, riding upon an English saddle, for, as he said, "a man ought to show his nationality," although in his case nature had stamped it on him both inside and out.

A hard-riding German, Frederick Vögel by name, but always known as Pancho Pájaro to the gauchos, was sure to join us, although his business was to sell sheep-dip to the estancieros. His name was a household word amongst the gauchos, for the long daring rides he had undertaken along the frontier.

Fair and square-built, fatigue of any kind was a thing unknown to him; so, I should think, was fear.

No one could want a better man beside him in a tough place, and when his off-stirrup happened to touch yours, you felt assured as long as he had life that Pancho Pájaro would not let you down.

These worthies and the brothers Milburn of the Sauce Grande, one a retired sea captain and the other, who was called lieutenant, perhaps because his brother was known as captain, for he had nothing military about him, and several settlers on the Napostá composed our company.

Most of them had been in Indian skirmishes and heard the pampa Indians yelling, striking their hands upon their mouths as they came on like a storm cloud, brandishing their spears.

Where they ride now is but a matter of conjecture; no one remembers them but I who write these lines, that I have written in memoriam, hoping that some day they will allow an old companion to ride with them, no matter where they ride.

GUALEGUAYCHÚ

The steamer glided from the yellow waters of the River Plate into a narrow channel overarched with trees, which almost swept her deck. A thick white mist rose from the stream, which shrouded both the banks and rose half up the masts and funnel, leaving the tops of trees hanging like islands in the air. Upon their highest branches cormorants and vultures sat asleep, which at the passing of the boat awoke and screamed, then dropped into the mist.

The channel narrowed, or appeared to do so, in the gloom which brooded on the river and its banks, although the moon shone brightly and the Southern Cross was hung above our heads, the black Magellan clouds looking like mouths of funnels in the sky, deep and mysterious. Capella was just rising, and the stars, though not so bright as in the northern hemisphere, seemed far more luminous and gleamed more yellow and more phosphorescent than do their sisters of the North. Carpinchos, startled from their sleep, plunged with a splash into the stream and swam for refuge to the reedy banks, their backs awash, and their flat heads stretched out upon the water, looking like giant prediluvian rats.

Moths, large as humming-birds, hung round the binnacle, making the helmsman curse, although his compass was a sinecure, as from the bow, the pilot, sounding with a cane, guided the vessel up the stream. From both the banks and from the islands with their feathery canes, the shrill mosquitoes' oboe piped its unpleasing tune. Nothing was heard but now and then the pilot's nasal cry as the stream shoaled, or the faint distant neigh of some wild stallion gathering up his mares. All was so still and ghostly that the snorting of the steam seemed like an outrage upon Nature, which wept great tears of dew upon the deck to see herself defiled.

Hours, which seemed long as days, went past, and still the steamer struggling with the current pressed into the night. At times she ran her nose against the bank, and from the trees the mist, congealed upon the leaves, poured down like rain upon the awnings and the shrouds. At times she grounded on a sandbank, backed, and was helped by all the crew, pushing her off with poles, then, shivering, swung into the stream, strove for a minute with the hurrying water, and once more glided through the mist.

Great wreaths of camalote floated past her sides, and now and then she swerved to let a tree come swirling lazily along. At last the mist grew lighter, and the moon, sinking below the trees, showed that the morning was at hand. The stars waxed paler and the air more chilly, and men, sleeping upon the deck beneath the awning, their heads upon their saddles with their long silver-handled knives close to their hands, stirred and drew close their ponchos in their sleep. Others sat up and lighted cigarettes, smoked silently and then lay down again, the white dew glistening on their blankets and their hair.

As the dawn brightened, and Capella fell behind the trees, the whistle sounded, echoing through the woods. The vessel edged into the bank, as if by instinct, and her sides rubbed against a pier made of rough planks and almost level with the stream. Some sleepy soldiers, smoking cigarettes, came through the mist like spectres and a man dressed in uniform stepped from the pier on to the deck, went down below, and in a little while came up again, wiping his lips, and with an air of having done his duty to the State.

The passengers, each with his hand-bag, or his saddle, as the case might be, stumbled ashore, and took their way through a rough path cut in the woods, which, after half a mile, came out upon a plain, and a short league away beheld the town, flat-roofed and white, silent and shining in the rising sun.

A diligence, which should have met the steamer, drawn by six horses driven, and one in front of which a ragged boy, half gaucho, half town loafer, rode, whirled in a cloud of dust towards them, and they, scaling it as it were a fortress, were jolted to the town.

Stuck like a chessboard on a table, on the plain, and with the streets all intersecting one another into squares, the houses all flat-topped and painted white, and with the towers called *miradores* looking like minarets, and the church dome resembling a mosque, it had a sort of Oriental look. The sandy unpaved streets, in which lean yellow dogs prowled after offal all the day, and howled at night in chorus at the moon, smacked also of the East. There the resemblance ended, and the line of posts, to almost every one of which a horse was tied, and the great stores, in front of which stood horses hobbled, for no one went on foot above two squares, was purely Argentine. Horses pervaded all the place, in every open space they fed attached to ropes, in all the yards they stood up to the fetlocks in black mud, or in hot dust, according to the season of the year, and ate alfalfa, or were led down to water by their owners, with the long picket rope known as a *mañador* curled like a lasso in the hand. Men dressed in loose black cashmere trousers, with high patent-leather boots, the tops all worked in patterns with red or yellow thread, their ponchos fluttering in the wind, rode past on silver-mounted saddles and with bits furnished with cups of silver on each side of the mouth, and with an eagle wrought in silver moving with every step below the horse's mouth. Their horses, with manes hogged to the middle of the neck, leaving upon the withers a long lock six inches wide to mount by, snorted and passaged at the strange sights of town, tried to whip round and spring across the street like goats, if a dog stirred, or a door fastened with a bang. Sometimes if they had eaten corn, a feat which often took them days to learn and which they only learned on being tied up without food, they trotted slowly at the *paso castellano*, their long tails squared off at the fetlock joints, swinging as if in rhythm to the short jogging trot. Their riders with their hats kept on by strings of silk with tassels underneath the chin, their bridle hand held high, and on the right their flat hide whips just dangling on their horse's quarters to keep him to the bit, assumed the far-off look of an ineffable content which horsemen, mounted on a horse that does them credit, put on quite naturally in every quarter of the world.

Wild and barefooted boys, on bare-backed ponies, careered

about the outskirts of the town, and the one beggar of the place, an old Canarian, rode a thin horse and when he saw a charitable face, took off his hat and mumbled, "For the love of God," receiving what was given, as his due, for alms are not a favour to the receiver, but to the giver, who thereby lays up for himself treasures beyond the skies, where beggars are not, and where horses, if they exist, are winged like Pegasus. It was a gaucho town that lived upon the "camp," as people styled the adjoining country in the pidgin-English of the place. A town in which all men went armed, their knives and pistols sticking out below their coats, and where, if you were so inclined, on any pretext you might fight with any one, no questions asked, and if you killed your man, get on your horse and ride into the "camp," secure of never being caught, so that you did not venture into town or run by accident into the hands of the police. During the hot hours of the day all slept, leaving the streets deserted and the stores wide open, so that a man could walk into them and knocking with his whip upon the counter or the door, find no one, till at last some sleepy shopman would appear and say that business was suspended, and retreat, cursing, to his bed. The sun declining put new life into the town, and in the various stores men sat and talked and criticised the horses and the women as they passed. Still later on, the evening brought the ladies of the place into the plaza, all dressed in Paris fashions of a year ago, to saunter up and down in groups beneath the orange trees, in which the fireflies flitted, making the heavy leaves seem all alive with light. As they passed by, a fire of compliments was turned on them, which they pretended not to hear, and yet were piqued if no one paid them, for as the saying was, even a compliment from a black man is better than indifference from a prince.

In the still air the tinkle of guitars sounded like Cupid's sheep-bells, and at the iron-grated windows on the streets men stood, flattening themselves against the bars, to talk to women, whom the judicious custom of the place only allowed to see their lovers with a stout iron railing set betwixt the two.

Between a male and female saint a wall of bricks and lime, the proverb says, but a stout iron bar aids virtue plaguily.

Although the streets were all deserted after ten, through the wide-open windows and the doors of patios you saw the richer people of the place, seated at tables playing cards or dancing, and at the window-bars the loafers stood, as at a theatre, but now and then giving forth their opinions of an ankle or a foot, not disrespectfully but with the freedom of the Spanish race which holds all men, as men, are equal, and that the want of money does not debar a man from being human, or its possession raise him to a god.

The lower classes congregated in the *pulperías*, and there drank gin and maté, danced the cielito, the gato, and the pericón, and not infrequently got drunk and fought with their long silver-handled knives. They played at monte, each producing his own pack, marked at the back (so that he knew each card as it was dealt), and striving to impose it on the rest. They, knowing well the trick, preferred a neutral pack, which, although marked, was yet unknown to any of the players, and having made a bank, they gambled desperately, so that a man, having begun well dressed, with silver-mounted arms and belt well stocked with dollars, not seldom left the place stripped to his trousers and his shirt.

The foreigners assembled at one of the hotels, either at Ellerman's or at the *Fonda del vapor*, kept by a Basque, Don Pedro, where they drank and sang, roaring the choruses of comic songs, after the fashion of boys at public schools or sailors in a port.

Don Pedro owned a long and flat-roofed house, built round a courtyard in which there was a well. Above the doorway hung a model of a steamboat made in wood, from which the *fonda* took its name. Broad in the beam, and painted blue and red, the funnel like a mast, and with enormous paddle-boxes, on one of which the captain, dressed in a general's uniform, girt with a sword, appeared to bellow through a speaking-trumpet to the stars, the model might have served for a museum in some inland capital, where none had seen the sea. But yet it was Don Pedro's pride, and pointing to it, he would say, "Steam—sí, señor, the steam is the great power which I have heard Prometheus stole from heaven; it means our life, for life is progress, and there can be no progress without steam." Not that, for all his aphorism, Don Pedro differed from his fellow-countrymen, who slow and steady, and as obstinate as a male mule, are able, it is said, to drive a nail into the door by beating on it with their heads, and then, when driven home, to draw it with their teeth.

The rooms all looked upon the patio, and it was well, after an evening of caña punch and song, to shut the door and put the candle out of sight, for the chief form of wit was shooting at the lights, and as you sat and read, a pistol shot was pretty sure to knock the plaster from the wall, close enough to your head to make things dangerous, as the man firing generally was drunk. The rooms were bare, but for a wooden folding-bed known as a *catre*, a chair, a table, and a washing-stand. Don Pedro's pride was centred in his dining-room, which was adorned with various French prints of hunting scenes, all highly coloured, in which the hunters in high-collared coats and bushy whiskers, girt about with knives, rode centaur-like. One was entitled "Fox-hunting to the Wild Boar," and showed a monstrous beast as bulky as a hippopotamus careering on the grass. The hunters to the boar rode after him, all clad in green, with high and shining boots, from their left sides there dangled cutlasses, and round their bodies horns like ophicleides. "Fox-hunting to the Deer" showed a strange animal much like an antelope, loping across the fields with a great company of beagles following at his heels, all lolling out their tongues. Last scene of all set forth the kill, which was enacted in a pigsty, wherein the deer had fled, and where a huntsman manfully butchered her with a cutlass; the pack of beagles, sitting on their hams, look like peccaries when they have run a man into a tree, and watch expectantly.

To the hotel there gravitated the more respectable of the young English cattle-farmers, a fair proportion of French bagmen, and some substantial Basques who, as Don Pedro was a countryman, gave him patronage. One or two wool-buyers from Buenos Aires, and an Italian engineer or two, who loafed about, waiting for contracts to build a bridge or make a railway to the moon, and several experts in what were known as fruits of the country, consisting of, in general, hides, with hoofs and horns, and salted beef to send to Cuba and to Brazil, to feed the slaves on the plantations, made the contingent commerce furnished to the house.

Science contributed two German lepidopterists, who in their rooms pursued their mystery in a strong smell of camphor, and at meals ate solidly, their knives and forks clinking upon their teeth like foils in a sharp bout. Captain McCandlish, too, was there, a worthy mariner, who, having lost his ship for drunkenness, passed all his life regretting the old days, when in the 'fifties he had had a brig in the South Seas. Much did he dwell upon the islands and the life: "Conceity folk, yon Kanakys, ye ken. The weemen too, sort of free living—juist vera leetle prejudice aboot them. I mind one o' them doon in Eromango—dod no, long before the missionaries cam', spoilin' the place. I cana' bear a Kanaky, in breeks, ye ken—seems to corrupt them—fine buirdly bodies, but European clothes mak's them upsettin'.

"Weel, this gurl, ye see; lads—I dinna care to mind aboot her, whiles I juist think I never should have left the islands—Awfu' easy life; taro, ye ken, is handy planted, handier far than tatties—a bonny climate too, and then the weemen. Man, I think I was a fool to leave the islands, and to fetch up in this mud turtle, round-bottomed sort o' a smouchin' toon, where everything is dear, and no a body kens the dogvane from the kingston valve. Hech, sirs, I think I was a fool."

Then he would snort in his red pocket-handkerchief, light up his pipe (he "couldna' stan' thae cigareets"), call for more whisky, and stagger down the street, lurching a little in his gait, as if he was at sea.

Within a square of the hotel was set the police-station and in a lane hard by some huts in which some half-caste *chinas*, with several mulatas, and two or three Hungarian and German girls, become too faded for the capital, sat painted at their doors. Vice was so unattractive, set as it was in a mud hovel, thatched with straw, that many, whom the love of virtue bound but lightly, yet were virtuous from disgust. Whether the moral gain was great, only the moralist can say, and he was an infrequent visitor in those days, either at Ellerman's or at the *Fonda del vapor*. In fact morality was looked at in the larger or the Latin way, with the result that on the whole life was far cleaner than in Anglo-Saxon lands, where nature being what it is, the same things happen but are rendered meaner by concealment; the homage, as they say, vice pays to virtue, but which makes virtue, as it were, compound a felony and smirches both of them.

Racing and cock-fights were the national sports, the former for short distances, two or three furlongs, with innumerable false starts, all of set purpose and with the object of tiring out the weaker horse before the race began. Barefooted and with silk handkerchiefs tied round their heads, a custom which they evidently took from the Indians, who tied a woollen string called *vicha* round their brows, and with their flat-thonged whips hung on their wrists, the riders made pretence to give their horses all their head, leaning well forward on their necks and shouting wildly, but all the time they held them well in hand. As all the starts were flying and by mutual consent, if one man saw his horse was but an inch behind the other's, or if he noticed that his adversary's horse (for all the races were confined to two) was getting out of hand, he stopped and, getting off, walked slowly back again up to the flag. This naturally upset the temper of a violent horse, who at the next attempt would rear and plunge, and break out sweating, and perhaps run half the course before he could be stopped. When at the last they got away, each shouted *"Vamos"*, and then they plied their whips, the horses close to one another, for if a man could bore the other rider off the course he won the race.

But at this game all gauchos were adepts, as well as that of trying to kick the opposing horse's chest, to put their feet below the other rider's heel and hurl him to the ground, all which was reckoned fair and part of racing, just as at cards they had a code of signs which were allowable, but in both cases tricks and signs were all conventional, and nothing might be done except what wont and immemorial use had rendered sanctified.

To a low building built in a circle and looking like a little bull-ring the sportsmen of the town repaired on Sundays, nearly all carrying cocks beneath their arms, or balanced on the pommels of their saddles as they rode. To show that nationality was no bar to sport, the committee had drawn up rules and invitations in several tongues; the one in English ran: "Sunday and other holly days there are large cock-fight. The native and the foreign cock is both accepted, and are accepted all kind of cock whatever his prevention." To make all clear, at the bottom of the page was written "The direction," which the composers of the document imagined had the same meaning in an English as in a Latin tongue. English or French or Spanish, or no matter what the tongue, all men were equal in the arena of the cocks. The love of blood and money, the two strongest passions, write what they please of love, levelled down most of them to a mere mass of animals, with bloodshot eyes, mouths open and their lips drawn back upon their teeth, sweating with interest, and following every wound the birds inflicted with their sharp steel spurs, all pity laid aside, and for the time savage as tigers, ready to quarrel with their brother if the red cock struck out the other's eye and he had criticised the stroke.

The remnant, those who cared not for the blood, and in whom the skill and fortitude of the trained cocks neither excited nor evoked compassion, called the odds with regularity, marking each turn in every combat, and when at last the victor dashed his spur down through the brains, and then himself fell dead beside his foe, just crowing out his victory as he fell, stretched out their hands to take the dollars, that their bird had gained them with his life, with a low chuckle of content.

But when in England or in South America did life, either of man or beast, stand any chance when there was money to be made? The only difference is that here we try to hide from others and ourselves the motives of our deeds, and there they stuff the dollars dripping red with blood into their pockets and light their cigarettes.

The town, such as it was, when first the little stern-wheel steamer groped through the mist, her decks swept by the dripping boughs of ñandubay and espinillo, no longer now exists.

No doubt the house in which they tortured Garibaldi,[1] hanging him by the thumbs and flogging him across the face with rawhide whips, has long made way, perhaps for a new church, perhaps for some smart bar-room in the Yankee style.

No longer in the shady lanes Paz and Dolores sit waiting for their customers, playing guitars, and with their pictures of a saint above their beds. Ladies from Paris and from Buda-Pesth, not so religious, but as superstitious to the full, no doubt adorn the town, driving their trade, and keeping their accounts by double entry, with the view of honourable retirement in their riper years when paint has failed and drink imparts no lustre to the eyes. The loafers cannot any longer stare in through the *rejas* on the ladies at a ball and criticise their clothes. Increasing wealth no doubt has set a bar betwixt the classes, making the poor man feel his poverty, and the rich know that isolation is the best weapon in the fight that he must wage. Who would allow a horse to stray about, now that no doubt his price is trebled, or to stand hobbled in a street, when all drive motors, and he would be in danger of his life? A vast and tin-roofed "terminus," in which the engines scream and whistle all the night, is the chief labarum of progress, and all who see it, with the smoke from its workshops hung across the sky, bow and adore it and are satisfied. Few still remain, who can recall the days, when taking horse a man could

---

[1] The great Italian liberator, Giuseppe Garibaldi (1807–82), went to Argentina and took part in the struggle against the dictator, Rosas.

ride to Corrientes without an obstacle to stop him on his way but flooded rivers, if it should chance to rain, or want of water if there was a drought.

Those were the days when on a journey man took no thought for food, for riding to a house, if by some chance there was no meat in the *galpón*, they said, "You have a *lazo*—eh? The cattle are but half a league away—out on the rise, beyond the round ombú. Well, go and kill a cow, take all the meat you want, but leave the hide; the owner does not like his brand to turn up in a parcel of strange stuff—and so—with God."

URUGUAY

Editor's Preface to the Uruguayan Sketches

The division between the pampas of Argentina and those of Uruguay is purely arbitrary, and I make it here only as a geographical convenience. For Graham and his kind, the pampas of the Banda Oriental (Uruguay, as we know it today) were merely an extension of the Argentinian pampas. It is not surprising that all the sketches are about horses, but in them we see several other aspects of Graham's writing—the realistic treatment of death, the unsurpassed powers of natural description, and the bitter attack on the evils of civilization and progress. This section ends with one of Graham's finest sketches, telling the story of an Englishman, who could have been Graham himself (the epitome of virility, a most important quality for the Latin American male), who forsakes England's green and fertile land to die in a *pulpería* brawl.

PREFACE TO HOPE

"Tyne hope, tyne a'!" the Scottish proverb says,[1] and it is right, for hope is like a northern hawthorn bush, late flowering but continuing long in bloom.

There is an element of speculation in it which faith quite lacks.

Thus, faith is for youth, hope for middle life, and charity, which only comes when faith and hope are dead, for age.

Sometimes, indeed, hope and her half-sister faith run almost into one another.

I remember once, in the Republic of the Banda Oriental del Uruguay, close to the frontier of Brazil, we came, my partner and myself, driving a troop of horses, to what in South America is called a "pass," that is, a ford. What was the river's name I cannot tell without an atlas, and that would be to put a slight upon my memory, so I refrain; but the ford was El Paso de los Novillos, and to get to it you had to ride down through a wood of espinillo de olor.

The trail that we followed to the pass was steep and sandy, and cut by the passage of the animals into deep ruts, leaving long hummocks here and there, called *albardones* (that is, pack-saddles), on which grew thorny shrubs. Great cactuses with their flat leaves, looking like gigantic seeds of honesty, white, gaunt, and sear, stood here and there, and seemed to guard the road. They had an almost human look, and report said, not very long before we passed, a band of robbers had stripped themselves,

---

[1] "Lose hope, and you lose everything!"

and standing naked by the whitish stems, were so invisible that they were able quietly to kill some travellers, who rode right into them before they were aware. Therefore we rode with care, hitching our pistols now and then round nearer to our hands as we urged on the troop, swinging our whips about our heads, and pressing close upon the driven horses to prevent their cutting back or separating when they came to the "pass." Hummingbirds fluttered like gigantic day-moths hung poised, with a thin whir of wings invisible, so that they seemed all body, then darted off so swiftly that no eye could follow them. In the hot air myriads of insects, seen and unseen, raised a shrill melody. Upon the trees black cormorants sat and discoursed, and herons, white, slate-coloured, and brown, stood fishing silently. Carpinchos, looking like little hippopotami, just showed their backs above the surface of the water as we came to the crossing of the stream. We closed upon the troop, Mansel, myself, Exaltación Medina, Raimundo Barragán, and the two peons; one of them rode a white and dun piebald, whose coat was curly as a sheep's. It had a strip of hide tied round the lower jaw to which the reins were fixed, for it was still unbitted. I see them now just as I saw them then, through a thin cloud of dust. The horses—there were about two hundred—entered the water in a bunch. The stream flowed strongly, yellow and turbid, and in the middle rose a low island, almost awash, long and grass-grown, and looking like one of those *albardones* in the road which I have spoken of before. The horses took the water well, and we stood back to give them space, so that they should not crowd upon each other and get choked.

How well I see them, their heads laid flat upon the stream, the lines made by their backs in the swift current, their tails spread out, and all of them swimming a little sideways, just as a carp swims sideways when he comes up for bread. Their eyes were fixed upon the bank, and in their wake a little wave as of a boat washed to the shore. We stood and gazed, watching a piebald mare, fat, strong, and wild, who led the troop. Her too I see and well remember, for she was barren and therefore just as good as is a horse. Moreover, though a natural pacer, she could bound forward like a deer when you but closed your legs upon her sides. *Linda la overa negra!*[2] Well, just as we were thinking about enter-

[2] "What a fine black piebald! " These are the opening words of Del Campo's *Fausto*, that Graham likes to quote occasionally. See note 2 in the sketch, "Facón Grande."

ing the stream ourselves, having taken off our clothes and piled them on our heads, cinched up our saddles a little forward, and with our boots and pistols round our necks, the spurs inside the boots, one of the peons cried out the mare was drowning. I, sitting sideways in my saddle, saw that the current, which ran strongly just below the island, had swept her on her side; perhaps she was a trifle fat to swim. Little by little she appeared to sink, her quarters dropping perpendicularly and then the water creeping up round her neck. Once for a moment her fore feet emerged, battling for life, her eyes were blue with terror, and then with a loud snort she disappeared.

One of us, I think it was Medina, exclaimed, "It was a pity of the mare, and she a barren mare as good as any horse—but God is not a bad man after all, the rest have landed safe." We crossed, the water lapping up almost to our mouths at the first plunge. I rode a horse that swam a little low, and on the other side we drove the troop into an open glade, and then dismounting, spread our clothes to dry.

The horses, after rolling, began to feed, guarded by a man who rode naked but for a light vicuña poncho, and we sat in the shade and boiled a kettle to take maté, in the lee of a fire of smoky wood to keep the flies away.

It may have been Raimundo or Exaltación, most certainly it was not either of the peons, who observed, "Life is a fandango," and received the answer, "Yes, but all do not dance."

This time I am almost sure it was Exaltación Medina who replied, "Yes, but all hope to dance."

As we sat thinking on his dictum, and also on the poor mare's death, one of those sudden panics that at times befall a *caballada* set our horses off.

When we had got them turned and we were riding slowly round them with the sun blistering our naked backs, I noticed that our feet were bleeding, for we had mounted barebacked in the hurry of the fright and ridden through the thorns.

LOS PINGOS

The amphitheatre of wood enclosed a bay that ran so far into the land it seemed a lake. The Uruguay flowed past, but the bay was so landlocked and so well defended by an island lying at its mouth that the illusion was complete, and the bay appeared to be cut off from all the world.

Upon the river twice a day passed steamboats, which at night-time gave an air as of a section of a town that floated past the wilderness. Streams of electric light from every cabin lit up the yellow, turgid river, and the notes of a band occasionally floated across the water as the vessel passed. Sometimes a searchlight falling on a herd of cattle, standing as is their custom after nightfall upon a little hill, made them stampede into the darkness, dashing through brushwood or floundering through a marsh, till they had placed themselves in safety from this new terror of the night.

Above the bay the ruins of a great building stood. Built scarcely fifty years ago and now deserted, the ruins had taken on an air as of a castle, and from the walls sprang plants, whilst in the deserted courtyard a tree had grown, amongst whose branches oven-birds had built their hanging nests of mud. Cypresses towered above the primeval hard-wood, which grew all gnarled and horny-looking, and nearly all had kept their Indian names, as ñandubay, chañar, tala and sarandí, molle, and many another name as crabbed as the trunks which, twisted and distorted, looked like the limbs of giants growing from the ground.

Orange trees had run wild and shot up all unpruned, and apple trees had reverted back to crabs. The trunks of all the fruit-trees in the deserted garden round the ruined factory were rubbed shiny by the cattle, for all the fences had long been destroyed or fallen into decay.

A group of roofless workmen's cottages gave an air of desolation to the valley, in which the factory and its dependencies had stood. They too had been invaded by the powerful sub-tropical plant life, and creepers covered with bunches of bright flowers climbed up their walls. A sluggish stream ran through the valley and joined the Uruguay, making a little natural harbour. In it basked cat-fish, and now and then from off the banks a tortoise dropped into the water like a stone. Right in the middle of what once had been the square grew a ceiba tree, covered with lilac flowers, hanging in clusters like gigantic grapes. Here and there stood some old ombús, their dark metallic leaves affording an impenetrable shade. Their gnarled and twisted roots, left half-exposed by the fierce rains, gave an unearthly, prehistoric look to them that chimed in well with the deserted air of the whole place. It seemed that man for once had been subdued, and that victorious nature had resumed her sway over a region wherein he had endeavoured to intrude, and had been worsted in the fight.

Nature had so resumed her sway that buildings, planted trees, and paths long overgrown with grass, seemed to have been decayed for centuries, although scarce twenty years had passed since they had been deserted and had fallen into decay.

They seemed to show the power of the recuperative force of the primeval forest and to call attention to the fact that man had suffered a defeat. Only the grass in the deserted square was still triumphant and grew short and green, like an oasis in the rough natural grasses that flowed nearly up to it, in the clearings of the woods.

The triumph of the older forces of the world had been so final and complete that on the ruins there had grown no moss, but plants and bushes with great tufts of grass had sprung from them, leaving the stones still fresh as when the houses were first built. Nature in that part of the New World enters into no compact with mankind, as she does over here in Europe to touch his work kindly and almost with a reverent hand, and blend it into something half compounded of herself. There bread is bread and wine is wine, with no half-tints to make one body of the whole. The one remaining evidence of the aggression of mankind, which still refused to bow the knee to the overwhelming genius of the place, was a round bunch of eucalyptus trees that stood up stark and unblushing, the colour of the trunks and leaves so harshly different from all around them that they looked almost vulgar, if such an epithet can be properly applied to anything but man. Under their exiguous shade were spread saddles and bridles, and on the ground sat men smoking and talking, whilst their staked-out horses fed, fastened to picket-pins by rawhide ropes. So far away from everything the place appeared that the group of men looked like a band of pioneers upon some frontier, to which the ruins only gave an air of melancholy, but did nothing to dispel the loneliness.

As they sat idly talking, trying to pass, or, as they would have said, trying to make time, suddenly in the distance the whistle of an approaching steamer brought the outside world into the little, lonely paradise. Oddly enough it sounded, in the hot, early morning air, already heavy with the scent of the mimosas in full bloom. Butterflies flitted to and fro or soared above the scrub, and now and then a wild mare whinnied from the thickets, breaking the silence of the lone valley through which the yellow, little stream ran to the Uruguay.

Catching their horses and rolling up the ropes, the men, who had been sitting underneath the trees, mounted, and following a little cattle trail, rode to a high bluff looking down the stream.

Panting and puffing, as she belched out a column of black smoke, some half a mile away, a tug towing two lighters strove with the yellow flood. The horsemen stood like statues with their horses' heads stretched out above the water thirty feet below.

Although the feet of several of the horses were but an inch or two from the sheer limit, the men sat, some of them with one leg on their horses' necks; others lit cigarettes, and one, with his horse sideways to the cliff, leaned sideways, so that one of his feet was in the air. He pointed to the advancing tug with a brown finger and exclaimed, "These are the lighters with the horses that must have started yesterday from Gualeguaychú, and ought to have been here last night." We had indeed been waiting all the night for them, sleeping round a fire under the eucalyptus grove, and rising often in the night to smoke and talk, to see our horses did not get entangled in their stake ropes, and to listen for the whistle of the tug.

The tug came on but slowly, fighting her way against the rapid current, with the lighters towing behind her at some distance, looking like portions of a pier that had somehow or another got adrift.

From where we sat upon our horses we could see the surface of the Uruguay for miles, with its innumerable flat islands buried in vegetation, cutting the river into channels; for the islands, having been formed originally by masses of water-weeds and drift-wood, were but a foot or two above the water, and all were elongated, forming great ribbons in the stream.

Upon the right bank stretched the green prairies of the State of Entre Ríos, bounded on either side by the Uruguay and Paraná. Much flatter than the land upon the Uruguayan bank, it still was not a sea of level grass as is the State of Buenos Aires, but undulating, and dotted here and there with white estancia houses, all buried in great groves of peach trees and of figs. On the left bank on which we stood, and three leagues off, we could just see Fray Bentos, its houses dazzlingly white, buried in vegetation, and in the distance like a thousand little towns in Southern Italy and Spain, or even in Morocco, for the tower of the church might in the distance just as well have been a minaret.

The tug-boat slowed a little, and a canoe was slowly paddled out to pilot her into the little haven made by the brook that flowed down through the valley to the Uruguay.

Sticking out like a fishing-rod over the stem of the canoe was a long cane, to sound with if it was required.

The group of horsemen on the bluff rode slowly down towards the river's edge to watch the evolutions of the tug, and to hold back the horses when they should be disembarked. By this time she had got so near that we could see the horses' heads looking out wildly from the sparred sides of the great decked lighters, and hear the thunderous noise their feet made tramping on the decks. Passing the bay, into which ran the stream, by about three hundred yards, the tug cast off one of the lighters she was towing in a backwater. There it remained, the current slowly bearing it backwards, turning round upon itself. In the wild landscape, with ourselves upon our horses forming the only human element, the gigantic lighter with its freight of horses looked like the ark, as set forth in some old-fashioned book on Palestine. Slowly the tug crept in, the Indian-looking pilot squatted in his canoe sounding assiduously with his long cane. As the tug drew about six feet of water and the lighter not much more than three, the problem was to get the lighter near enough to the bank, so that when the hawser was cast off she would come in by her own way. Twice did the tug ground, and with furious shoutings and with all the crew staving on poles was she got off again. At last the pilot found a little deeper channel, and coming to about some fifty feet away, lying a length or two above the spot where the stream entered the great river, she paid her hawser out, and as the lighter drifted shorewards, cast it off, and the great ark, with all its freight, grounded quite gently on the little sandy beach. The Italian captain of the tug, a Genoese, with his grey hair as curly as the wool on a sheep's back, wearing a pale pink shirt, neatly set off with horseshoes, and a blue gauze necktie tied in a flowing bow, pushed off his dirty little boat, rowed by a negro sailor and a Neapolitan who dipped their oars into the water without regard to one another, either as to time or stroke.

The captain stepped ashore, mopping his face with a yellow pocket-handkerchief, and in the jargon between Spanish and Italian that men of his sort all affect out in the River Plate, saluted us and cursed the river for its sandbanks and its turns, and then having left it as accursed as the Styx or Periphlegethon, he doubly cursed the Custom House, which, as he said, was all composed of thieves, the sons of thieves who would be certainly begetters of the same. Then he calmed down a little, and drawing out a long Virginia cigar, took out the straw with seriousness and great dexterity, and then allowed about a quarter of an inch of it to smoulder in a match, lighted it, and sending out a cloud of smoke, sat down upon the grass, and fell a-cursing, with all the ingenuity of his profession and his race, the country, the hot weather, and the saints.

This done, and having seen the current was slowly bearing down the other lighter past the sandy beach, with a last hearty curse upon God's mother and her Son, whose birth he hinted not obscurely was of the nature of a mystery, in which he placed no credence, got back into his boat, and went back to his tug, leaving us all amazed, both at his fluency and faith.

When he had gone and grappled with the other lighter which was slowly drifting down the stream, two or three men came forward in the lighter that was already in the little river's mouth, about a yard or so distant from the edge, and calling to us to be ready, for the horses had not eaten for sixteen hours at least, slowly let down the wooden landing-flap. At first the horses craned their necks and looked out on the grass but did not venture to go down the wooden landing-stage; then a big roan, stepping out gingerly and snorting as he went, adventured, and when he stood upon the grass, neighed shrilly and then rolled. In a long string the others followed, the clattering of their unshod feet upon the wood sounding like distant thunder.

Byrne, the porteño, stout and high-coloured, dressed in great thigh boots and baggy breeches, a black silk handkerchief tied loosely round his neck, a black felt hat upon his head, and a great silver watchchain, with a snaffle-bridle in the middle of it, contrasting oddly with his broad pistol belt, with its old silver dollars for a fastening, came ashore, carrying his saddle on his back. Then followed Doherty, whose name, quite unpronounceable to men of Latin race, was softened in their speech to Duarte, making a good Castilian patronymic of it. He too was a porteño, although of Irish stock. Tall, dark, and dressed in semi-native clothes, he yet, like Byrne, always spoke Spanish when no foreigners were present, and in his English that softening of the consonants and broadening of the vowels was discernible, that makes the speech of men such as himself have in it something, as it were, caressing, strangely at variance with their character. Two or three peons of the usual gaucho type came after them, all carrying saddles, and walking much as an alligator waddles on the sand, or as the Medes whom Xenophon describes, mincing upon their toes, in order not to blunt the rowels of their spurs.

Our men, García the innkeeper of Fray Bentos, with Pablo Suárez, whose negro blood and crispy hair gave him a look as of a Roman emperor of the degenerate times, with Pancho Arrellano and Miguel Paralelo, the gaucho dandy, swaying upon his horse with his toes just touching his heavy silver stirrups with a crown underneath them, Vélez and El Pampita, an Indian who had been captured young on the south pampa, were mounted ready to round the horses up.

They did not want much care, for they were eating ravenously, and all we had to do was to drive them a few hundred yards away to let the others land.

By this time the Italian captain in his tug had gently brought the other lighter to the beach, and from its side another string of horses came out on the grass. They too all rolled, and, seeing the other band, by degrees mixed with it, so that four hundred horses soon were feeding ravenously on the sweet grass just at the little river's mouth that lay between its banks and the thick belt of wood.

Though it was early, still the sun was hot, and for an hour we held the horses back, keeping them from the water till they had eaten well.

The Italian tugmaster, having produced a bottle of trade gin (the Anchor brand), and having drunk our health, solemnly wiped the neck of the bottle with his grimy hand and passed it round to us. We also drank to his good health and voyage to the port, that he pronounced as if it were written "Bono Airi," adding, as it was war-time, "*Avanti Savoia*"[1] to the toast. He grinned, and with a gesture of his thick, dirty hand, adorned with two or three coppery-looking rings, as it were, embedded in the flesh, pronounced an all-embracing curse on the Tedeschi, and went aboard the tug.

When he had made the lighters fast, he turned down stream, saluting us with three shrill blasts upon the whistle, and left us and our horses thousands of miles away from steam and smoke, blaspheming skippers, and the noise and push of modern life.

Humming-birds poised themselves before the purple bunches of the ceiba flowers, their tongues thrust into the calyx and their iridescent wings whirring so rapidly you could see the motion, but not mark the movement, and from the yellow balls of the mimosas came a scent, heady and comforting.

Flocks of green paroquets flew shrieking over the clearing in which the horses fed to their great nests, in which ten or a dozen seemed to harbour, and hung suspended from them by their claws, or crawled into the holes. Now and then a few locusts, wafted by the breeze, passed by upon their way to spread destruction in the plantations of young poplars and of orange trees in the green islands in the stream.

An air of peace gave a strange interest to this little corner of a world plunged into strife and woe. The herders nodded on their horses, who for their part hung down their heads, and now and then shifted their quarters so as to bring their heads into the shade. The innkeeper, García, in his town clothes, and perched upon a tall grey horse, to use his own words, "sweated blood and water like Our Lord" in the fierce glare of the ascending sun.

---

[1] "Onwards, Savoy!" War cry used against the Tedeschi (the Germans) in 1914–18 War.

Suárez and Paralelo pushed the ends of the red silk handkerchiefs they wore tied loosely round their necks, with two points like the wings of a great butterfly hanging upon their shoulders, under their hats, and smoked innumerable cigarettes, the frontiersman's specific against heat or cold. Of all the little company only the pampa Indian showed no sign of being incommoded by the heat. When horses strayed he galloped up to turn them, now striking at the passing butterflies with his heavy-handled whip, or, letting himself fall down from the saddle almost to the ground, drew his brown finger on the dust for a few yards, and with a wriggle like a snake got back into his saddle with a yell.

The hours passed slowly, till at last the horses, having filled themselves with grass, stopped eating and looked towards the river, so we allowed them slowly to stream along towards a shallow inlet on the beach. There they stood drinking greedily, up to their knees, until at last three or four of the outermost began to swim.

Only their heads appeared above the water, and occasionally their backs emerging just as a porpoise comes to the surface in a tideway, gave them an amphibious air, that linked them somehow or another with the classics in that unclassic land.

Long did they swim and play, and then, coming out into the shallow water, drink again, stamping their feet and swishing their long tails, rise up and strike at one another with their feet.

As I sat on my horse upon a little knoll coiling my *lazo*, which had got uncoiled by catching in a bush, I heard a voice in the soft, drawling accents of the inhabitants of Corrientes say, *"Pucha, pingos."*

Turning, I saw the speaker, a gaucho of about thirty years of age, dressed all in black in the old style of thirty years ago. His silver knife, two feet or more in length, stuck in his sash, stuck out on both sides of his body like a lateen.

Where he had come from I had no idea, for he appeared to have risen from the scrub behind me. "Yes," he said, *"Puta, pingos,"* giving the phrase in the more classic, if more unregenerate style, "how well they look, just like the garden in the plaza at Fray Bentos in the sun."

All shades were there, with every variegation and variety of colour, white, and fern noses, chestnuts with a stocking on one leg up to the stifle joint, horses with a ring of white right round their throats, or with a star as clear as if it had been painted on the hip, and *tuvianos*, that is, brown, black, and white, a colour justly prized in Uruguay.

Turning half round and offering me a cigarette, the Correntino spoke again. "It is a paradise for all those *pingos* here in this *rincón*: grass, water, everything that they can want, shade, and shelter from the wind and sun."

So it appeared to me—the swiftly flowing river with its green islands; the pampas grass along the stream; the ruined buildings, half-buried in the orange trees run wild; grass, shade, and water: "*Pucha*, no—*Puta, pingos*, where are they now?"

BOPICUÁ

The great corral at Bopicuá was full of horses. Greys, browns, bays, blacks, duns, chestnuts, roans (both blue and red), skewbalds and piebalds, with claybanks, calicos, buckskins, and a hundred shades and markings, unknown in Europe, but each with its proper name in Uruguay and Argentina, jostled each other, forming a kaleidoscopic mass.

A thick dust rose from the corral and hung above their heads. Sometimes the horses stood all huddled up, gazing with wide distended eyes and nostrils towards a group of men that lounged about the gate. At other times that panic fear, that seizes upon horses when they are crushed together in large numbers, set them a-galloping. Through the dust-cloud their footfalls sounded muffled, and they themselves appeared like phantoms in a mist. When they had circled round a little they stopped, and those outside the throng, craning their heads down nearly to the ground, snorted, and then ran back, arching their necks and carrying their tails like flags. Outside the great corral was set Parodi's camp, below some China trees, and formed of corrugated iron and hides, stuck on short uprights, so that the hides and iron almost came down upon the ground, in gipsy fashion. Upon the branches of the trees were hung saddles, bridles, halters, hobbles, *lazos*, and *boleadoras*, and underneath were spread out saddle-cloths to dry. Pieces of meat swung from the low gables of the hut, and under the low eaves was placed a *catre*, the canvas scissor-bedstead of Spain and of her colonies in the New World. Upon the *catre* was a heap of ponchos airing in the sun, their bright and startling colours looking almost dingy in the fierce light of a March afternoon in Uruguay. Close to the camp stood several bullock-carts, their poles supported on a crutch, and their reed-covered tilts giving them an air of huts on wheels. Men sat about on bullocks' skulls, around a smouldering fire, whilst the maté circulated round from man to man after the fashion of a loving-cup—Parodi, the stiff-jointed son of Italian parents, a gaucho as to clothes and speech, but still half-European in his lack of comprehension of the ways of a wild horse; Arena, the *capataz* from Entre Ríos, thin, slight, and nervous, a man who had, as he said, in his youth known how to read and even guide the pen; but now "things of this world had turned him quite unlettered, and made him more familiar with the *lazo* and the spurs." The mulatto Pablo Suárez, active and cat-like, a great race-rider and horse-tamer, short and deep-chested, with eyes like those of a black cat, and toes, prehensile as a monkey's, that clutched the stirrup when a wild colt began to buck, so that it could not touch its flanks. They and Miguel Paralelo, tall, dark, and handsome, the owner of some property, but drawn by the excitement of a cowboy's life to work for wages, so that he could enjoy the risk of venturing his neck each day on a *bagual*, with other peons as El Correntino and Venancio Báez, were grouped around the fire. With them were seated Martín el Madrileño, a Spanish horse-coper, who had experienced the charm of gaucho life together with Silvestre Ayres, a Brazilian, slight and olive-coloured, well-educated, but better known as a dead pistol-shot than as man of books. They waited for their turn at maté, or ate great chunks of meat from a roast cooked upon a spit, over a fire of bones. Most of the men were tall and sinewy, with that air of taciturnity and self-equilibrium that their isolated lives and Indian blood so often stamp upon the faces of those centaurs of the plains. The camp, set on a little hill, dominated the country for miles on every side. Just underneath it, horses and more horses grazed. Towards the west it stretched out to the woods that fringe the Uruguay, which, with its countless islands, flowed between great tracks of forest, and formed the frontier with the Argentine.

Between the camp and the corrals smouldered a fire of bones and ñandubay, and by it, leaning up against a rail, were set the branding-irons that had turned the horses in the corral into the property of the British Government. All round the herd enclosed, ran horses neighing, seeking their companions, who were to graze no more at Bopicuá, but be sent off by train and ship to the battlefields of Europe to die and suffer for they knew not what, leaving their pastures and their innocent comradeship with one another till the judgment day. Then, I am sure, for God must have some human feeling after all, things will be explained to them, light come into their semi-darkness, and they will feed in prairies where the grass fades not, and springs are never dry, freed from the saddle, and with no cruel spur to urge them on they know not where or why.

For weeks we had been choosing out the doomed five hundred. Riding, inspecting, and examining from dawn till evening, till it appeared that not a single equine imperfection could have escaped our eyes. The gauchos, who all think that they alone know anything about a horse, were all struck dumb with sheer amazement. It seemed to them astonishing to take such pains to select horses that for the most part would be killed in a few months. "These men," they said, "certainly all are doctors at the job. They know even the least defect, can tell what a horse thinks about and why. Still, none of them can ride a horse if he but shakes his ears. In their bag surely there is a cat shut up of some kind or another. If not, why do they bother so much in the matter, when all that is required is something that can carry one into the thickest of the fight?"

The sun began to slant a little, and we had still three leagues to drive the horses to the pasture, where they had to pass the night for the last time in freedom, before they were entrained. Our horses stood outside of the corral, tied to the posts, some saddled with the *recado*, its heads adorned with silver, some with the English saddle, that out of England has such a strange unserviceable look, much like a saucepan on a horse's back. Just as we were about to mount, a man appeared, driving a point of horses, which, he said, "to leave would be a crime against the sacrament." "These are all *pingos*," he exclaimed, "fit for the saddle of the Lord on High, all of them are bitted in the Brazilian style, can turn upon a spread-out saddle-cloth, and all of them can gallop round a bullock's head upon the ground, so that the rider can keep his hand upon it all the time." The speaker by his accent was a Brazilian. His face was olive-coloured, his hair had the suspicion of a kink. His horse, a cream-colour, with black tail and mane, was evidently only half-tamed, and snorted loudly as it bounded here and there, making its silver harness jingle and the rider's poncho flutter in the air. Although time pressed, the man's address was so persuasive, his appearance so much in character with his great silver spurs just hanging from his heel, his jacket turned up underneath his elbow by the handle of his knife, and, to speak truth, the horses looked so good and in such high condition that we determined to examine them, and told their owner to drive them into a corral.

Once again we commenced the work that we had done so many times of mounting and examining. Once more we fought, trying to explain the mysteries of red tape to unsophisticated minds, and once again our *domadores* sprang lightly, barebacked, upon the horses they had never seen before, with varying results. Some of the Brazilian's horses bucked like antelopes, El Correntino and the others of our men sitting them barebacked as easily as an ordinary man rides over a small fence. To all our queries why they did not saddle up we got one answer, "To ride with the *recado* is but a pastime only fit for boys." So they went on, pulling the horses up in three short bounds, nostrils aflame and tails and manes tossed wildly in the air, only a yard or two from the corral. Then, slipping off, gave their opinion that the particular *bayo*, *zaino*, or *gateao* was just the thing to mount a lancer on, and that the speaker thought he could account for a good tale of Boches if he were over there in the Great War. This same great war, which they called "barbarous," taking a secret pleasure in the fact that it showed Europeans not a whit more civilised than they themselves, appeared to them something in the way of a great pastime from which they were debarred.

Most of them, when they sold a horse, looked at him and remarked, "*Pobrecito*, you will go the Great War," just as a man looks at his son who is about to go, with feelings of mixed admiration and regret.

After we had examined all the Brazilian's *tropilla* so carefully that he said, "By Satan's death, your graces know far more about my horses than I myself, and all I wonder is that you do not ask me if all of them have not complied with all the duties of the Church," we found that about twenty of them were fit for the Great War. Calling upon Parodi and the *capataz* of Bopicuá, who all the time had remained seated round the smouldering fire and drinking maté, to prepare the branding-irons, the peons led them off, our head man calling out *"Artillería"* or *"Caballería,"* according to their size. After the branding, either on the hip for cavalry and on the neck for the artillery, a peon cut their manes off, making them as ugly as a mule, as their late owner said, and we were once more ready for the road, after the payment had been made. This took a little time, either because the Brazilian could not count, or perhaps because of his great caution, for he would not take payment except horse by horse. So, driving out the horses one by one, we placed a roll of dollars in his hand as each one passed the gate. Even then each roll of dollars had to be counted separately, for time is what men have the most at their disposal in places such as Bopicuá.

Two hours of sunset still remained, with three long leagues to cover, for in those latitudes there is no twilight, night succeeding day, just as films follow one another in a cinematograph. At last it all was over, and we were free to mount. Such sort of drives are of the nature of a sport in South America, and so the Brazilian drove off the horses that we had rejected, a half a mile away, leaving them with a negro boy to herd, remarking that the rejected were as good or better than those that we had bought, and, after cinching up his horse, prepared to ride with us. Before we started, a young man rode up, dressed like an exaggerated gaucho, in loose black trousers, poncho, and a *golilla* round his neck, a *lazo* hanging from the saddle, a pair of *boleadoras* peeping beneath his *cojinillo*, and a long silver knife stuck in his belt. It seemed he was the son of an estanciero who was studying law in Buenos Aires, but had returned for his vacation, and hearing of our drive had come to ride with us and help us in our task. No one on such occasions is to be despised, so, thanking him for his good intentions, to which he answered that he was a "partizan of the Allies, lover of liberty and truth, and was well on in all his studies, especially in International Law," we mounted, the gauchos floating almost imperceptibly, without an effort, to their seats, the European with that air of escalading a ship's side that differentiates us from man less civilised.

During the operations with the Brazilian, the horses had been let out of the corral to feed, and now were being held back *en pastoreo*, as it is called in Uruguay, that is to say, watched at a little distance by mounted men. Nothing remained but to drive out of the corral the horses bought from the Brazilian, and let them join the larger herd. Out they came like a string of wild geese, neighing and looking round, and then instinctively made towards the others that were feeding, and were swallowed up amongst them. Slowly we rode towards the herd, sending on several well-mounted men upon its flanks, and with precaution—for of all living animals tame horses most easily take fright upon the march and separate—we got them into motion, on a well-marked trail that led towards the gate of Bopicuá.

At first they moved a little sullenly, and as if surprised. Then the contagion of emotion that spreads so rapidly amongst animals upon the march seemed to inspire them, and the whole herd broke into a light trot. That is the moment that a stampede may happen, and accordingly we pulled our horses to a walk, whilst the men riding on the flanks forged slowly to the front, ready for anything that might occur. Gradually the trot slowed down, and we saw as it were a sea of manes and tails in front of us, emerging from a cloud of dust, from which shrill neighings and loud snortings rose. They reached a hollow, in which were several pools, and stopped to drink, all crowding into the shallow water, where they stood pawing up the mud and drinking greedily. Time pressed, and as we knew that there was water in the pasture where they were to sleep, we drove them back upon the trail, the water dripping from their muzzles and their tails, and the black mud clinging to the hair upon their fetlocks, and in drops upon their backs. Again they broke into a trot, but this time, as they had got into control, we did not check them, for there was still a mile to reach the gate.

Passing some smaller mud-holes, the body of a horse lay near to one of them, horribly swollen, and with its stiff legs hoisted a little in the air by the distension of its flanks. The passing horses edged away from it in terror, and a young roan snorted and darted like an arrow from the herd. Quick as was the dart he made, quicker still El Correntino wheeled his horse on its hind legs and rushed to turn him back. With his whip whirling round his head he rode to head the truant, who, with tail floating in the air, had got a start of him of about fifty yards. We pressed instinctively upon the horses; but not so closely as to frighten them, though still enough to be able to stop another of them from cutting out. The Correntino on a half-tamed grey, which he rode with a rawhide thong bound round its lower jaw, for it was still unbitted, swaying with every movement in his saddle, which he hardly seemed to grip, so perfect was his balance, rode at a slight angle to the runaway and gained at every stride. His hat blew back and, kept in place by a black ribbon underneath his chin, framed his head like an aureole. The red silk handkerchief tied loosely round his neck fluttered beneath it, and as he dashed along, his *lazo* coiled upon his horse's croup, rising and falling with each bound, his eyes fixed on the flying roan, he might have served a sculptor as the model for a centaur, so much did he and the wild colt he rode seem indivisible.

In a few seconds, which to us seemed minutes, for we feared the infection might have spread to the whole *caballada*, the Correntino headed and turned the roan, who came back at three-quarter speed, craning his neck out first to one side, then to the other, as if he still thought that a way lay open for escape.

By this time we had reached the gates of Bopicuá, and still seven miles lay between us and our camping-ground, with a fast-declining sun. As the horses passed the gate we counted them, an operation of some difficulty when time presses and the count is large. Nothing is easier than to miss animals, that is to say, for Europeans, however practised, but the lynx-eyed gauchos never are at fault. "Where is the little brown horse with a white face, and a bit broken out of his near forefoot?" they will say, and ten to one that horse is missing, for what they do not know about the appearance of a horse would not fill many books. Only a drove road lay between Bopicuá and the great pasture, at whose faraway extremity the horses were to sleep. When the last animal had passed and the great gates swung to, the young law student rode up to my side, and, looking at the "great *tropilla*," as he called it, said, "*Morituri te salutant.*[1] This is the last time they will feed in Bopicuá." We turned a moment, and the falling sun lit up the undulating plain, gilding the cottony tufts of the long grasses, falling upon the dark-green leaves of the low trees around Parodi's camp, glinting across the belt of wood that fringed the Uruguay, and striking full upon a white estancia house in Entre Ríos, making it appear quite close at hand, although four leagues away.

Two or three hundred yards from the great gateway stood a little native hut, as unsophisticated, but for a telephone, as were the gaucho's huts in Uruguay, as I remember them full thirty years ago. A wooden barrel on a sledge for bringing water had

---

[1] "They who are about to die salute you." This is a variation of the death salute of the condemned in the imperial arenas of ancient Rome.

been left close to the door, at which the occupant sat drinking maté, tapping with a long knife upon his boot. Under a straw-thatched shelter stood a saddled horse, and a small boy upon a pony slowly drove up a flock of sheep. A blue, fine smoke that rose from a few smouldering logs and bones blended so completely with the air that one was not quite sure if it was really smoke or the reflection of the distant Uruguay against the atmosphere.

Not far off lay the bones of a dead horse, with bits of hide adhering to them, shrivelled into mere parchment by the sun. All this I saw as in a camera-lucida, seated a little sideways on my horse, and thinking sadly that I, too, had looked my last on Bopicuá. It is not given to all men after a break of years to come back to the scenes of youth, and still find in them the same zest as of old. To return again to all the cares of life called civilised, with all its littlenesses, its newspapers all full of nothing, its sordid aims disguised under high-sounding nicknames, its hideous riches and its sordid poverty, its want of human sympathy, and, above all, its barbarous war brought on it by the folly of its rulers, was not just at that moment an alluring thought, as I felt the little *malacara* that I rode twitching his bridle, striving to be off. When I had touched him with the spur he bounded forward and soon overtook the *caballada*, and the place which for so many months had been part of my life sank out of sight, just as an island in the tropics fades from view as the ship leaves it, as it were, hull down.

When we had passed into the great enclosure of La Pileta, and still four or five miles remained to go, we pressed the *caballada* into a long trot, certain that the danger of a stampede was past. Wonderful and sad it was to ride behind so many horses, trampling knee-high through the wild grasses of the camp, snorting and biting at each other, and all unconscious that they would never more career across the plains. Strange and affecting, too, to see how those who had known each other all kept together in the midst of the great herd, resenting all attempts of their companions to separate them.

A *tropilla* that we had bought from a Frenchman called Leon, composed of five brown horses, had ranged itself around its bell mare, a fine chestnut, like a bodyguard. They fought off any of the other horses who came near her, and seemed to look at her both with affection and with pride.

Two little bright bay horses, with white legs and noses, that were brothers, and what in Uruguay are known as *seguidores*, that is, one followed the other wherever it might go, ran on the outskirts of the herd. When either of them stopped to eat, its companion turned its head and neighed to it, when it came galloping up. Arena, our head man, riding beside me on a skewbald, looked at them, and, after dashing forward to turn a runaway, wheeled round his horse almost in the air and stopped it in a bound, so suddenly that for an instant they stood poised like an equestrian statue, looked at the *seguidores*, and remarked, "*Patrón*, I hope one shell will kill them both in the Great War if they have got to die." I did not answer, except to curse the Boches with all the intensity the Spanish tongue commands. The young law student added his testimony, and we rode on in silence.

A passing sleeve of locusts almost obscured the declining sun. Some flew against our faces, reminding me of the fight Cortés had with the Indians not far from Vera Cruz, which, Bernal Díaz[2] says, was obstructed for a moment by a flight of locusts that came so thickly that many lost their lives by the neglect to raise their bucklers against what they thought were locusts, and in reality were arrows that the Indians shot. The effect was curious as the insects flew against the horses, some clinging to their manes, and others making them bob up and down their heads, just as a man does in a driving shower of hail. We reached a narrow causeway that formed the passage through a marsh. On it the horses crowded, making us hold our breath for fear that they would push each other off into the mud, which had no bottom, upon either side. When we emerged and cantered up a little hill, a lake lay at the bottom of it, and beyond it was a wood, close to a railway siding. The evening now was closing in, but there was still a good half-hour of light. As often happens in South America just before sundown, the wind dropped to a dead calm, and passing little clouds of locusts, feeling the night approach, dropped into the long grass just as a flying-fish drops into the waves, with a harsh whirring of their gauzy wings.

The horses smelt the water at the bottom of the hill, and the

[2]Bernal Díaz del Castillo (c. 1495–1584), *Historia verdadera de la conquista de Nueva España*, translated into English by A. P. Maudslay as *True History of the Conquest of New Spain* (New York and London, 1928, 1956; also by J. M. Cohen, Penguin, Harmondsworth, 1963).

whole five hundred broke into a gallop, manes flying, tails raised high, and we, feeling somehow the gallop was the last, raced madly by their side until within a hundred yards or so of the great lake. They rushed into the water and all drank greedily, the setting sun falling upon their many-coloured backs, and giving the whole herd the look of a vast tulip field. We kept away so as to let them drink their fill, and then, leading our horses to the margin of the lake, dismounted, and, taking out their bits, let them drink, with the air of one accomplishing a rite, no matter if they raised their heads a dozen times and then began again.

Slowly Arena, El Correntino, Paralelo, Suárez, and the rest drove out the herd to pasture in the deep lush grass. The rest of us rode up some rising ground towards the wood. There we drew up, and looking back towards the plain on which the horses seemed to have dwindled to the size of sheep in the half-light, some one, I think it was Arena, or perhaps Pablo Suárez, spoke their elegy: "Eat well," he said; "there is no grass like that of La Pileta, to where you go across the sea. The grass in Europe all must smell of blood."

CHARLIE THE GAUCHO

The *pulpería* stood on a little rise, surrounded by a peach orchard. Its whitewashed walls, flat roof, and door studded with iron nails, gave it a look as of the houses in Utrera, Ecija or any of the towns in the land of María Santísima. There the resemblance stopped, a side door opened into a room, half-store, half-bar. Hanging from pegs were stirrups, girths, spurs, bits, bridles and horse gear of all kinds. Upon the shelves were rolls of gaudy cotton goods, and ponchos made in Birmingham. Bottles of cheap scent, in those days generally of Agua de Florida, in tall thin flasks, with elongated necks. They had a picture of a red-cheeked girl, with eyes like saucers, and an air of super-harlotry, that to be honest I never have observed amongst the daughters of the Banda Oriental, the name, in those days, of the republic of Uruguay.

Above the wooden bar were rows of bottles: gin, caña, hesperidina de Bagley, vermouth, and various syrups, cassis, naranjada, and orchata, known locally as *refrescos*, and much consumed by the fair, or more properly the brown sex.

A wooden palisade running up almost to the roof, protected the proprietor, when what was styled *"un barullo de Jesucristo,"* that may be translated or rather paraphrased as "Hell's own Row" arose, after a quarrel, either between two rival guitar players, or two gauchos as to the brand one or the other remembered on a horse, ten or twelve years ago. Then the proprietor would retire, and close the wicket through which he served the drinks in stout and heavy glasses with enormously thick bottoms, that I never saw again till I arrived years afterwards in Corpus Christi, Texas. There so to speak he "stood by," grasping a bottle, ready to throw, for there was always a good pile of empty bottles to serve as missiles in the like emergencies.

Outside at a stout post of hard-wood, called a *palenque*, were tied the horses of the customers; browns, blacks and chestnuts, duns, sorrels, greys of all shades from steel to dappled, and every kind of piebald and of skewbald, wild-eyed, and looking only fit for "perches for a hawk," as ran the gaucho saying, stood looking nervously about at the least noise, or if they happened to be tame, patiently waiting in the sun with half-closed eyes, head hanging down, and resting a hind leg.

Their owners, dressed in the *chiripá*, that curious garment, consisting of a long piece of cloth or linen, held round the waist by a silk, knotted sash, and passed between the legs to form a trouser, with the front lap tucked underneath the sash, that they must have taken in old times from the native Indians; they either had a jacket of some sort or other, a pleated woollen overshirt, or a cheap, reach-me-down alpaca coat. All of them had ponchos that they either carried on one arm, or wore, their long-handled knife sticking them out just as a boom spreads out a sail. Their hats were very small, and seemed to balance on their shock heads of hair, coarse as a horse's tail, and were kept in their place, when the wind blew, by a black ribbon from which hung two tassels, generally greasy from long wear. Their wearers, when they dismounted, waddled like alligators upon land, clanking their enormous spurs, known as *lloronas* or as *nazarenas*, on the ground.

They called for gin, or caña, striking the counter with their whips, or the flat of their long knives. The etiquette was to invite the company, and in all cases to hand the glass to the man nearest to the drinker, who touched it with his lips, handing it back, with a grave *"gracias, caballero,"* or *"amigo,"* as the case might be.

A pack of hungry-looking dogs, that usually rushed out to seize the horse's tail of any passer-by, guarded the house, and helped to bring the cattle up into the corral.

An empty bullock cart, straw-thatched and with the heavy pole sticking up like a mast, served as a roosting place or shelter from the sun, to the wild, stringy-looking chickens, or to a game-cock fastened by a string.

As the house stood not far from where a flying raft conveyed the horses of the travellers or troops of cattle over the river Yi, several straw huts inhabited either by Indian-looking girls, or women, who could no longer get a living in the capital, were the abode of those who dealt in "love."

The country people always spoke of them as *las quitanderas*; no one was able to explain the name, so it remains a problem for philologists.

Over the place, upon that morning of Saint Rose of Lima, a season when in Uruguay the country people always expect a storm, there was an air of tension and unusual quiet, such as in every country of the world seems to take hold of people after a tragedy. The side door of the *pulpería* was deserted, no groups of gauchos stood at the bar, gravely discoursing of the next revolution, that was certain to break out if the accursed Blancos or Colorados, as the case might be, remained too long in power. No tinkle of a guitar, its strings mended and supplemented by strips of hide cut almost as fine as wire, floated out into the still heavy air. No high-pitched falsetto voice was heard, singing a triste, or some such artless effort of a local bard, as "At the door of my house, there is a plate of vinegar. Who laughs at me, laughs at his mother."

No one sat on the ground drawing, or as they called it, "painting" the brands of horses with his finger in the dust, or scratching them upon the door with the point of his *facón* to clinch his argument. Three or four grave men of middle age, but without a silver hair in their black heads, stood talking in subdued tones to the proprietor.

The shrill laughter of the *quitanderas* was subdued, and now and then, one of them, with her face unpainted, and a black shawl around her shoulders, peeped out from her rancho as timidly as some wild animal peers out from its lair.

"*Che*, friend Azcoitia," said one of the group of men who stood about the door of the *pulpería*, conversing in low voices, "the commissary has not hurried much. The *chasqui* that you sent off at daybreak this morning, after the 'misfortune,' on your best horse, that *zaino* that you got from the Brazilian for a pair of silver spurs, two dollars, and a flask of rum, with orders to the lad Ramón, not to spare the *rebenque* or the spurs, could not have taken more than two hours at the most to arrive at the *Estancia de los sarandís*, where the commissary lives."

"I know," said the proprietor, "but then the law always walks with a leaden foot."

"Perhaps they could not find the horses, or perhaps news of the revolution had arrived, God alone knows, and He, although He knows, never informs us what He knows, so that to us it matters little what He knows."

"Heretics," said one of the gauchos with a smile, and then, holding his hand, as brown as if it had been cut out of mahogany, before his eyes, exclaimed, "*Caray, amigo*,[1] I see three horsemen on the far-off *loma* galloping this way."

In spite of all his efforts the Basque proprietor saw nothing for at least half a minute, though Don Fulgencio, the old gaucho, kept on muttering, "Sí, señor, it is the commissary. *Lindo el lobuno!*[2] What a fine gallop, the two poor soldiers with their crop-eared jades keep their *rebenques* going like the handle of a pump, to keep them up with him."

The figures of the men and horses by degrees got more distinct, until at last even the proprietor of the *pulpería* could see them plainly. Enveloped in a cloud of dust, they neared the house, rode up to the *palenque* and dismounted from their beasts.

Don Exaltación Rodríguez, commissary of the department of Porongos and the Yi, got slowly off his horse. In early middle age and with the stoutness that office always lends to men in Oriental countries, in South America, and Spain already coming on, he yet was a fine figure on his horse, a dun with a black stripe right down its back, and markings like a zebra on its hocks. He handed his long white well-plaited rawhide reins, with silver rings at spaces of six inches or a foot, to one of his wild-looking soldiers, who had forced his horse up to the *palenque* of the *pulpería* rejoicing in the appellation of *La flor de mayo*, with curses and with blows of his flat whip. The proprietor, a Spanish Basque, strong, muscular, his black hair contrasting strangely with his dark blue eyes, dressed as a gaucho of the better class in the loose black merino Turkish trouser known as *bombachas* in the republic of Uruguay, a light alpaca coat, white hemp-soled alpargatas on his feet, and on his head the national blue bonnet of the Basque provinces, came out to greet the representative of the law's authority.

"Good morning, Don Exaltación" he said, "come in and have your eleven hours, I have the finest caña from Brazil, vermouth,

---

[1] A vulgar exclamation of surprise or disgust, similar to *caramba*.
[2] "What a fine horse (wolf-colored)!"

gin of the Palm Tree brand, dry wine of Spain, and a butt of the best Carlón from Catalonia."

Gravely the Comisario, who had put on *une tête de circonstance*,[3] returned his greeting, thanked him and said, "First I must see the dead. I hope that no one has touched the body, as the laws of the republic, in these cases, charge its citizens."

"All is in order, Don Exaltación, the man lies where he fell, for though the fight took place inside the house, he staggered out to the *galpón*, holding his intestines up with his left hand, still grasping his *facón*, and died without a word, just as the *tigre* dies, when he is cornered by the dogs, after a dozen wounds."

"Enough, friend," rejoined the man in authority, "you seem to have not badly of the 'syrup of the beak' for one of your nationality, but men of your calling all learn it in the trade."

Without more words the storekeeper led the way to the *galpón*. Three or four gauchos, whose horses sat back on their halters, as the little cortege passed, [moved,] making the Comisario's horse, that stood hobbled and with the reins tied to the cantle of the *recado* arching his neck and looking like the knight in chess, rattle his silver gear.

The gauchos' great iron spurs, trailing on the ground, completed the orchestra.

The air was heavy, the sky lowering, and now and then short gusts of wind raised dust in whirls like little waterspouts, a sure sign that the *pampero* was on its way, from the far southern plains.

Signing with his hand for all to stand back, the Comisario, taking off his hat, crossed himself furtively, threw away his black, Brazilian cigarette and drew away the white embroidered cotton handkerchief that someone, perhaps a *quitandera*, had placed upon the dead man's face, in defiance of the law. Azcoitia had spoken truly when he said the man lay just as he had fallen. Dressed in the clothes of a poor gaucho, a cotton *chiripá*, dirty white cotton drawers, his feet, that stuck up in the appealing way the feet of those who have died violent deaths so often take, were shod in boots made from the skin of a calf's hind leg, leaving the toes bare.

The man had fallen with his right arm underneath his head. His left still was in the attitude of holding up the intestines,

---

[3] A face to suit the particular situation.

although the fingers were relaxed, and underneath his cotton *chiripá* the lump was plainly visible where the bowels had escaped and stained his soiled white drawers with blood. Another gaping wound above the heart, that had not bled much, and was already drying on his white pleated shirt, had been the final stroke. Tall, thin, and muscular, his long fair hair was spread over his shoulders, for in those days gauchos all wore long hair, and took a pride in it. His chestnut beard and sunburned face showed that he was a European, but one who had lived long upon the plains of Uruguay. His face was calm, save for a little rictus that displayed his teeth, strong and as white as ivory. His hands were muscular and brown, showing several old scars he might have got in other fights during the course of a wild life.

His staring, wide-opened eyes were grey, and you divined at once that they were eyes accustomed to great open spaces, by the contraction of the muscles at the corners. Flies had begun to buzz about them.

Gravely the Comisario looked at the dead man, almost with admiration, and said, "*Pucha,* what wounds; see where the hilt of the *facón* has left a mark upon his shirt; it must have been sufficient to have killed a bullock. How long has he been dead, Azcoitia? Tell me his name, and how he got his death." The Basque, in the curious jargon so many of them speak in Spanish, using feminine adjectives with masculine nouns and vice versa, took up his parable. Three or four gauchos, the two ragged soldiers, and several of the *quitanderas,* who had overcome their fear, stood by to listen to him.

"Señor Comisario, this was a brave man. Everyone knew him as Carlitos el Inglés. For years he wandered up and down the republic, working occasionally as a *tropero,* or as a horse-breaker despite his five-and-forty years; for him no horse was wild."

A gaucho interrupted, "No, señor, it seemed a lie to see him on a colt, with or without a saddle—*pucha, gringo lindo!*[4] He was really more gaucho than ourselves, and knew more of the camp than *Satanás* himself, who, you know, knows more, for that he is old, than because he is *Satanás.*"

The other gauchos who stood round about the body, nodded their heads in affirmation, remarking, "Sí señor, Fulgencio only speaks the truth."

[4] "What a handsome gringo! "

"Enough," said the Comisario, who had been taking what he called "dates" in a little dog-eared pocket-book, with a greasy pencil-stump that was as often in his mouth as on the paper, looked up and turning to the Basque Azcoitia, said, "Tell me the manner of his death?"

Azcoitia took up his parable: "Señor Comisario, this Carlitos, who although he was a man of education, knowing the pen, and reading his own tongue, the Castilian, and the French, better than any *doctorcillo* of them all, liked to live with the gauchos and be one of them. He, as Don Fulgencio has said, was a great horse-breaker, threw the lasso, and the *boleadoras* better than any of them, but his chief pride was in his skill with the *facón*. When he heard of some *valentón* he would ride leagues to meet him, and when they met, usually at a *pulpería*, Carlitos would salute him as courteously as if he had been an old friend, and leave him generally stretched out, showing his navel, as we say here in the Department of the Yi."

The Comisario, a man who had bad fleas, as say the gauchos, cut him short, impatiently. "Jesus! what a tongue, long as a lasso! Friend, you should have stayed at home and been a friar. Tell me without flourishes and rodeos, how this Carlitos died, and who it was that killed him; but not here—one should respect the dead."

As they adjourned towards the *pulpería*, one of the *quitanderas* walked into the shed, covered the dead man's face with a silk handkerchief, knelt down, and saying, "Carlitos was a generous man, and valiant; if he had money no one was freer with it." That was his epitaph. Generous and valiant, what more can man desire to be said of him after death?

Crossing herself both on the breast and mouth, she muttered a short prayer, scarce audible, after the fashion of the country. Then rising to her feet, she draped herself in her black shawl, taking on for a moment the dignity that sincerity imparts. Then with a courteous salutation to the Comisario, she walked out of the *galpón*. As they turned towards the horses, the long-threatened storm broke suddenly. Lightning played continuously, a low green arch that had formed on the horizon was dissolved into a furious rain that ran along the parched-up soil like hail. The thunder seemed to shake the world. The wind swept everything before it. The horses tied to the *palenque* turned their quarters to the rain, lowered their heads, and stood looking like caricatures of what they had been but a few minutes before the *pampero* had caught them and all their little world in its fell sweep. Almost as if by magic the country seemed to become a lake, and through the water, already several inches deep, the Comisario and the rest scuttled to safety, their heavy spurs clanking like fetters on the ground.

When they had shaken the rain from their soaked clothes and had had a glass of caña or of gin, Azcoitia was once more about to start his parable. "No," said the Comisario, "let a son of the country speak and tell us how this Carlitos died, for this man is as long-winded as a well-trained racehorse." The Basque laughed, but, as goes the saying, with "the laugh of a rabbit," that is, a rabbit that is going to be killed.

"It is this way, señor Comisario," a quiet-looking gaucho, Eustaquio Medina, began. "Carlitos came into the *pulpería* last evening, not drunk but with enough gin under his belt to make him foolish. He rode a *pangaré*, half tamed, but that already knew the bit. *"Vaya un fletón."* [5] He had hardly tied him to the *palenque* than *El Ñato* Vargas de Correntino, a real alligator, like most of his compatriots, who was standing at the door—he had an eye, that Indian, in his scrunched-up face!—walked up to the *inglés*, and called out, 'That is my *pangaré*. He has the mark of Sigismundo Pérez in the Cuchilla de Haedo, from whom I bought him as a colt.' 'You lie,' replied Carlitos, 'he has another brand, a little like that of Don Sigismundo, but different.' 'Yes,' cried *El Ñato*, 'but you have altered it; see where the scar has scarcely healed.' Before a man could say Jesús, a terrible *bochinche* started. Both of them *tigres*, both men to whom the *facón* was as familiar as is the pen to a *cagatinta* of the law. Carlitos was the stronger of the two, the Correntino quicker on his feet. With their light summer ponchos wrapped round their left arms, their heads held low, to protect their bellies, they circled round each other like two cats, or fighting cocks. *Pucha*! their *facóns* flashed through the air like torches! There was no trick they left untried; but both of them were old hands at the game. Not two old bulls, señor Comisario, when they met at the edge of a rodeo, or alone in a clearing of the *monte*, were more cunning or more fierce. Carlitos first drew blood. Stooping down low he scooped up dust with his left hand, and threw it in *El Ñato's* eyes, crossing his face with a *jabeque*, that he will carry to the grave. Time after time, they came together with their hands meeting in the air, only to jump yards back-

[5] "What a horse!"

wards, and to come on guard again, panting, and glaring, watching each other's every move. At last Carlitos, who had been drinking, began to tire. *El Ñato* drove him backwards, and with a slash opened his belly, but Carlitos, holding up his guts with his left hand, still came at him, like a tiger, till, weakened as he was, *El Ñato* drove his *facón* into his chest, till the hilt clinked on the breast-bone. Then, as you know, Carlitos staggered out to the *galpón* and died without a word. *El Ñato*, with his face opened like a water-melon, a finger gone from his left hand, and all the poncho that had covered his left arm cut into lace, mounted his horse, and with the *pangaré, de tiro*, galloping beside him, went off, perhaps to his own *pago* in Corrientes, or perhaps to hide himself in some island in the Uruguay."

" 'Tis well," the Comisario remarked, "we can do nothing, but the man must be buried like a Christian."

Azcoitia promised that it should be done and that next morning he would take the body into town, in his own bullock cart, and pay for a mass for the repose of the soul of the dead man.

After an interval the Comisario got upon his horse. The gauchos mounted, like drops of water sliding down a pane of glass, saluted one another gravely, and struck into the clockwork gallop of the plains towards their separate ranchos, gradually disappearing into the horizon, their ponchos waving in the wind, and their right arms moving mechanically as they just touched their horses' flanks with their *rebenques* to keep them to their stride.

The Comisario, as he rode past the *galpón*, where lay the body of Carlitos el Inglés, who had been both the admiration and the terror of the district, raised his forefinger to his hat, murmuring, "Of all the animals God has created, the male Christian is the wildest, but He knew best when He created him," touched his horse with the spur and, followed by his ragged soldiers, breasted a little hill and disappeared.

What I have written, I, sinner that I am, did not see with these eyes the earth will eat, but three days afterwards I passed the *pulpería*, halted to buy a box of sardines, raisins of Málaga, and bread; and as I drank a glass of caña, heard the story; heard and forgot it, though no doubt it stayed fixed in the brain, just as a photograph is dormant on the gelatine or glass before it is revealed.

Everyone in the Banda Oriental knew Charlie the Gaucho, at least by reputation. His adventures, fights, flights from justice, disappearances into hiding, some said amongst the Indians of the Chaco, and others that he knew of an uninhabited island in the Uruguay, to which he would retire until pursuit had been abandoned. There were not wanting those who were convinced he used to plunge into the depths of the Laguna Yberá in Corrientes, in whose recesses, as every gaucho knew, there lived a race of dwarfs, unseen but yet believed in fervently, for faith alone works miracles, has done so since the beginning of the world and will do so to the last day that it exists. There with the hypothetic dwarf, lighted at night by the ipétatá, the bird that bears a lantern in its tail, living on game, Carlitos was believed to pass a month or two, and then emerge, to resume his usual life, as justice in those days was little retrospective, and no one troubled to bring criminals to account, after the immediate scandal had died down. In fact they held that, in the words of the old Spanish saw, "the dead and the absent have no friends," to which they might have added, "and no enemies."

Little by little, the fight upon the margin of the Yi, Charlie the Gaucho, even the story that Azcoitia used to tell, with endless repetitions, had become legendary.

No one could tell me anything of Gaucho Charlie's previous life. He seemed to have come into the world of Uruguay armed at all points, just as Minerva issued from the head of Jove. No one remembered him as a poor rider, an indifferent thrower of the *lazo* or the *boleadoras*, or before he spoke Spanish perfectly. No one had seen him possessed of any visible means of support, except such money as he earned by breaking in horses and working as a vaquero with the herds of cattle that in those days were always passing to Brazil. Still he had always money to spend at all the *pulperías*, or lavish on *las quitanderas*, and at all race meetings he was certain to appear.

At times well dressed, in gaucho fashion, his horse adorned with silver and he himself trailing great silver spurs that dangled from the high-heeled boots the gauchos used to wear, at others in the clothes in which he died, poncho and *chiripá*, with potro boots upon his feet, and a bandana handkerchief tied round his head beneath his hat.

Years passed, and even in that country of long memories, Charlie the Gaucho's exploits gradually grew dim. Although I always thought "there was a cat shut up in the bag," and that there must have been a mystery in the life of an educated Englishman, who for years roamed about amongst the gauchos, speaking their language perfectly with all its turns of slang, and met his death in a fight, in an obscure *boliche*, about a horse that it appeared that he had stolen, no one I met could solve or even throw a light upon it.

In my case fate was kind. Long afterwards, business called me to the capital.

A Mr. Beckeridge was, I think, our vice-consul in those half-forgotten days. Short, rather stout, with thick dark whiskers, drink had bestowed a nose upon him as red as a beefsteak. The gauchos, always apt at nicknames, called him *"El Farolito,"* that is, the little lantern. He seemed as proud of the designation as a Habsburg might be proud of his long chin.

Spanish he spoke as easily as English, with all the verbs in the infinitive, and no regard to genders, but understood it perfectly, although his accent was most formidable, so that one never knew, without attention, which language he was speaking, for he had formed a jumble of the two, almost inextricable.

I found him in his dusty office, unswept and strewed with ends of cigarettes, half torn-up letters, and all the flotsam and the jetsam of an untidy bachelor, seated for greater comfort in his shirt-sleeves, smoking a Brazilian cigar. His desk was piled with invoices, bills of lading, deeds of charter-party and matters of the kind, and on the walls hung the announcements of ships' sailings, arrivals at the port, rates of exchange, advertisements for missing British subjects, and all the multifarious affairs that in those days, for miserable pay, fell to a consul's lot. Withal a gentleman, both in his bearing and his speech, and, as I found when he began to talk, not inefficient at his job.

He welcomed me, as was the fashion of the country and those days, as if we had been friends from boyhood. My trifling business soon dispatched, we fell a-talking over a glass or two of hesperidina, a liquor fashionable at the time throughout the River Plate, concocted and retailed by an American called Bagley, who had made a fortune out of it. Long did we talk on local topics, the coming revolution, and that just ended, the want of water for the camps, the locusts, and how a Mr. Walker rode from the Estancia de Las Arias to "Montyviddeó" as he pronounced the word, two hundred miles at least, in two-and-twenty hours.

These subjects palling, although we did them ample justice, I mentioned Gaucho Charlie, said I just missed his death, and asked the consul if he had ever heard about him. At last I had struck oil. "Charlie the Gaucho!" exclaimed the consul, throwing away the stump of his cigar, and tossing off another glass of the pale yellow hesperidina from one of the little barrel-shaped bottles that I so well remember in every *pulpería*. "Yes, many's the time he has sat in the chair in which you now are sitting. You are right in thinking that he had a curious history. I will read you what the French call his dossier." So saying, he took from a bookshelf a volume bound in soft brown calf. He mopped his face, settled his glasses well on his red nose, poured out another glass, mixed this time with soda water and Angostura bitters, and was about to read. Then, interrupting himself, he said: "All that I am going to read to you I had from Charlie's lips. After his death one of his family corroborated all that he had said. "Charles Edward Mitchell was born in Yorkshire of a good family. His family were county gentry, of considerable wealth. Charles, a fine lad, high-spirited and generous, but subject all his life to sudden fits of rage, was sent into the Navy. " 'He did well there, and as a midshipman of about sixteen was on board a frigate, lying at the time the tragedy occurred at a little port in Uruguay, upon the River Plate. She lay in-shore, not far from land, and, as the weather was extremely hot, with all her ports open.'

"You remember the old-fashioned gun-rooms in the frigates of those days; dark, low, and smelling of stale rum and cockroaches, with candles stuck in empty gin bottles?"

I did, having seen many of them, with their air of frowsiness, the midshipmen asleep on benches, the steward in a striped linen jacket, and their well-remembered smell.

"What happened only himself could tell with accuracy, but in some argument a furious quarrel arose. Young Mitchell felled his antagonist with a gin bottle, and thinking he was dead, without reflection rushed to the open port and plunged into the sea. As the ship only lay three or four hundred yards off-shore, escape was easy for him. After a search the vessel sailed without him, for he had disappeared, like a stone disappears dropped into the pitch lake of Trinidad, leaving no trace behind.

"Several years passed and the affair was quite forgotten, when one day a tall young man dressed as a gaucho, pretty well-to-do, walked in, and introduced himself to me. His English had grown rusty with disuse, and it was some time before I took in what he had to say, for he spoke very slowly, bringing the words out from the recesses of his brain in jerks, and asking me in Spanish now and then if I understood him properly.

"He told me he was the midshipman who, as he thought, had killed one of his brother officers and deserted from his ship. When he had swum ashore, still in a panic, he had walked till he was tired, thinking he was pursued. After a night's rest in a wood, he took the road again till he arrived at an estancia.

"The owner took pity on the frightened, hungry boy and treated him more as a long lost son than as a lad who had come penniless to ask for food. He sent and found the ship had sailed, after a prolonged search for the fugitive, and that the other midshipman had recovered from the blow."

The consul halted in his reading, filled up his glass and said sententiously: "The wild goat always seeks the wood, and so it happened with young Mitchell in this case. From the first day he liked the wild life of the gauchos, learned to ride a wild horse, and *lazo*, with the wildest of the lads upon the place. The language seemed to come to him naturally. He let his hair grow long, after the gaucho fashion of the time, adopted all their ways, dressed as they dressed, and in a year or two left the estancia, to the regret of the kind owners of the place, who, being childless, wished to adopt him, to take up the life of a wandering gaucho, working at sheep-shearings, breaking in horses and going now and then as a peon with troops of cattle to Brazil. That, in essentials," said the consul, "was his tale."

He closed the book, put it back more carefully than I expected in the shelf, and after lighting a black Brazilian cigarette, resumed: "But the tale had a *llapa*, as the gauchos call the last six feet of their *lazo*, that as you know is made of a finer plait than the whole body of the rope. As Charlie talked, gradually his English became more fluent, and he was not obliged to think for words.

"I asked him, 'Why did you never write home to your people, in all the years since you had left the ship?' 'Well,' he said, 'in the first place, I was afraid that there might be trouble with the authorities, and as we say in Spanish, "Justice, but not in my house." Then I forgot all about my life in England. You see, I am a gaucho now. Their ways of life are mine, and though I often thought of going home, working my passage before the mast, I never did so, and I suppose would have forgotten all about England and that I had ever been a midshipman, brass buttons, and a dirk, *lindo no más*,'[6] he said, as if the midshipman had not

[6] "Not a dandy any longer! "

been the midshipman in question, but some young officer off a British ship whom he had seen in Montevideo, and whose dress he had admired.

"Last week I was at an estancia near Paysandú, belonging to an Englishman, working as a *domador*, a horse-breaker, you know. It was years since I had read an English newspaper, and I turned it over listlessly, as nothing interested me. What did I care for Whigs and Tories, for cricket, or for races I should never look at, or the Court Circular! I was glad, for sure, that Queen Victoria was still alive. Her name has a good sound about it, especially in Spanish, and aboard ship we always used to drink her health at dinner-time. I was just putting down the paper, the famous *Times*, I think, when in the corner I came on my own name.'"

He took out of a pocket-book, bought at some *pulpería*, greasy and ragged-looking, a piece of newspaper, unrolled it carefully, smoothed it on the table, and gave it to me to read. "Jesús, María!" the consul exclaimed, "it was a *llapa*, with a vengeance, and took my breath away."

The little cutting contained an advertisement, asking Charles Edward Mitchell, once a midshipman in the Royal Navy, to apply to a firm of solicitors if he were still alive, as he was sole heir to his uncle's estate. The uncle had been dead for full three months.

"*La puta*! What an occurrence, as they say hereabouts."

Both bottle and cigars were finished, and the consul rose from his chair, looked at himself critically in the looking-glass that hung upon the wall, and after passing a comb through his hair and whiskers, hummed in a low voice: "Jolly red nose. Jolly red nose. How did you come by that jolly red nose?" A song he may have heard at a Victorian music-hall on his last visit home.

His feelings thus relieved, he went back to his tale, saying: "There is little more to tell. I facilitated Charlie, as we say, enough money to pay his passage home. Wonderful to tell, by the next mail I got a cheque from him, with something over to pay the interest, as he said, and a gold watch. Yes, yes, oh, yes, the watch I still have it, and after what you tell me I shall have his name engraved on it, and the date when he was killed. Did I hear any more about him? Well, he wrote once or twice, to say he was the owner of a pretty large estate, member of several clubs in London, and that he rather liked the life. He added, 'The horses have infernally hard mouths.' Years passed, eight, nine or ten, I don't remember—where in hell do the years go when they pass—*Labuntur anni*,[7] as we used to say at school?"

I had no answer to the query Postumus[8] seems to have left unanswered, but waited for him to take up his parable again.

"He told me," said the consul, "that the life in England had become intolerable to him, and that he knew there was no other life for him but with gauchos on the plains. He said: 'I passed over the estate to a first cousin, for a sum of money, intending to return at once to Uruguay. In London, I fell in with several old friends, and [spent] two years there, till women, drink, and gambling had run away with the most of my capital. I still have several hundred pounds, and by the first boat to-morrow I shall go back to Paysandú.'

"Years had not touched him in the least except to take away his sunburn, and make him thinner than he was. His English had come back to him entirely, but his eyes, that always looked beyond you, as if they looked across the plains, showed that his spirit was unchanged. We had a night together, and painted 'Montyviddeó' vermilion, and in the morning I saw him to the boat. That was the last time that I set eyes upon him, though of his exploits I heard plenty, and the name Carlitos el Inglés was known to everyone from the Brazilian frontier to the Uruguay."

The consul stopped suddenly, just as a horse stops in his stride when galloping at night, when he sees something that has startled him. He took his hat down from the peg where it was hanging, set it squarely on his head, lighted another cigarette, and said: "What say you to a *paseo*, to the Quilombo, to see if any camp men have come into town?"

I did not go with him, having ridden twenty leagues since sunrise, although the Quilombo was in those days our general rendezvous and club.

"So long!" the consul said, and left me wondering whether, if after all Charlie the Gaucho had not chosen wisely when he went back to *chiripá*, poncho and potro boots.

Then I reflected that the gauchos say the potro boot is not for everybody.

[7] "How the years glide on!"

[8] A friend of Horace, to whom the poet addressed his Ode II, xiv, "*Eheu fugaces, Postume, Postume,*" on the passage of time, from which the above quotation is taken.

PARAGUAY

Editor's Preface to the Paraguayan Sketches

When Graham writes of Paraguay, he usually treats three themes—the Jesuits, the dictator López, and horses. Though not a religious man himself, in the sense that he did not belong to any organized church (he once called himself a Christian unattached), Graham wrote a great deal on the Jesuit *reducciones*. He was extremely fair to the Jesuits, correcting the excesses of other Anglo-Saxon historians like Prescott and Robertson, and did much to redress the balance of the *leyenda negra*, highlighting the good qualities of this much maligned order.[1]

[1]See R. B. Cunninghame Graham, *A Vanished Arcadia*.

IN THE TARUMENSIAN WOODS

Strange that reason should so often go astray, but that digestion should be unerring. So it is, though. The greatest minds have fallen into error. There is no recorded instance of even a congenital idiot having deceived his digestion. It may be then, that, after all, reason is not the highest attribute of humanity.

Be that as it may, reason, in its eternal conflict with faith, seldom comes off so badly as when it encounters prejudice. So inveterate is prejudice and so shamefaced is reason, that one sometimes wonders whether faith and prejudice are not synonymous.

Few prejudices are so inveterate, and therefore on few questions is so little reason displayed, as on the subject of the Jesuits.

To be a member of the Society of Jesus conveys to many excellent people the impression that a sort of baccalaureate of lying, of chicanery, and of casuistry has been attained. It would seem that a Jesuit is a man perpetually, for no particular object, endeavouring to deceive the world, and even himself. Machiavelli[1] is his favourite author, Suárez[2] his dearest study, and his political ideal that of Ezzelino da Romano or Malatesta of Rimini.[3] In history, when a king was murdered or dethroned, a

[1] Niccoló Machiavelli (1469–1527), famous Italian statesman and political writer, author of *The Prince* (1513).

[2] Francisco Suárez (1548–1617), eminent Spanish Jesuit theologian and philosopher.

[3] Ezzelino da Romano (1194–1259), cruel despot who was lord of Verona, Vicenza and Padua. Sigismondo Pandolfo Malatesta (1417–68), profligate, cruel lord of Rimini, reputedly guilty of the most horrible crimes.

queen poisoned, a conspiracy hatched, or a revolution attempted, the blame was thrown upon the Jesuits, with or without proof, in the same impartial way as it is now thrown upon the anarchists. In both cases no doubt the desired result was attained, and a scapegoat acquired on which to lay the sins of others. Humanity dearly loves a scapegoat.

Nothing in all the Mosaic Dispensation appears to me to show more clearly the profound knowledge of the human heart possessed by its compiler than the institution of the sin-bearing quadruped. If the people were worth the sacrifice of the goat appears doubtful after a perusal of their history, and it might have been prudent, one would have thought, to hesitate before sacrificing the unoffending animal.

The Jesuits were said to be self-seekers in the Indies and schemers in Europe.

True, St. Francis Xavier was a Jesuit; and few, after reading his life, would accuse him of being a schemer or a self-seeker, and, after reading his hymn, I should imagine that the doubts of any one would be removed. Still, perhaps he was the exception that proved the rule; though how exceptions prove rules has not been vouchsafed to us at present.

By a curious fatality, not only Catholics and Protestants, but also freethinkers, were united against them, and their only defenders were Rousseau, Raynal, Mably, and Montesquieu.[4] Even Félix de Azara,[5] impartial as he was on most matters, and amiable, as his celebrated dedication to his History of Paraguay clearly shows him to have been, became a violent partisan when writing of the Jesuits. That in Paraguay, at all events, the Jesuits were not all self-seekers and plotters, that they accomplished much good, endured great perils and hard-ships, and were the only people whose mere presence did not bring mortality amongst the Indians, I hope to try to prove at some length at the proper time and place.[6] Meanwhile I have to deal with the adventures of one particular Jesuit, a kindly, honest, simple-minded man, whose lot was thrown in strange places, and who fortunately has preserved for us a record of his undertakings.

On the eve of St. John, but without chronicling the year, except

---

[4] All French philosophers of the eighteenth century.
[5] See note 8 to "A Vanishing Race."
[6] See Graham's book *A Vanished Arcadia*.

more or less (*año de 1756 más o menos*), did he, so to speak, strike the Gospel trail from San Joaquín in Paraguay, accompanied by some Guaraní neophytes; but this demands a little explication.

In the last century the Jesuits had gathered most of the Guaraní Indians in Paraguay, and what has now become the Argentine province of Corrientes, into some thirty little towns or missions, known to the country people as *capillas*, and extending from Guayrá, near the cataract of the Paraná, to Yapeyú, on the Uruguay. On this somewhat stony vineyard they worked unceasingly, instilling not only theology, but some tincture of civilisation, into the Guaranís.

The Tobás, the Guaycurús, the Mocobíos, then as now roamed the swampy wilderness of the Gran Chaco, the Great Hunting Ground (Chaco in Guaraní signifies a hunting-ground) of the remnant of the tribes who fled from Peru and Chile on the advance of Almagro and Pizarro, and from Bolivia and the Argentine Republic before Solís and the Mendozas,[7] to wander in its recesses. In the little town of San Joaquín, called Tarumá by the Jesuits, on account of the forests of tarumá-trees which surrounded it, there dwelt the chronicler of the following little episode.

He was a member of the crafty, scheming Society of Jesus, it should be remembered, so that no doubt his writings had an esoteric meaning. From his youth he had been engaged in missionary work.

Like Moffat and like Livingstone,[8] he burned with zeal to change the faith of men who had done him no previous injury, and, like them, having begun his labours, his humanity rose superior to his dogma. In those days no paragraphs in newspapers, no plaudits from a close-packed audience in Exeter Hall, at intervals of a year or two, no testimonials, no pious teas; nothing but drudgery amongst savages, but journeys, ridings by night and day, sleeping amongst swamps, fightings and preachings, and death at last of fever, or by Indian club or arrow.

---

[7] Diego de Almagro (c. 1475–1538), Spanish conquistador who was with Francisco Pizarro (c.1474–1541) at the bloody conquest of Peru. Juan Díaz de Solís (1470–1516) was an early Spanish explorer of the River Plate estuary, while Pedro de Mendoza (1487–1537) was the first governor of the Plate region and founder of Buenos Aires.

[8] Robert Moffat (1795–1883), Scottish missionary in Africa. His daughter married David Livingstone (1813–73), also a missionary and explorer in Africa.

For all reward, calumny and misconception and a notice in the appendix of a book written by a member of the Society, in this wise:—

Padre Julián Lizardi, a Biscayan, caught by the Chiriguanos, tied to a stake, and shot to death with arrows.

Diego Herrera, pierced with a spear.

Lucas Rodríguez, slain at the altar by the Mocobíos.

Gaspar Osorio, killed and eaten by the Payaguás.

In those days a missionary, even a Jesuit, had to bear his cross; not that the missionary of to-day does not ascend his little Calvary, but still I fancy that the pebbles in the road are not so lumpy, and that the road itself is better fit for bicycles. Thrice had my Jesuit crossed the pampas from Buenos Aires to Mendoza, as he tells us. Often had he travelled amongst the Tobás and the Abipones; amongst the Guaycurús, "most turbulent of heathen, who extract their eyelashes to better see the Christians, and to slay them; their bodies painted many colours; worshipping no gods, except, perhaps, their horses, with whom they are more truly of one flesh than with their wives." In perils oftentimes amongst the Payaguás, "those pirates of the Paraná, disdaining gods, destroying man, staining their faces with the juice of the caraguatá, a purple like that of Tyre; having a vulture's wing dependent from their ears; very hard of heart, and skilled in paddling a canoe, and striking fish with arrows, like themselves alone."

Languages so hard as to appear impossible to Europeans, "so do they snort and sneeze and cough their words," had to be overcome; speaking both Guaraní and Mocobío, "with the Latin and some touch of Greek and Hebrew." Though brought up as a priest, he had become a horseman; riding with the gauchos day and night, though, as he tells us, never quite so much at home upon a horse of Paraguay as on a horse of Europe; for it appears "a horse of Paraguay" (and this I have observed myself, though not a Jesuit) "is apt to shy and bound, and if the bridle be neglected, lift his head up in the air, and, arching his back, give with his rider (*dar con el jinete*) on the ground."

Medio chapetón el padre, as I think I see.[9]

[9]"Not a very good horseman, the priest!" See *chapetón* in the glossary.

This was the sort of training a Jesuit missionary underwent in Paraguay, and for which it may be that Salamanca, Rome, Coimbra, or even Paris, fitted him but moderately.

San Joaquín itself could not have been a place of residence to be called luxurious. Like all the Jesuit missions in Paraguay, it must have been a little place built round a square, enclosing a bright green lawn; a kind of island lost in the sea of forest. A well-built church of stone in the Jesuit style of architecture, the college with its storerooms for hides and wool and maté. On each side the church a date palm, waving like a bulrush. A long low row of wooden houses, with deep verandahs, thatched with palm leaves. An air of calm and rest and melancholy over the place, a sort of feeling as if you had landed (and been left) in Juan Fernández. Sun and more sun, heat and more heat, and a whitish vapour stealing at evening time over the woods, wrapping the town within its folds, and giving the bell of the Angelus a muffled sound.

In the daytime women, in white clothes, with baskets on their heads of maize and mandioca, hair like horses' tails cut square across the forehead and hanging down their backs, clustered like bees in the centre of the square, and chattered Guaraní in under-tones, like Indians always use. The men in white duck trousers, barefooted, and with cloaks of red *bayeta*, lounged about, doubt-less, when the Jesuits were not looking, as they do to-day.

Before the houses, posts of heavy wood, to which from sunrise till sunset horses ready saddled stood fastened; horses which seemed to sleep, unless an unwary passer-by approached too near them, when they sprang back into life, snorting with terror, sat back upon their *jáquimas*, causing their owners to leave their maté, and to bound like cats to quiet them, with cries of "*Jesús*," "*Ba eh picó*," and other things less fitting to record, even in Guaraní. Outside the town the forest stretching into distance. Forests of viraró, of urunday, tarumá, araguay, and zamaú, of every strange and iron-hearted wood that Europe never hears of, even to-day. Trees which grow, and fall and rot, and spring up bound with lianas like thick cordage, and through which the bell-bird calls, the guacamayos flutter and tucanes dart; and where the spotted tiger creeps (that Jesuit of the jungle) beside some pool covered with leaves of the Victoria Regia.

The college itself, no doubt a cheerless place enough, dazzling with whitewash on the outside, and in the interior dark and heavy, with an aroma of tobacco-smoke to serve as incense. For furniture a *catre* of wood, with strips of hide for bedstraps, or a white cotton hammock swung from an iron ring let into the beams. A shelf or two of books, chiefly on medicine or engineering or architecture; for your Jesuit was doctor, music-master, architect, and sometimes military instructor to the community. Two or three chairs, roughly cut out of solid wood and seated with stamped leather in the Spanish style; a table or two, a porous water-jar; in the corner the padre's saddle on a trestle, and on a nail a gun; for at times a Jesuit *capilla* became a place to fight as well as pray in.

In the forests scattered families of Indians lived, remnants of tribes destroyed by small-pox or by wars; and it was the dream of every self-respecting, able-bodied Jesuit to find and mark these sheep wandering in the wilderness without a shepherd. What they underwent in hardships, lack of food, attacks of Indians, crossing swamps, and rivers, by heat and cold, Guevara and Lozano, Ruiz Montoya and Father Dobrizhoffer,[10] have set forth with pious pride, and more or less dog Latin.

News having come to San Joaquín that the trail of Indians had been crossed near to the town, he sallied forth, and having found and marked his sheep, compiled the following description, in which he tells, besides the story, what kind of man he was himself; and proves beyond a doubt that, following the words of Santa Teresa, he "was only fit for God."

On the eve of the Evangelist Blessed St. John the Baptist I took a guide and entered the Tarumensian woods accompanied by some neophytes. I crossed the Río Empalado, and having carefully explored all the woods of the river Monday Miní, and discovering at length on the third day a human footstep, we tracked it to a little dwelling where an old woman with her son and daughter, a youth and maiden of fifteen and twenty years, were dwelling.

Being asked where the other Indians were to be found, the mother replied that no one dwelt in the woods but herself, her son and daughter, and that all the rest had died of small-pox.

Perceiving us doubtful as to the truth of this, the son said, "You may believe my mother, for I have looked for a wife up and down these woods for leagues, but never met a human being."

Nature had taught the young savage that it was not lawful to marry his sister.

---

[10] All Jesuit historians and missionaries in eighteenth-century Paraguay.

I exhorted the mother to remove to my town, where she would be more comfortable.

She declared herself willing to do so, but there was one objection: "I have," she said, "three peccaries which I have brought up. They follow us wherever we go, and I am afraid, if they are exposed to the sun in a dry plain, unshaded by trees, they will soon die."

Pray be no longer anxious," I said; "I shall treat these dear little animals with due kindess. Lakes, rivers, and marshes will aways be at hand to cool your favourites."

Here I detect the cloven foot for the first and last time in this worthy man's career, for round San Joaquín there are no rivers or lakes, and I fear his anxiety to mark the sheep rendered him careless of the little peccaries.

Induced by these promises, she set out with us, and reached the town on the first of January.

No date is given, but I fancy in San Joaquín time was what they had most to dispose of.

And now it will be proper to give an account of the dwelling of the mother and her children. Their hut consisted of the branches of the palm-tree and their drink of muddy water.

To this day the majority of huts in Paraguay are of palm-leaves, and for the muddy water, it grits yet (in dreams) between my teeth.

Fruits, antas, rabbits, and birds, maize, and mandioca were their food, a cloth woven of the leaves of the caraguatá their bed and clothing. They delighted in honey, which abounds in the hollow trees. The smoke of tobacco the old woman inhaled day and night through a reed. The son constantly chewed tobacco-leaves. The youth wore a cloak of caraguatá, reaching to the knees. The girl wore a short net by day, which she used as a hammock by night. This appearing to me too transparent, I gave her a cotton towel to cover her more effectually. The girl, folding up the towel, put it on her head; but at the desire of her mother wrapped herself in it. I gave the youth, too, some linen clothes to wrap himself in. Before putting on these he had climbed the trees, agile as a monkey, but his wrapper impeded him so that he could hardly move a step.

Whether my author thinks it an advantage that of a happy

climbing faun he had made a being who could not move a step, I do not know. But "all was conscience and tender heart" with him, for he observes immediately:

In such extreme need, in such penury, I found them, experiencing the rigours of the anchorites of old without discontent, vexation, or disease. The mother and son were tall and good-looking, but the daughter had so fine and elegant a countenance that a poet would have taken her for a nymph or dryad. She united a becoming cheerfulness with great courtesy, and did not seem at all alarmed at our arrival.

When one reads an account like this, and reflects that Cook, Cabeza de Vaca, de Bougainville, Columbus,[11] and others, all unite in describing similar people; and when one has even seen them oneself, it seems a pity that villainous saltpetre should have been digged, more villainous whisky distilled, and that Bible-peddling should have become a trade.

As this insulated family had no intercourse with any but themselves, their Guaraní was much corrupted. The youth had never seen a woman but his mother and his sister. The girl had seen no man but her brother, her father having been torn to pieces by a tiger before she was born. Not to go unattended [*sin compañero*], she had a little parrot and a small monkey on her arm.

The new proselytes were quickly clothed in the town, and food supplied them. *L'ultimo lasso! de' lor giorni allegri.*[12]

I also took care that they should take frequent excursions to the woods to enjoy the shade and pleasant freshness of the trees, to which they had been used, for we found by experience that savages removed to towns often waste away from the change of food and air, and from the heat of the sun, accustomed as they have been to moist, shady, and cool groves.
The same was the fate of the mother, son and daughter.

One hardly knows whether to laugh or cry. Hamlet has put the

[11] All famous discoverers: Captain James Cook (1728–79), British sailor who explored New Zealand; Alvar Núñez Cabeza de Vaca (c.1490–c.1560), Spanish explorer with expedition to Florida and other adventures; Louis Antoine de Bougainville (1729–1811), French explorer in the Pacific, colonizer of the Falkland Islands; and Christopher Columbus (c.1451–1506), first discoverer of the New World.
[12] Alas! the last of their happy days!

folly of falling a-cursing in such a light that perhaps not to *raggionar* is best, but silently to pass.

A few months after their arrival they were afflicted with a heaviness and universal rheum, to which succeeded pains in the eyes and ears and deafness. Lowness of spirits and disgust to food at length wasted their strength to such a degree that an incurable consumption followed. After languishing some months the old mother, who had been properly instructed [one feels relieved] in the Christian religion and baptized, delivered up her spirit with a mind so calm, so acquiescent with the Divine will, that I cannot doubt but that she entered into a blessed immortality.

I would fain hope so too, so that at least the unhappy sufferer had some practical set-off against the clothes and baptism which were her apparent ruin.

The girl, who had entered the town full of health and beauty, soon lost all resemblance to herself. Enfeebled, withering by degrees like a flower, her bones hardly holding together, she followed her mother to the grave, and, if I be not deceived, to heaven.

Again I hope the good and worthy muddlehead was right in his conjecture, though there is no mention of baptism or religious instruction in this case.

The brother still surviving was attacked by the same malady, but being of a stronger constitution overcame it. The measles, which made great havoc in the town [another blessing in disguise], left him so confirmed in health that he seemed beyond danger. He was of a cheerful nature, went to church daily [*pobrecito*], learnt the doctrines of Christianity with diligence, was gentle and compliant to all, and in everything discovered marks of future excellence. Nevertheless, to put his perseverance to the proof, I thought best to delay his baptism. At this time a rich and Christian Indian, who at my request had received the catechumen into his house, came and said to me: "Father (pai), our wood Indian is in perfect health of body, but is a little astray in mind. He makes no complaints, but says sleep has deserted him: his mother and sister appearing to him every night and saying, "Suffer thyself to be baptized."

I wonder a little at this, when they knew how fatal baptism had proved in their own case.

"We shall return to take thee when thou dost not expect it." This vision, he says, takes away his sleep. "Tell him," I answered, "to be of good cheer, for that the melancholy remembrance of his mother and sister is the cause of his dreams, and they, as I think [O Pai Yponá, were you not certain then?], are gone to heaven, and have nothing more to do with this world."

A few days after the same Indian returned, giving the same account. Suspecting there was something in it, I hastened to the house, and found him sitting up in bed. On my asking for his health, he answered, "I am well and free from pain," but that he could not sleep, from the vision of his mother and sister telling him to be baptized, and saying they were ready for him. This he told me prevented him from getting any rest. I thought it probable that this was a mere dream, and worthy of neglect. Mindful, however, that dreams have often been Divine admonitions, and oracles of God, as appears from Holy Writ, it seemed advisable in a matter of such moment to consult the security and tranquility of the catechumen. Being assured of his constancy and of his acquaintance with the chief heads of religion by previous interrogation, I soon after baptized him by the name of Luis. This I did on the 23rd of June, the eve of St. John, about the hour of ten in the morning, by the sand clock.

On the evening of the same day, without a symptom of disease or apoplexy, he quietly expired.

This event, a fact well known to the whole town, and which I am ready to attest on oath, astonished every one.

I should have only looked on it as certain to occur after the fateful effects of the previous treatment (and *interrogatorios*) on the mother and sister.

I leave my reader to form his own opinion, but in my own mind I could never deem the circumstance merely accidental. I attributed it to the exceeding compassion of the Almighty that these three Indians were discovered by me in the recesses of the woods; that they so promptly complied with my exhortations to enter my town and embrace Christianity, and that they closed their lives after receiving baptism. The remembrance of my expeditions to the Empalado, though attended by many dangers and hardships, is still most grateful to my heart; insomuch as it proved highly fortunate to the three wood Indians, and advantageous to the Spaniards. These last having been certified by me that no more savages [sic] remained, collected many thousand pounds of yerba maté, from which they derived an amazing profit.

This much of the Guaraní town of Tarumaá. If on this subject [says our pious author] I appear to have written too much, let the reader be told that I have passed over many remarkable things in silence.

The above history almost seems to show that there were Jesuits and Jesuits even in Paraguay.

Why has their rule, then, called forth such censure, and gained them such an evil reputation? Why have both Catholics and Protestants combined to write them down? It could not be their wealth in Paraguay, for at their expulsion, when all their colleges were ransacked, only a small sum was found. It could not be that the luxurious lives they led excited envy, for the little episode I have commented on is but one of many scattered through the lives of all of them, and recorded in various tongues from Latin to Guaraní. It may be that the viceroys feared an *imperium in imperio* in Paraguay; though how some thousands of such Indians as those who suffered baptism and death in the old priest's story could shake an empire is difficult to understand. It may have been that the Mission priests in Paraguay paid for the sins of Jesuit intriguers at the Courts of Europe. Theology does not, I think, reject vicarious punishment. Certain it is that mention of Paraguay and the Missions never fails to call forth talk of despotism and tyranny, and complaints of Indians turned to mere machines by the too paternal government of the Jesuits. This may have been so. It may have been that their scheme of government would not have satisfied Sir Thomas More, Karl Marx, or Plato.[13] Still, there were then Indians to govern. Where are they now? Where are the thirty towns, the 80,000 or 100,000 inhabitants, the flocks and herds, the domestic cattle ("with wild ones innumerable"), spoken of in the report of the suppression of the Missions, by Bucareli, viceroy to Charles the Third?[14]

Where are the well-built churches, and the happy simple folk who worshipped in them, believing all things?

Take horse from Itapua, ride through San Cosme, the Estero-Neembucú, or San Ignacio Miní, and look for Indians, look for churches, look for cattle, or any sign of agriculture; you will find all dead, gone, desolate, deserted, or fallen to ruin. Sleep in the deserted towns, and perhaps, as I did, camping in the plaza of La Trinidad alone, my horse tied to a tuft of grass beside me, you

[13] All noted political and social writers: Sir Thomas More (1478–1535), the English saint and scholar, wrote *Utopia*; Karl Marx (1818–83), the German philosopher of history, wrote *Capital*; and Plato (c.428–348 B.C.), the Greek philosopher and political thinker, wrote *The Republic*.

[14] Antonio María Bucareli y Ursúa (1717–79), viceroy of New Spain (modern Mexico).

may see a tiger steal in the moonlight out of the deserted church, descend the steps, and glide into the forest.

Azara and Bonpland[15] say that the communistic rule of the Society rendered the Indians thriftless and idle; though this is difficult to reconcile with their further statement that they were well-nigh worked to death. The Indians themselves were not aggrieved at communism; for, in their petition to the viceroy at the expulsion of the Jesuits, they complain of "liking not the fashion of living of the Spaniards, in which no man helps the other." It may have been that the Spanish settlers in Paraguay wanted the Indians to slave for them in their plantations, and that the Jesuits withstood them. But when the ruin of an institution or of an individual is decreed, reasons are never wanting. The Jesuits in Europe may have deserved their fate. In Paraguay, in spite of writers none of whom saw the Missions under their rule, the Jesuits did much good, mixed with some folly, as is incidental to mankind.

If only on the principle that a living dog is of more value than a dead king, the policy of isolation the Jesuits pursued was not a bad one, for it left them at least Indians to govern. Be all this as it may, I have no doubt that many learned men, skilled in the Greek and Latin (but not in Guaraní), have written and will write of the Jesuits in Paraguay, and prove to demonstration that it is fruit for self-congratulation that the Indians of the Missions are free and non-existent. Still, I sometimes wish that I had seen the Missions full of Indians, and stocked with cattle, instead of desolate and fallen into decay. And for the amiable and apostolic priest who told the story of his labours in the Tarumensian wilds, and chronicled in execrable Spanish the discovery, death, and baptism of his three victims, I have only one complaint to make, and that is, that he did not tell us if town life proved fatal to the three little peccaries.

[15] Aimé Jacques Alexandre Bonpland (1773–1858), French naturalist who accompanied Humboldt to South America and eventually stayed there.

A JESUIT

It was, I think at the little port of the *esquina* in Corrientes that he came on board. A priest at first sight, yet not quite similar to other priests, at least to those whose mission is only for mass and meat. A Spaniard, too, at first sight, with the clean-cut features of Old Castile, the bony hands that mark the man of action, and feet as square as boxes. Withal not commonplace, though unassuming, but with a look of that intensity of purpose which many saints have shared with bulldogs. All day the steamer had been running between the myriad islets of the Paraná. Sometimes it seemed impossible she could thread her way between the mass of floating camalote which clogged the channel.

Now and then the branches of the tall lapachos and urundays swept the deck as the vessel hugged the shore. On every side a mass of vegetation, feathery palms, horny mimosas, giant cacti, and all knotted together with lianas like cordage of a ship, stretching from tree to tree. The river, an enormous yellow flood, flowing between high banks of rich alluvial soil ever slipping with a dull splash into the stream. On every side Nature overwhelming man and making him feel his littleness.

Such a scene as Hulderico Schmidel, Alvar Núñez, or Solís[1] may have gazed on, with the exception that now and then wild

[1] Some of the earliest explorers of the River Plate region: Hulderico Schmidel was a Fleming or German who accompanied Pedro de Mendoza (see Graham's sketch "Hulderico Schmidel" in *His People*); for Alvar Núñez Cabeza de Vaca and Juan Díaz de Solís, see notes 11 and 7 respectively of previous sketch.

horses came into sight and snorted as the steamer passed; or a gaucho, wilder than the horse he rode, with flowing hair and floating poncho, cantered along the plain where the banks were low, his *pingo* galloping like a piece of clockwork. In the slack water, under the lee of the islands, alligators lay like trunks of trees and basked. In the trees the monkeys and parrots chattered and howled, and *picaflores* flitted from flower to flower; and once between the islands a tiger appeared swimming in pursuit of some carpinchos. The air was full of the filmy white filaments like cobwebs which the north wind always brings with it in those countries, and which clung from every rope and piece of rigging, making the steamer look as if she had run through a cotton manufactory. In every cabin mosquitoes hummed and made life miserable.

On board the steamer everything was modern of the modern, but modern seen through a Spanish medium—no door would shut, no bolt would draw, and nothing made to slide would work; engines from Barrow-in-Furness, or from Greenock, but the brass-plate which set forth the place of their manufacture was so covered with patina as to leave the name a matter of conjecture. The captain was from Barcelona, and fully impressed with the importance of his native province and city; the crew, Italians and Spanish Basques; the pilot, a Correntino, equally at home in the saddle or in a schooner, and knowing every turn and bend of the river in the nineteen hundred miles from Buenos Aires to Cuyabá. The passengers, chiefly Bolivians and Brazilians, hating one another, but indistinguishable to the undiscerning foreigner; an Argentine *tropero*, going to Corrientes; a Spanish merchant or two from Buenos Aires; the ambulant troop of Italian opera singers, without which no river steamer in South America ever seems to leave a port; a gambler or two in pursuit of their daily avocation; some Paraguayans with innumerable children and servants and birds in cages, all chattering in Guaraní, like the Christian Indians they are; some English business men, looking as business-like as if in London. On the lower deck a group of gauchos with their *capataz*. Seated all day long they played at *truco* with cards as greasy as bits of hide, and so well marked upon the back that the anxiety of the dealer to conceal their faces seemed a work of supererogation. These were the only passengers who thoroughly enjoyed themselves. Lounging on the deck when tired of playing cards, or when tobacco failed or maté was unprocurable, they talked of horses and scratched their marks upon the deck, to the annoyance of the captain, with the points of their *facones*. Had the voyage endured a month they would not have complained, so long as meal-times came in regular succession and there was room to stretch their *recados* upon the deck at night to sleep. Mosquitoes troubled them not, and though they never seemed to look at anything, not a bend of the stream or a tree, still less a horse, escaped their observation. If there was a guitar procurable, they sang to it for hours in the moonlight, but in such quiet fashion as to disturb no one, least of all themselves. Their songs were chiefly of melancholy love affairs or of the prowess of famous horses. If the first-class passengers danced upon the deck at night, the gauchos sauntered up and criticised them, as if they had been cattle at a *saladero*.

At the *esquina*, the usual mild bustle of a South American riverine port was soon over. The captain of the port, after a full hour's waiting, rode leisurely to the pier, got off his horse, lighted his cigarette, and sauntered to his boat. The Italian boatmen were galvanised into a little life, and stood and grinned, and tried to look as if they were at Naples or at Genoa. After much talking of yellow fever and the perennial revolution, and inquiries if such and such a one had had his throat cut, the passengers surrendered themselves to be cheated by the boatmen and went ashore. As the vessel slid away and the little city baking like a white oven in the sun, with the Argentine flag with its bars of blue and white flapping against the flagstaff, and the horses tied to the *palenque* in front of the houses in the plaza, faded out of sight, our interest centred on the only passenger who had come aboard. Nobody knew him, and he did not seem to be a man of much importance. The stewards, observing that all his luggage consisted of a newspaper which he carried under his arm, turned from him with disdain. The traders and the gamblers saw he was not of them. Even the gauchos looked a little scornful, and remarked that he was most probably a *maturrango*. In their vocabulary *maturrango*, meaning a bad rider, is the most contemptuous term of them all. Amongst them, a philosopher who touched his horse with his toe in mounting would have no acceptation. As for the itinerant opera company, even the basso (always the wit of an Italian opera troupe) had nothing to say about him.

Still, after a little time, and as the steamer skirted the city of Corrientes and entered the Paraguay, passing Humaitá with the church a ruin still from the time of the war, and left Curupaity behind her, passing into the regions of dense forests where the Bermejo and the Pilcomayo, after running through the Chaco, fall into the Paraguay, it was clear that the lonely passenger had become a favourite. Why, was not apparent at first sight. Certainly he knew the river better in some respects than the Correntino pilot, and could point out the various places where, in bygone times, such or such a missionary had met his fate by Indian spear or arrow. "Just between that tuft of palms under the mountain in the distance, Father Julián Lizardi, a Biscayan, received his martyr's crown in 1735 at the hands of the Chiriguanos. Beside his body, pierced with arrows, was found his breviary open at the office for the dead, as if, poor soul, he had been trying to read his own funeral service. *In pace requiescat.* There, where you see the broken tower and ruined walls, the *tapera,* as they call it here in these countries, the Jesuits had a town amongst the Guaycurús. This was before the Philistines prevailed against them, and withdrew them from their work and light from the souls of the poor Indians."

Thus discoursing and smoking cigarettes perpetually, for the newspaper contained nothing but paper and tobacco, he wound himself into our hearts. The traders swore by him; even the Englishmen, when he said he was a Jesuit, replied that they did not care, he was a damned good fellow, and he smiled, not understanding but seeing they were pleased. The Brazilians in the morning asked for his blessing on the sly, though all freethinkers when talking in the smoking-room. The opera troupe were his devoted slaves, and he used to sit and hear their grievances and settle their quarrels. Even the gauchos, before they went ashore at Asunción, chatted familiarly with him, and asked him if he knew the Pope, and told him of the "deaths they owed," and wondered if one of them who never was baptized and, therefore, had no saint, could go to heaven; to which he answered: "Yes, my son, on All Saints' Day."

We left Asunción with its towers and houses hidden in orange gardens, and the great palace, in the style of Palladio,[2] by the river's edge. Asunción, the capital of the viceroyalty of Paraguay—in the Spanish times a territory about as large as Europe,

[2] Andrea Palladio (1518–80), great Italian architect from Vicenza in northern Italy.

and now a sleepy semi-Indian village, after having endured the three successive tyrannies of Francia and the two López—[3] looks over the Chaco at the great desert, still an unknown wilderness of swamps and forests. Then the river narrows and all traces of civilisation are left behind. Here the Jesuit, for all had now begun to call him nothing else, seemed to brighten up as if he expected something, and his stories of the Jesuits of old times became more frequent. Little by little his own history came out, for he was not communicative, at least about himself. Near the Laguna de los Xarayes it appeared that the Company of Jesus had secretly started a mission amongst the Guasarapos, and he was of it. Never since the days of the Jesuits' glory in America had any missionary been bold enough to make the experiment. Fernández and Alvar Núñez, in times past, had written of their fierceness and intractability. Nuflo de Chaves, the bold adventurer, who founded the town of Sta. Cruz de la Sierra, had met his death close to their territory.[4] At long intervals they had been known to come to the mission of El Santo Corazón, or sometimes to wander even as far as that of Reyes in the district of the Moxos, while, throughout the region of the upper Paraguay, stories of their outrages and murders were rife. In the long hot nights, as the vessel drew near to Corumbá, the passengers would sit and listen to the tales the Jesuit told. Seated in a cane chair, dressed in rusty black, a *jipijapa* hat, nothing about him priestly but his breviary and *alzacuello*, without an atom of pose, he held us spellbound. Even the Catalonian captain, nurtured to show his Liberalism by hating priests of all degrees, Catholic and Protestant, grew quite friendly with the "little crow," as he called him, and promised to put him ashore as near the mission as he could. "Mission, Señor Captain! there is no mission, that is, now. I am the mission, that is, all that now remains of it."

Such was the case, for it appeared that the Indians, either tired of missions or bored by preaching or because they wished to kill a white man, had risen some months ago and burnt the church and buildings, killed the priests, with the exception of our pas-

[3] Doctor Gaspar Rodríguez Francia (1766–1840); Carlos Antonio López (1790–1862), dictator of Paraguay from 1844 til 1862; Francisco Solano López (1826–70), son of Carlos Antonio, responsible for Paraguayan disaster in the War of the Triple Alliance (1865–70) against Argentina, Brazil, and Uruguay.

[4] Spanish colonizer, who went with Cabeza de Vaca to Brazil and Paraguay, where he became viceroy before being murdered by the Indians in 1567.

senger, and returned to wander in the forests. "Those who are dead are now in glory," our Jesuit observed, "and the Indians will find some other pastors more successful, though none more self-devoted." Every one on board the steamer protested, and the little man smiled as he informed us that he had escaped and made his way to a settlement, had gone to Buenos Aires, whence he had telegraphed to Rome for orders, and the one word had come: "Return."

Next day, after much protestation from the captain, the steamer stopped at a sort of clearing in the forest, lowered a boat, and the Jesuit went ashore, his newspaper well filled with cigarettes. Stepping ashore, he stood for an instant, a little figure in rusty black, a midget against the giant trees, a speck against the giant vegetation. The steamer puffed and snorted, swung into the stream, the Jesuit waved his hand, took up his newspaper of cigarettes and, as the passengers and crew stood staring at him from the decks and rigging, walked into the forest.

FEAST DAY IN SANTA MARÍA MAYOR

The great *capilla*, the largest in the Jesuit reductions of Paraguay, was built round a huge square, almost a quarter of a mile across.

Upon three sides ran the low, continuous line of houses, like a "row" in a Scotch mining village or a phalanstery designed by Prudhon or St. Simon in their treatises;[1] but by the grace of a kind providence never carried out, either in bricks or stone.

Each dwelling-place was of the same design and size as all the rest. Rough tiles made in the Jesuit times, but now weathered and broken, showing the rafters tied with rawhide in many places, formed the long roof, that looked a little like the penthouse of a tennis court.

A deep verandah ran in front, stretching from one end to the other of the square, supported on great balks of wood, which, after more than two hundred years and the assaults of weather and the all-devouring ants, still showed the adze marks where they had been dressed. The timber was so hard that you could scarcely drive a nail into it, despite the flight of time since it was first set up. Rings fixed about six feet from the ground were screwed into the pillars of the verandah, before every door, to fasten horses to, exactly as they are in an old Spanish town.

Against the wall of almost every house, just by the door, was set a chair or two of heavy wood, with the seat formed by strips of

---

[1] Pierre Joseph Proudhon (1809–65) and Comte de Saint-Simon (1760–1825) were both French socialist writers and thinkers, with revolutionary ideas on industry and the working classes.

hide, on which the hair had formerly been left, but long ago rubbed off by use or eaten by the ants.

The owner of the house sat with the back of the strong chair tilted against the wall, dressed in a loose and pleated shirt, with a high turned-down collar open at the throat, and spotless white duck trousers, that looked the whiter by their contrast with his brown, naked feet.

His home-made palm-tree hat was placed upon the ground beside him, and his cloak of coarse red baize was thrown back from his shoulders, as he sat smoking a cigarette rolled in a maize leaf, for in the Jesuit *capillas* only women smoked cigars.

At every angle of the square a sandy trail led out, either to the river or the woods, the little patches planted with mandioca, or to the maze of paths that, like the points outside a junction, eventually joined in one main trail, that ran from Itapua on the Paraná up to Asunción.

The church, built of wood cut in the neighbouring forest, had two tall towers, and followed in its plan the pattern of all the churches in the New World built by the Jesuits, from California down to the smallest mission in the south. It filled the fourth side of the square, and on each side of it there rose two feathery palms known as the tallest in the Missions, which served as landmarks for travellers coming to the place, if they had missed their road. So large and well-proportioned was the church, it seemed impossible that it had been constructed solely by the Indians themselves, under the direction of the missionaries.

The overhanging porch and flight of steps that ran down to the grassy sward in the middle of the town gave it an air as of a cathedral reared to nature in the wilds, for the thick jungle flowed up behind it and almost touched its walls.

Bells of great size, either cast upon the spot or brought at vast expense from Spain, hung in the towers. On this, the feast day of the Blessed Virgin, the special patron of the settlement, they jangled ceaselessly, the Indians taking turns to haul upon the dried lianas that served instead of ropes. Though they pulled vigorously, the bells sounded a little muffled, as if they strove in vain against the vigorous nature that rendered any work of many puny and insignificant in the Paraguayan wilds.

Inside, the fane was dark, the images of saints were dusty, their paint was cracked, their gilding tarnished, making them look a little like the figures in a New Zealand pah, as they loomed through the darkness of the aisle. On the neglected altar, for at that time priests were a rarity in the reductions, the Indians had placed great bunches of red flowers, and now and then a humming-bird flitted in through the glassless windows and hung poised above them; then darted out again, with a soft, whirring sound. Over the whole *capilla*, in which at one time several thousand Indians had lived, but now reduced to seventy or eighty at the most, there hung an air of desolation. It seemed as if man, in his long protracted struggle with the forces of the woods, had been defeated, and had accepted his defeat, content to vegetate, forgotten by the world, in the vast sea of green.

On this particular day, the annual festival of the Blessed Virgin, there was an air of animation, for from far and near, from Jesuit *capilla*, from straw-thatched huts lost in the clearings of the primeval forest, from the few cattle ranches that then existed, and from the little town of Itapua, fifty miles away, the scanty population had turned out to attend the festival.

Upon the forest tracks, from earliest dawn, long lines of white-clad women, barefooted, with their black hair cut square across the forehead and hanging down their backs, had marched as silently as ghosts. All of them smoked great, green cigars, and as they marched along, their leader carrying a torch, till the sun rose and jaguars went back to their lairs, they never talked; but if a woman in the rear of the long line wished to converse with any comrade in the front, she trotted forward till she reached her friend and whispered in her ear. When they arrived at the crossing of the little river they bathed, or, at the least, washed carefully, and gathering a bunch of flowers, stuck them into their hair. They crossed the stream, and on arriving at the plaza they set the baskets, which they had carried on their heads, upon the ground, and sitting down beside them on the grass, spread out their merchandise. Oranges and bread, called *chipa*, made from mandioca flour and cheese, with vegetables and various homely sweetmeats, ground nuts, rolls of sugar done up in plantain leaves, and known as *rapadura*, were the chief staples of their trade. Those who had asses let them loose to feed; and if upon the forest trails the women had been silent, once in the safety of the town no flight of parrots in a maize field could have chattered louder than they did as they sat waiting by their wares. Soon the square filled, and men arriving tied their horses in the shade, slackening their broad hide girths, and piling up before them heaps of the leaves of the palm called *pindó* in Guaraní, till they were cool enough to eat their corn. Bands of boys, for in those days most of the men had been killed off in the past war,[2] came trooping in, accompanied by crowds of women and of girls, who carried all their belongings, for there were thirteen women to a man, and the youngest boy was at a premium amongst the Indian women, who in the villages, where hardly any men were left, fought for male stragglers like unchained tigresses. A few old men came riding in on some of the few native horses left, for almost all the active, little undersized breed of Paraguay had been exhausted in the war. They, too, had bands of women trotting by their sides, all of them anxious to unsaddle, to take the horses down to bathe, or to perform any small office that the men required of them. All of them smoked continuously, and each of them was ready with a fresh cigarette as soon as the old man or boy whom they accompanied finished the stump he held between his lips. The women all were dressed in the long Indian shirt called a *tupoi*, cut rather low upon the breast, and edged with coarse black cotton lace, which every Paraguayan woman wore. Their hair was as black as a crow's back, and quite as shiny, and their white teeth so strong that they could tear the ears of corn out of a maize cob like a horse munching at his corn.

Then a few Correntino gauchos next appeared, dressed in their national costume of loose black merino trousers, stuffed into long boots, whose fronts were all embroidered in red silk. Their silver spurs, whose rowels were as large as saucers, just dangled off their heels, only retained in place by a flat chain, that met upon the instep, clasped with a lion's head. Long hair and brown vicuña ponchos, soft black felt hats, and red silk handkerchiefs tied loosely round their necks marked them as strangers, though they spoke Guaraní.

They sat upon their silver-mounted saddles, with their toes resting in their bell-shaped stirrups, swaying so easily with every movement that the word riding somehow or other seemed inapplicable to men who, like the centaurs, formed one body with the horse.

As they drew near the plaza they raised their hands and touched their horses with the spur, and, rushing like a whirlwind

[2]War of the Triple Alliance. See note 3 of previous sketch.

right to the middle of the square, drew up so suddenly that their horses seemed to have turned to statues for a moment, and then at a slow trot, that made their silver trappings jingle as they went, slowly rode off into the shade.

The plaza filled up imperceptibly, and the short grass was covered by a white-clad throng of Indians. The heat increased, and all the time the bells rang out, pulled vigorously by relays of Indians, and at a given signal the people turned and trooped towards the church, all carrying flowers in their hands.

As there was no one to sing Mass, and as the organ long had been neglected, the congregation listened to some prayers, read from a Book of Hours by an old Indian, who pronounced the Latin, of which most likely he did not understand a word, as if it had been Guaraní. They sang "*Las flores a María*" all in unison, but keeping such good time that at a little distance from the church it sounded like waves breaking on a beach after a summer storm.

In the neglected church, where no priest ministered or clergy prayed, where all the stoops of holy water had for years been dry, and where the Mass had been well-nigh forgotten as a whole, the spirit lingered, and if it quickeneth upon that feast day in the Paraguayan missions, that simple congregation were as uplifted by it as if the sacrifice had duly been fulfilled with candles, incense, and the pomp and ceremony of Holy Mother Church upon the Seven Hills.

As every one except the Correntinos went barefooted, the exit of the congregation made no noise except the sound of naked feet, slapping a little on the wooden steps, and so the people silently once again filled the plaza, where a high wooden arch had been erected in the middle, for the sport of running at the ring.

The vegetable sellers had now removed from the middle of the square, taking all their wares under the long verandah, and several pedlars had set up their booths and retailed cheap European trifles such as no one in the world but a Paraguayan Indian could possibly require. Razors that would not cut, and little looking-glasses in pewter frames made in Thuringia, cheap clocks that human ingenuity was powerless to repair when they had run their course of six months' intermittent ticking, and gaudy pictures representing saints who had ascended to the empyrean,[3] as it appeared, with the clothes that they had worn in life, and all bald-headed, as befits a saint, were set out side by side with handkerchiefs of the best China silk. Sales were concluded after long-continued chaffering—that higgling of the market dear to old-time economists, for no one would have bought the smallest article, even below cost price, had it been offered to him at the price the seller originally asked.

Enrique Clerici, from Itapua, had transported all his *pulpería* bodily for the occasion of the feast. It had not wanted more than a small wagon to contain his stock-in-trade. Two or three dozen bottles of square-faced gin of the Anchor brand, a dozen of heady red wine from Catalonia, a pile of sardine boxes, sweet biscuits, raisins from Málaga, esparto baskets full of figs, and sundry pecks of apricots dried in the sun and cut into the shape of ears, and hence called *orejones*, completed all his store. He himself, tall and sunburnt, stood dressed in riding-boots and a broad hat, with his revolver in his belt, beside a pile of empty bottles, which he had always ready, to hurl at customers if there should be any attempt either at cheating or to rush his wares. He spoke the curious lingo, half-Spanish, half-Italian, that so many of his countrymen use in the River Plate; and all his conversation ran upon Garibaldi, with whom he had campaigned in youth, upon *Italia Irredenta*,[4] and on the time when anarchy should sanctify mankind by blood, as he said, and bring about the reign of universal brotherhood.

He did a roaring trade, despite the competition of a native Paraguayan, who had brought three demi-johns of caña, for men prefer the imported article the whole world over, though it is vile, to native manufactures, even when cheap and good.

Just about twelve o'clock, when the sun almost burned a hole into one's head, the band got ready in the church porch, playing upon old instruments, some of which may have survived from Jesuit times, or, at the least, been copied in the place, as the originals decayed.

Sackbuts and psalteries and shawms were there, with ser-

---

[3] Empyrean was originally the name for the outermost and highest sphere, and came to mean the highest heaven in the Christian authors. In the nineteenth and twentiety centuries it sometimes means vaguely cosmic space.

[4] Unredeemed Italy. Irredentism was the name given to the movement, after Italian unification, to win back all the territories that should have belonged to Italy, but were separated from it.

pents, gigantic clarionets, and curiously twisted oboes, and drums, whose canvas all hung slack and gave a muffled sound when they were beaten, and little fifes, earpiercing and devilish, were represented in that band. It banged and crashed "*La palomita*," that tune of evil-sounding omen, for to its strains prisoners were always ushered out to execution in the times of López, and as it played the players slowly walked down the steps.

Behind them followed the *alcalde*, an aged Indian, dressed in long cotton drawers, that at the knees were split into a fringe that hung down to his ankles, a spotless shirt much pleated, and a red cloak of fine merino cloth. In his right hand he carried a long cane with a silver head—his badge of office. Walking up to the door of his own house, by which was set a table covered with glasses and with home-made cakes, he gave the signal for the running at the ring.

The Correntino gauchos, two or three Paraguayans, and a German married to a Paraguayan wife, were all who entered for the sport. The band struck up, and a young Paraguayan started the first course. Gripping his stirrups tightly between his naked toes, and seated on an old *recao*, surmounted by a sheepskin, he spurred his horse, a wall-eyed skewbald, with his great iron spurs tied to his bare insteps with thin strips of hide. The skewbald, only half-tamed, reared once or twice and bounded off, switching its ragged tail, which had been half-eaten off by cows. The people yelled, a *mosqueador!*—that is, a "fly-flapper," a grave fault in a horse in the eyes in Spanish Americans—as the Paraguayan steered the skewbald with the reins held high in his left hand, carrying the other just above the level of his eyes, armed with a piece of cane about a foot in length.

As he approached the arch, in which the ring dangled from a string, his horse, either frightened by the shouting of the crowd or by the arch itself, swerved and plunged violently, carrying its rider through the thickest of the people, who separated like a flock of sheep when a dog runs through it, cursing him volubly. The German came the next dressed in his Sunday clothes, a slop-made suit of shoddy cloth, riding a horse that all his spur-ring could not get into full speed. The rider's round, fair face was burned a brick-dust colour, and as he spurred and plied his whip, made out of solid tapir hide, the sweat ran down in streams upon his coat. So intent was he on flogging, that as he neared the ring he dropped his piece of cane, and his horse, stopping suddenly just underneath the arch, would have unseated him had he not clasped it round the neck. Shouts of delight greeted this feat of horsemanship, and one tall Correntino, taking his cigarette out of his mouth, said to his fellow sitting next to him upon his horse, "The very animals themselves despise the gringos. See how that little white-nosed brute that he was riding knew that he was a *maturrango*, and nearly had him off."

Next came Hijinio Rojas, a Paraguayan of the better classes, sallow and Indian-looking, dressed in clothes bought in Asunción, his trousers tucked into his riding-boots. His small black hat, with the brim flattened up against his head by the wind caused by the fury of the gallop of his active little roan with four white feet, was kept upon his head by a black ribbon knotted underneath his chin. As he neared the arch his horse stepped double several times and fly-jumped; but that did not disturb him in the least, and, aiming well, he touched the ring, making it fly into the air. A shout went up, partly in Spanish, partly in Guaraní, from the assembled people, and Rojas, reining in his horse, stopped him in a few bounds, so sharply that his unshod feet cut up the turf of the green plaza as a skate cuts the ice. He turned and trotted gently to the arch, and then, putting his horse to its top speed, stopped it again beside the other riders, amid the *"Vivas"* of the crowd. Then came the turn of the four Correntinos, who rode good horses from their native province, had silver horse gear and huge silver spurs, that dangled from their heels. They were all gauchos, born, as the saying goes, "amongst the animals." A dun with fiery eyes and a black stripe right down his back, and with black markings on both hocks, a chestnut skewbald, a *doradillo*, and a horse of that strange mealy bay with a fern-coloured muzzle, that the gauchos call a *pangaré*, carried them just as if their will and that of those who rode them were identical. Without a signal, visible at least to any but themselves, their horses started at full speed, reaching occasionally at the bit, then dropping it again and bridling so easy that one could ride them with a thread drawn from a spider's web. Their riders sat up easily, not riding as a European rides, with his eyes fixed upon each movement of his horse, but, as it were, divining them as soon as they were made. Each of them took the ring, and all of them checked their horses, as it were, by their volition, rather than the bit, making the silver horse gear rattle and their great silver spurs jingle upon their feet. Each waited for the other at the far side of the arch, and then turning in a line they started with a shout, and as they passed right through the middle of the square at a wild gallop, they swung down sideways from their saddles and dragged their hands upon the ground. Swinging up, apparently without an effort, back into their seats, when they arrived at the point from where they had first started, they reined up suddenly, making their horses plunge and rear, and then by a light signal on the reins stand quietly in line, tossing the foam into the air. Hijinio Rojas and the four centaurs all received a prize, and the *alcalde*, pouring out wineglasses full of gin, handed them to the riders, who, with a compliment or two as to the order of their drinking, emptied them solemnly.

No other runners having come forward to compete, for in those days horses were scarce throughout the Paraguayan Missions, the sports were over, and the perspiring crowd went off to breakfast at tables spread under the long verandahs, and silence fell upon the square.

The long, hot hours during the middle of the day were passed in sleeping. Some lay face downwards in the shade. Others swung in white cotton hammocks, keeping them in perpetual motion, till they fell asleep, by pushing with a naked toe upon the ground. At last the sun, the enemy, as the Arabs call him, slowly declined, and white-robed women, with their *tupois* slipping half off their necks, began to come out into the verandahs, slack and perspiring after the midday struggle with the heat.

Then bands of girls sauntered down to the river, from whence soon came the sound of merry laughter as they splashed about and bathed.

The Correntinos rode down to a pool and washed their horses, throwing the water on them with their two hands, as the animals stood nervously shrinking from each splash, until they were quite wet through and running down, when they stood quietly, with their tails tucked in between their legs.

Night came on, as it does in those latitudes, no twilight intervening, and from the rows of houses came the faint lights of wicks burning in bowls of grease, whilst from beneath the orange trees was heard the tinkling of guitars.

Enormous bats soared about noiselessly, and white-dressed couples lingered about the corners of the streets, and men stood talking, pressed closely up against the wooden gratings of the windows, to women hidden inside the room. The air was heavy with the langorous murmur of the tropic night, and gradually the lights one by one were extinguished, and the tinkling of the guitars was stilled. The moon came out, serene and glorious, showing each stone upon the sandy trails as clearly as at midday. Saddling their horses, the four Correntinos silently struck the trail to Itapua, and bands of women moved off along the forest tracks towards their homes, walking in Indian file. Hijinio Rojas, who had saddled up to put the Correntinos on the right road, emerged into the moonlit plaza, his shadow outlined so sharply on the grass it seemed it had been drawn, and then, entering a side street, disappeared into the night. The shrill neighing of his horse appeared as if it bade farewell to its companions, now far away upon the Itapua trail. Noises that rise at night from forests in the tropics sound mysteriously, deep in the woods. It seemed as if a population, silent by day, was active and on foot, and from the underwood a thick white mist arose, shrouding the sleeping town.

Little by little, just as a rising tide covers a reef of rocks, it submerged everything in its white, clinging folds. The houses disappeared, leaving the plaza seething like a lake, and then the church was swallowed up, the towers struggling, as it were, a little, just as a wreath of seaweed on a rock appears to fight against the tide. Then they too disappeared, and the conquering mist enveloped everything. All that was left above the sea of billowing white were the two topmost tufts of the tall, feathery palms.

A MEETING

It was, if I remember rightly, for it is more than thirty years ago, in the great stretch of forest between Caraguatá-Guazú and Caballero Punta, that the meeting which I think brought joy, at least for a short time, to one of those concerned, took place. For miles the track ran through the woods; the trail worn deep into the red and sandy soil looked like a ribbon, dropped underneath the dark, metallic-foliaged trees.

At times a great fallen log, round which the parasitic vegetation had wrapped itself, turned the path off, just as a rock diverts the current of a stream. In places the road, opened long ago, most likely by the Jesuits, ran almost in the dark, under the intertwining ceibas and urandays. Again, it came out on a clearing, in which a straw-thatched hut or two, with a scant patch of mandioca, an orange grove, and a thick bunch of plantains, marked a settlement. The fences were all broken, and peccaries had rooted up the crops. The oranges lay rotting underneath the trees, and as you passed along the solitary trail and came out on the clearings, flocks of green parakeets took wing from where they had been feeding in the deserted fields, and troops of monkeys howled. The four years' war had laid the country waste, and villages were left deserted, or at the best inhabited by women and by girls. In all that long, mosquito-haunted ride, that I remember, just as if I had ridden it a week ago, through the old Jesuit missions, between the Paraná and Paraguay, it was the rarest thing to meet a man, and rarer still to meet a horse. Occasionally you might come upon a family living alone amongst the woods, upon the edge of some old clearing; but if you did, they had no animals about the house but fowls.

At intervals you might chance to cross some wandering Correntino, dressed in the poncho and the *bombachas* of the gaucho, journeying towards Asunción; more rarely a Brazilian on his mule; but all the natives were on foot, most of the horses having been killed in the long war. The legend was that López met his death on the last native Paraguayan horse, a little roan; but be that as it may, horses were rare to find, and the fierce nature of the tropics had so reconquered all the cultivated land that there was little grass for them to eat. Fields that had once borne mandioca were indistinguishable under a tangle of rank grass, dwarf palms, and scrubby plants, whilst maize plantations had remained unsown, bearing but a few straggling plants, grown from the falling ears. Even the pathways through the woods had become impassable, through the thick growth of gnarled and knotty lianas, which, like a web of cordage, barred the way. Tigers abounded and killed the few remaining horses, if they could catch them sleeping near the woods. Bats and mosquitoes, with enormous ticks, combined with several distempers, which the natives said had only come after the war, and when the country had begun to go back to the primeval forest, rendered a horse's life unbearable, and made him difficult to keep.

Those Paraguayans who had a horse cherished him as the apple of their eye, covering him up at night against the vampire bats, and bathing him at sunrise and at sunset to keep away ticks and mosquitoes and a thousand other crawling and flying plagues. Even with these precautions there yet remained the fear of snakes and poisonous weeds, so that a man who had a horse became a slave, and passed his time in caring for him and ministering to his welfare and his health. So as I jogged, that is, of course, walked, for the forest trails were far too deeply worn into the soil to jog with safety, I passed long strings of women, dressed in their low-cut sack-like garment, embroidered round the neck with black embroidery. Their hair, cut square across the forehead and hanging down their backs, gave them a mediaeval air. All were barefooted, and all smoked thick cigars, which they kept lighted at the torch their leader carried in her hand to scare the jaguars. Upon their heads they carried baskets full of oranges, of mandioca, and of maize. Sometimes they all saluted, sometimes they only smiled and showed their teeth, and sometimes one of them would say, amidst the laughter of the rest, "We all want husbands," and added something else in Guaraní that made a laugh run rippling down the line.

Occasionally a crashing in the bushes near the trail told of the passage of a tapir through the underwood, and once, as I came to a little clearing, a tiger lay stretched flat upon a log, watching the fish in some dark backwater, just as a cat lies on the garden wall to watch the birds. Butterflies floated lazily about, scarce moving their broad, velvet wings, reminding one somehow of owls, flitting across a grass ride in a wood, noiseless, but startling by their very quietness.

The snakes, the humming-birds, the alligators basking in the creeks, the whir of insects, and the metallic croaking of the frogs, the air of being in the grip of an all-powerful vegetation, reduced a man, travelling alone through the green solitude, to nothingness. One felt as if, in all that wealth of vegetation and strange birds and beasts, one's horse were the one living thing that was of the same nature as oneself.

Had Balaam only heard his ass's voice in such a place, it would have sounded comforting to him, and might have cheered him on his way.[1] The heat which poured down from the sun, in the few places where the track was open overhead, met the heat rising from the red, sandy soil and focussed on one's face, drying the blood that the innumerable flies had drawn, into hard, sticky flakes. After interminable hours of heat and intervals of dozing from which one woke but just in time to save one's balance and to remember, shuddering, what would occur, if by mischance one fell and let the horse escape, alone, and miles away from any human habitation, the trail led out upon a little clearing in the sea of woods. Smoke curled from a fire under some orange trees, between whose branches hung a cotton hammock, with the fringe sweeping on the ground, as it swung to and fro, impelled by a brown foot.

To my astonishment my horse neighed shrilly, and was answered by a horse, which on first coming to the clearing I had over-looked. As I rode up, repeating, as I rode, the formula,

---

[1]A reference to the biblical story in the Book of Numbers of the prophet Balaam, who disobeyed God and would have been killed by an avenging angel if his ass had not saved him. When he beat his ass, God spoke through the ass and reproached him.

"Hail, blessed Virgin," being answered by the man who had been lying in the hammock, "Without sin conceived," I saw the horse was a red roan, fat and in good condition, and branded with the sign of Aries, set rather low upon the hip. The Paraguayan welcomed me, and bringing out two solid, wooden chairs with cowhide seats, tilted them up against the wall of his mud and straw-thatched hut, and we sat down to talk. His clothes were simple, and yet adequate enough considering the place. Upon his head he wore a home-made hat plaited from fibre of a palm-leaf, and round his waist a leather apron, held in its place by two old, silver coins. With the exception of hide sandals on his feet, and a red cloak of baize hung loosely on one shoulder, he was as naked as the day on which he first drew breath upon the earth. For all that, in his bearing he was dignified enough, and after placing a long-barrelled gun, which he had snatched up hastily when I approached his house, against the wall, but well within his reach, he sat down and motioning me to the other chair began to talk as a man talks who has been long alone. Where had I come from? and how was it that I was dressed like a Correntino, being as he imagined, a foreigner, perhaps a Spaniard, or some other "nation," that spoke no Guaraní?

My horse, he did not know the brand, looked like a horse from the low countries down the river. I had better be careful of him, especially at night, or else the vampire bats would suck his blood. The tigers, too, were specially attracted to a white animal, but then white was such a colour for a gentleman, especially white with a black skin, suitable too for Paraguay, as a white horse is certain to swim well, and the old boat upon the Tebicuari had never been replaced, and I should have to cross in a canoe.

"Tell me," he said, "what are the 'nations' doing in Asunción? Is there a government, and who is president? What, General Caballero? Ah, I remember him, a barefoot boy, running about till López took his pretty sister to live with him. Madama Lynch was not well pleased at it—but then a president is just like God. What he wants, that he will have, be sure of it." It seemed his wife was dead or lost during the war, and when I pointed to some women, one pounding maize in a tall mortar, another picking oranges, and a third swinging in a white cotton hammock, he said, "Yes, women, as you see. In these times the poor things have got no husbands, and Christians have to do their best, out of pure charity."

Much did we talk about things interesting to men in Paraguay, the price of cattle and the like, the increase of tigers in the land, whether the road was open from Corrientes to Asunción through the Estero Ñembucú, and if the Indians in the Chaco had been at what he called "their own," now that there was no law. On all these points I satisfied him as far as I was able, striving to make such news, as I had gleaned upon my way, exact but palatable.

When we had drunk a little maté, which after the Paraguayan country fashion was served quite cold, my host said, "By this time your horse's back must have got cool; one of the girls shall take him down to bathe."

As the girl led him past the roan, both neighed, and my host's horse reared and strove to break his rope.

When in a little [while] the girl came back leading my horse all dripping from his bath, the roan with a wild plunge snapped his hide halter, and came galloping to meet my white, and, circling round him, at last stood with his red, wide-open nostrils close against his nose.

The horses seemed to talk, and mine plunged and would certainly have broken loose had not I run to him. My host, who had looked on with interest, told me his horse had been six months without once seeing another of his kind. "Let your horse loose," he said, "to play with him. Neither is shod, and they can do no harm to one another; let him loose, then, to play." Placing some canes and brushwood to block the road, he said, "Now they are safe; they cannot get away, and horses never go into the thick woods, and if they did they cannot possibly go far."

Somewhat reluctantly I let my horse run loose, leaving his headstall with a *lazo* trailing on the ground, knowing a horse in South America, once loose, is never willing to be caught.

The Paraguayan smiled, and as my horse passed by him, caught and undid the *lazo* saying, "I answer for him with my head, and in the galloping that they will make, the rope would be a danger to them; besides, your horse will never try to get away."

For hours the horses played, leaping about like lambs, galloping to and fro, now rearing up and now coming down with their legs across each other's shoulders on their backs. At nightfall we caught and tied them close to each other, and after feeding them with maize cut down bundles of green *pindó*, heaping it up before them for the night. When we had had our supper, which, if I remember after thirty years, was a rough stew of rice and *charqui*, which we ate using our long knives for spoons, we sat against the corner of the house, swinging our tilted chairs. The women brought us green cigars, and one of them, taking a cracked guitar, some of whose strings were mended up with copper wire and some with bits of hide, sang what is called a *triste*, as the fireflies flitted through the trees.

"Don Rigoberto," said my host (for my own name was unfamiliar to him, and to pronounce it with more ease he altered it, perhaps for euphony), "look at the animals." I looked, and they had finished eating and stood with their heads resting on each other's shoulders, like the advertisement of Thorley's food for cattle, which I remember in my youth at railway stations. "Two years," he said, "I was in prison in Asunción, in the time of López, not the one that José Diabo killed at Tacurupitá, but his old father Don Antonio. Days passed, and weeks and years, and all the time I never saw a man, for they let down my food and water by a string. When I got out, the first man that I met was to me as a long-lost brother—I went and kissed him in the street. Therefore, Don Rigoberto, I know what my horse feels alone here in this *roza*, with not a soul of his own kind to say a word to him. This day has been a fiesta for him, and now let us repeat the rosary, and then to bed—Tomorrow is another day."

I fear the part I took in the repetition of the simple prayers was fragmentary; but at the break of day, or, to be accurate, about an hour before the dawn, I saddled up and bade my host good-bye. As I rode out into the dewy trail a thick white mist enveloped everything. It blotted out the lonely clearing in the first few yards. It dulled the shrill, high neighings of the roan, who plunged and reared upon his rope. Through the long, silent alleys of the primeval forest they sounded fainter as I rode, until at last they ceased, leaving their sadness stll echoing after thirty—or is it five-and-thirty?—years, fixed in my memory.

BRAZIL

Editor's Preface to the Brazilian Sketches

Here we see something of the keen rivalry between Spanish and Portuguese from the earliest days of conquest and discovery. The bull of Pope Alexander VI in 1493 and the Treaty of Tordesillas in 1494 were supposed to settle the territorial disputes over border demarcation. We are again reminded of the Old World–New World theme in "Uno Dei Mille," in which we take a look at the cosmopolitanism of Brazil, with its huge influx of Europeans in the late nineteenth and early twentieth century—in this case, Italians, whom we also saw in "Los Pingos," where the seamen talk a mixture of Spanish and Italian called *cocoliche*. Apart from the linguistic aspect, the sociological and psychological problems of the Italian immigrants can be seen in *La gringa*, by the Uruguayan playwright Florencio Sánchez (1875–1910), who, incidentally, died in Italy.

HEREDITY

Right along the frontier between Uruguay and Río Grande, the southern province of Brazil, the Spanish and the Portuguese sit face to face, as they have sat for ages, looking at, but never understanding, one another, both in the Old and the New World.

In Tuy and Valenza, Monzón and Salvatierra, at Poncho Verde and Don Pedrito, Rivera and Santa Ana do Libramento, and far away above Cruz Alta, where the two clumps of wood that mark old camps of the two people are called O Matto Castelhano and O Matto Português, the rivalry of centuries is either actual or at least commemorated on the map.

The border-line, that once made different peoples of the dwellers at Floriston and Gretna, still prevails in the little castellated towns, which snarl at one another across the Minho, just as they did of old.

"Those people in Valenza would steal the sacrament," says the street urchin playing on the steps of the half-fortalice, half-church, that is the cathedral of Tuy on the Spanish side.

His fellow in Valenza spits towards Tuy and remarks, "From Spain come neither good marriages nor the wholesome winds."

So on to Salvatierra and Monzón, or any other of the villages or towns upon the river, and in the current of the native speech there still remains some saying of the kind, with its sharp edges still unworn after six centuries of use. Great is the power of artificial barriers to restrain mankind. No proverb ever penned is more profound than that which sets out, "Fear guards the vineyard, not the fence around it."

231

So Portuguese and Spaniards in their peninsula have fought and hated and fought and ridiculed each other after the fashion of children that have quarrelled over a broken toy. Blood and an almost common speech, for both speak one Romance when all is said, have both been impotent against the custom-house, the flag, the foolish dynasty, for few countries in the world have had more foolish kings than Spain and Portugal.

That this should be so in the Old World is natural enough, for the dead hand still rules, and custom and tradition have more strength than race and creed; but that the hatred should have been transplanted to America, and still continue, is a proof that folly never dies.

In the old towns on either side of the Minho the exterior life of the two peoples is the same.

In the stone-built, arcaded plazas women still gather around the fountain and fill their iron-hooped water-barrels through long tin pipes, shaped like the tin valences used in wine stores. Donkeys stand at the doors, carrying charcoal in esparto baskets, whether in Portugal or Spain, and goats parade the streets driven by goatherds, wearing shapeless, thickly-napped felt hats and leather overalls.

The water-carrier in both countries calls out "*agua-a-a*," making it sound like Arabic, and long trains of mules bring brushwood for the baker's furnace (even as in Morocco), or great nets of close-chopped straw for horses' fodder.

At eventide the girls walk on the plaza, their mothers, aunts, or servants following them as closely as their shadows on a sunny afternoon. In quiet streets lovers on both sides of the river talk from a first-floor balcony to the street, or whisper through the window-bars on the ground floor. The little shops under the low arches of the arcaded streets have yellow flannel drawers for men and petticoats of many colours hanging close outside their doors, on whose steps sleep yellow dogs.

The jangling bells in the decaying lichen-grown old towers of the churches jangle and clang in the same key, and, as appears, without a touch of *odium theologicum*.[1] The full bass voices boom from the choirs, in which the self-same organs in their walnut cases have the same rows of golden trumpets sticking out into the aisle.

[1] Theological hatred.

One faith, one speech, one mode of daily life, the same sharp "green" wine, the same bread made of maize and rye, and the same heaps of red tomatoes and green peppers glistening in the sun in the same market-places, and yet a rivalry and a difference as far apart as east from west still separates them.

In both their countries the axles of the bullock-carts, with solid wheels and wattled hurdle sides, like those upon a Roman coin, still creak and whine to keep away the wolves.

In the soft landscape the maize fields wave in the rich hollows on both sides of the Minho.

The pine woods mantle the rocky hills that overhang the deep-sea lochs that burrow in both countries deep into the entrails of the land.

The women, with their many-coloured petticoats and handkerchiefs, chaffer at the same fairs to which their husbands ride their ponies in their straw cloaks.

At *romerías* the peasantry dance to the bagpipe and the drum the self-same dances, and both climb the self-same steep grey steps through the dark lanes, all overhung with gorse and broom, up to the Calvaries, where the three crosses take on the self-same growth of lichen and of moss. Yet the *boyero* who walks before the placid oxen, with their cream-coloured flanks and liquid eyes of onyx, feels he is different, right down to the last molecule of his being, from the man upon the other side.

So was it once, and perhaps is to-day, with those who dwell in Liddes or Bewcastle dales. Spaniard and Portuguese, as Scot and Englishman in older times, can never see one matter from the same point of view. The Portuguese will say that the Castilian is a rogue, and the Castilian returns the compliment. Neither have any reason to support their view, for who wants reason to support that which he feels is true.

It may be that the Spaniard is a little rougher and the Portuguese more cunning; but if it is the case or not, the antipathy remains and has been taken to America.

From the Laguna de Merín to the Cureim, that is to say, along a frontier of two hundred leagues, the self-same feeling rules upon both sides of the line. There, as in Portugal and Spain, although the country, whether in Uruguay or in Brazil, is little different, yet it has suffered something indefinable by being occupied by members of the two races so near and yet so different from one another.

Great rolling seas of waving grass, broken by a few stony hills, are the chief features of the landscape of the frontiers in both republics. Estancia houses, dazzlingly white, buried in peach and fig groves, dot the plains, looking like islands in the sea of grass. Great herds of cattle roam about, and men on horseback, galloping like clockwork, sail across the plains like ships upon a sea. Along the river-banks grow strips of thorny trees, and as the frontier line trends northward palm-trees appear, and monkeys chatter in the woods. Herds of wild asses, shyer than antelopes, gaze at the passing horsemen, scour off when he approaches, and are lost into the haze. Stretches of purple borage, known as *la flor morada*, carpet the ground in spring and early summer, giving place later on to red verbena; and on the edges of the streams the tufts of the tall pampa grass recall the feathers on a pampa Indian's spear.

Bands of grave ostriches feed quietly upon the tops of hills, and stride away when frightened, down the wind, with wings stretched out to catch the breeze.

Clothes are identical, or almost so; the poncho and the loose trousers stuffed into high patent-leather boots, the hat kept in its place by a black ribbon with two tassels, are to be seen on both sides of the frontier. Only in Brazil a sword stuck through the girth replaces the long knife of Uruguay. Perhaps in that one item all the differences between the races manifest themselves, for the sword is, as it were, a symbol, for no one ever saw one drawn or used in any way but as an ornament. It is, in fact, but a survival of old customs, which are cherished both by the Portuguese and the Brazilians as the apple of the eye.

The vast extent of the territory of Brazil, its inaccessibility and the enormous distances to be travelled from the interior to the coast, and the sense of remoteness from the outer world, have kept alive a type of man not to be found in any other country where the Christian faith prevails. Risings of fanatics still are frequent; one is going on to-day in Paraná, and that of the celebrated Antonio Conselheiro, twenty years ago, shook the whole country to its core.[2] Slavery existed in the memory of people still alive. Women in the remoter towns are still secluded almost as with the Moors. The men still retain something of the Middle Ages in their love of show. All in the province of Río

[2] Treated by Graham at length in *A Brazilian Mystic*.

Grande are great horsemen, and all use silver trappings on a black horse, and all have horses bitted so as to turn round in the air, just as a hawk turns on the wing.

The sons of men who have been slaves abound in all the little frontier towns, and old grey-headed negroes, who have been slaves themselves, still hang about the great estates. Upon the other side, in Uruguay, the negro question was solved once and for all in the Independence Wars, for then the negroes were all formed into battalions by themselves and set in the forefront of the battle, to die for liberty in a country where they all were slaves the month before. War turned them into heroes and sent them out to die.

When once their independence was assured, the Uruguayans fell into line like magic with the modern trend of thought. Liberty to them meant absolute equality, for throughout the land no snob is found to leave a slug's trail on the face of man by his subserviency.

Women were held free, that is, as free as it is possible for them to be in any Latin-peopled land. Across the line, even to-day, a man may stay a week in a Brazilian country house and never see a woman but a mulata girl or an old negro crone. Still he feels he is watched by eyes he never sees, listens to voices singing or laughing, and a sense of mystery prevails.

Spaniards and Portuguese in the New World have blended just as little as they have done at home. Upon the frontier all the wilder spirits of Brazil and Uruguay have congregated. There they pursue the life, but little altered, that their fathers led full fifty years ago. All carry arms, and use them on small provocation, for if an accident takes place the frontier shields the slayer, for to pursue him usually entails a national quarrel, and so the game goes on.

So Jango Chavez, feeling inclined for sport, or, as he might have said, to *brincar un bocadinho*,[3] saddled up his horse. He mounted, and, as his friends were looking on, ran it across the plaza of the town, and, turning like a sea-gull in its flight, came back to where his friends were standing, and stopped it with a jerk.

His silver harness jingled, and his heavy spurs, hanging loosely on his high-heeled boots, clanked like fetters, as his

---

[3] "To play around a little."

active little horse bounded into the air and threw the sand up in a shower.

The rider, sitting him like a statue, with the far-off look horsemen of every land assume when riding a good horse and when they know they are observed, slackened his hand and let him fall into a little measured trot, arching his neck and playing with the bit, under which hung a silver eagle on a hinge. Waving his hand towards his friends, Jango rode slowly through the town. He passed through sandy streets of flat-roofed, whitewashed houses, before whose doors stood hobbled horses nodding in the sun.

He rode past orange gardens surrounded by brown walls of sun-baked bricks with the straw sticking in them, just as it had dried. In the waste the castor-oil bushes formed little jungles out of which peered cats, exactly as a tiger peers out of a real jungle in the woods.

The sun poured down, and was reverberated back from the white houses, and on the great gaunt building, where the captain-general lived, gloated the green-and-yellow flag of the republic, looking like a bandana handkerchief. He passed the negro ranchería, without which no such town as Santa Ana do Libramento is complete, and might have marked, had he not been too much used to see them, the naked negro children playing in the sand. Possibly, if he marked them, he referred to them as *cachorrinhos pretos*,[4] for the old leaven of the days of slavery is strongly rooted in Brazil. So he rode on, a slight and graceful figure, bending to each movement of his horse, his mobile, olive-coloured features looking like a bronze masque in the fierce downpour of the sun.

As he rode on, his whip, held by a thong and dangling from his fingers, swung against his horse's flanks, keeping time rhythmically to its pace. He crossed the rivulet that flows between the towns and came out on the little open plain that separates them. From habit, or because he felt himself amongst unfriendly or uncomprehended people, he touched his knife and his revolvers, hidden beneath his summer poncho, with his right hand, and with his bridle arm held high, ready for all eventualities, passed into just such another sandy street as he had left behind.

[4] "Little black dogs."

Save that all looked a little newer, and that the stores were
better supplied with goods, and that there were no negro huts,
the difference was slight between the towns. True that the
green-and-yellow flag had given place to the barred blue-and-
white of Uruguay. An armed policeman stood at the corners of
the main thoroughfares, and water-carts went up and down at
intervals. The garden in the plaza had a well-tended flower-
garden.

A band was playing in the middle of it, and Jango could not fail
to notice that Rivera was more prosperous than was his native
town.

Whether that influenced him, or whether it was the glass of
caña which he had at the first *pulpería*, is a moot point, or
whether the old antipathy between the races brought by his
ancestors from the peninsula; anyhow, he left his horse untied,
and with the reins thrown down before it as he got off to have his
drink. When he came out, a policeman called to him to hobble it
or tie it up.

Without a word he gathered up his reins, sprang at a bound
upon his horse, and, drawing his mother-of-pearl-handled pistol, fired at the policeman almost as he sprang. The shot threw up
a shower of sand just in the policeman's face, and probably saved
Jango's life. Drawing his pistol, the man fired back, but Jango,
with a shout and pressure of his heels, was off like lightning,
firing as he rode, and zigzagging across the street. The policeman's shot went wide, and Jango, turning in the saddle, fired
again and missed.

By this time men with pistols in their hands stood at the doors
of all the houses; but the Brazilian passed so rapidly, throwing
himself alternately now on the near side, now on the off side of
his horse, hanging by one foot across the croup and holding with
the other to the mane, that he presented no mark for them to hit.

As he passed by the *jefatura* where the *alcalde* and his friends
were sitting smoking just before the door, he fired with such
good aim that a large piece of plaster just above their heads fell,
covering them with dust.

Drawing his second pistol and still firing as he went, he dashed
out of the town, in spite of shots from every side, his horse
bounding like lightning as his great silver spurs ploughed deep
into its sides. When he had crossed the little bit of neutral

ground, and just as a patrol of cavalry appeared, ready to gallop after him, a band of men from his own town came out to meet him.

He stopped, and shouting out defiance to the Uruguayans, drew up his horse, and lit a cigarette. Then, safe beyond the frontier, trotted on gently to meet his friends, his horse shaking white foam from off its bit, and little rivulets of blood dripping down from its sides into the sand.

UNO DEI MILLE[1]

A veil of mist, the colour of a spider's web, rose from the oily river. It met the mist that wrapped the palm-trees and the unsubstantial-looking houses painted in light blue and yellow ochre, as it descended from the hills. Now and then, through the pall of damp, as a light air was wafted up the river from the sea, the bright red earth upon the hills showed like a stain of blood; canoes, paddled by men who stood up, balancing themselves with a slight movement of the hips, slipped in and out of sight, now crossing just before the steamer's bows and then appearing underneath her stern in a mysterious way. From the long line of tin-roofed sheds a ceaseless stream of snuff- and butter-coloured men trotted continuously, carrying bags of coffee to an elevator, which shot them headlong down the steamer's hold. Their naked feet pattered upon the warm, wet concrete of the dock side, as it were stealthily, with a sound almost alarming, so like their foot-fall seemed to that of a wild animal.

The flat-roofed city, buried in sheets of rain that spouted from the eaves of the low houses on the unwary passers-by, was stirred unwontedly. Men, who as a general rule lounged at the corners of the streets, pressing their shoulders up against the houses as if they thought that only by their own self-sacrifice the walls were kept from falling, now walked up and down, regardless of the rain.

[1] "One of the Thousand." Graham refers here to the thousand volunteers who accompanied Garibaldi to recapture Sicily.

In the great oblong square, planted with cocoa-palms, in which the statue of Cabral stands up in cheap Carrara marble, looking as if he felt ashamed of his discovery,[2] a sea of wet umbrellas surged to and fro, forging towards the Italian Consulate. Squat Genoese and swarthy Neapolitans, with sinewy Piedmontese, and men from every province of the peninsula, all had left their work. They all discoursed in the same tone of voice in which no doubt their ancestors talked in the Forum, even when Cicero was speaking, until the lictors forced them to keep silence, for their own eloquence is that which in all ages has had most charm for them. The reedy voices of the Brazilian coloured men sounded a mere twittering compared to their full-bodied tones. *"Viva l'Italia"* pealed out from thousands of strong throats as the crowd streamed from the square and filled the narrow streets; fireworks that fizzled miserably were shot off in the mist, the sticks falling upon the umbrellas of the crowd. A shift of wind cleared the mist off the river for a moment, leaving an Italian liner full in view. From all her spars floated the red and white and green, and on her decks and in the rigging, on bridges and on the rail, men, all with bundles in their hands, clustered like ants and cheered incessantly. An answering cheer rose from the crowd ashore of "Long live the Reservists! *Viva l'Italia,"* as the vessel slowly swung into the stream. From every house excited men rushed out and flung themselves and their belongings into boats, and scrambled up the vessel's sides as she began to move. Brown hands were stretched down to them as they climbed on board. From every doorstep in the town women with handkerchiefs about their heads came out, and with the tears falling from their great, black eyes and running down their olive cheeks, waved and called out, *"Addio Giuseppe; addio Gian Battista, abbasso i Tedeschi,"* [3] and then turned back into their homes to weep. On every side Italians stood and shouted, and still, from railway station and from the riverside, hundreds poured out and gazed at the departing steamer with its teeming freight of men.

Italians from the coffee plantations of São Paulo, from the mines of Ouro Preto, from Goyaz, and from the far interior, all young and sun-burnt, the flower of those Italian workmen who have built the railways of Brazil, and by whose work the strong

[2] Pedro Alvares Cabral (c.1467–c.1520), the "official" discoverer of Brazil.
[3] "Goodbye, Giuseppe! Goodbye, Gian Battista! Down with the Germans!

foundations of the prosperity of the Republic have been laid, were out, to turn their backs upon the land in which, for the first time, most of them had eaten a full meal. Factories stood idle, the coasting schooners all were left unmanned, and had the coffee harvest not been gathered in, it would have rotted on the hills. The Consulate was unapproachable, and round it throngs of men struggled to enter, all demanding to get home. No rain could damp their spirits, and those who, after waiting hours, came out with tickets, had a look in their eyes as if they just had won the chief prize in the lottery.

Their friends surrounded them, and strained them to their hearts, the water from the umbrellas of the crowd trickling in rivulets upon the embracer and the embraced.

Mulatto policemen cleared the path for carriages to pass, and, as they came, the gap filled up again as if by magic, till the next carriage passed. Suddenly a tremor ran through the crowd, moving it with a shiver like the body of a snake. All the umbrellas which had seemed to move by their own will, covering the crowd and hiding it from view, were shut down suddenly. A mist-dimmed sun shone out, watery, but potent, and in an instant gaining strength, it dried the streets and made a hot steam rise up from the crowd. Slouched hats were raised up on one side, and pocket-handkerchiefs wrapped up in paper were unfolded and knotted loosely round men's necks, giving them a look as of domestic bandits as they broke out into a patriotic song, which ceased with a long drawn-out "*Viva*," as the strains of an approaching band were heard and the footsteps of men marching through the streets in military array.

The coloured policemen rode their horses through the throng, and the streets, which till then had seemed impassable, were suddenly left clear. Jangling and crashing out the Garibaldian hymn, the band debouched into the square, dressed in a uniform half-German, half-Brazilian, with truncated *pickelhauben* on their heads, in which were stuck a plume of gaudy feathers, apparently at the discretion of the wearer, making them look like something in a comic opera; a tall mulatto, playing on a drum with all the seriousness that only one of his colour and his race is able to impart to futile actions, swaggered along beside a jet-black negro playing on the flute. All the executants wore brass-handled swords of a kind never seen in Europe for a hundred years. Those who played the trombone and the ophicleide blew till their thick lips swelled, and seemed to cover up the mouth-pieces. Still they blew on, the perspiration rolling down their cheeks, and a black boy or two brought up the rear, clashing the cymbals when it seemed good to them, quite irrespective of the rest. The noise was terrifying, and had it not been for the enthusiasm of the crowd, the motley band of coloured men, arrayed like popinjays, would have been ridiculous; but the dense ranks of hot, perspiring men, all in the flower of youth, and every one of whom had given up his work to cross the ocean at his country's call, had something in them that turned laughter into tears. The sons of peasants, who had left their homes, driven out from Apulean plains or Lombard rice-fields by the pinch of poverty, they now were going back to shed their blood for the land that had denied them bread in their own homes. Twice did the band march round the town whilst the procession was getting ready for a start, and each time that it passed before the Consulate, the Consul came out on the steps, bare-headed, and saluted with the flag.

Dressed in white drill, tall, grey-haired, and with the washed-out look of one who has spent many years in a hot country, the Consul evidently had been a soldier in his youth. He stood and watched the people critically, with the appraising look of the old officer, so like to that a grazier puts on at a cattle market as he surveys the beasts. "Good stuff," he muttered to himself, and then drawing his hand across his eyes, as if he felt where most of the "good stuff" would lie in a few months, he went back to the house.

A cheer at the far corner of the square showed that the ranks were formed. A policeman on a scraggy horse, with a great rusty sabre banging at its side, rode slowly down the streets to clear the way, and once again the parti-coloured band passed by, playing the Garibaldian hymn. Rank upon rank of men tramped after it, their friends running beside them for a last embrace, and women rushing up with children for a farewell kiss. Their merry faces set with determination, and their shoulders well thrown back, three or four hundred men briskly stepped along, trying to imitate the way the Bersaglieri march in Italy.[4] A shout went up of "Long live the Reservists," as a contingent, drawn from every class of the

[4] The Bersaglieri, literally "the marksmen," were the select light infantry of the Italian army, famous for their plumed hats and rapid marching.

Italian colony, passed along the street. Dock-labourers and pale-faced clerks in well-cut clothes and unsubstantial boots walked side by side. Men burnt the colour of a brick by working at the harvest rubbed shoulders with Sicilian emigrants landed a month or two ago, but who now were going off to fight, as poor as when they left their native land, and dressed in the same clothes. Neapolitans, gesticulating as they marched, and putting out their tongues at the Brazilian negroes, chattered and joked. To them life was a farce, no matter that the setting of the stage on which they moved was narrow, the fare hard, and the remuneration small. If things were adverse they still laughed on, and if the world was kind they jeered at it and at themselves, disarming both the slings of fortune and her more dangerous smiles with a grimace.

As they marched on, they now and then sketched out in pantomime the fate of any German who might fall into their hands, so vividly that shouts of laughter greeted them, which they acknowledged by putting out their tongues. Square-shouldered Liguresi succeeded them, with Lombards, Sicilians, and men of the strange negroid-looking race from the Basilicata, almost as dark-skinned as the Brazilian loungers at the corners of the streets.

They all passed on, laughing, and quite oblivious of what was in store for most of them—laughing and smoking, and, for the first time in their lives, the centre of a show. After them came another band; but this time of Italians, well-dressed, and playing on well-cared-for instruments. Behind them walked a little group of men, on whose appearance a hush fell on the crowd. Two of them wore uniforms, and between them, supported by silk handkerchiefs wrapped round his arms, there walked a man who was welcomed with a scream of joy. Frail, and with trembling footsteps, dressed in a faded old red shirt and knotted handker-chief, his parchment cheeks lit up with a faint flush as the veteran of Marsala[5] passed like a phantom of a glorious past. With him appeared to march the rest of his companions who set sail from Genoa to call into existence that Italy for which the young men all around him were prepared to sacrifice their lives.

To the excited crowd he typified all that their fathers had

[5]Marsala is the seaport in Sicily where Garibaldi landed with his "one thousand" to begin the campaign.

endured to drive the stranger from their land. The two Cairoli, Nino Bixio, and the heroic figure, wrapped in his poncho, who rides in glory on the Janiculum,[6] visible from every point of Rome, seemed to march by the old man's side in the imagination of the crowd. Women rushed forward, carrying flowers, and strewed them on the scant grey locks of the old soldier, and children danced in front of him, like little Baccahanals. All hats were off as the old man was borne along, a phantom of himself, a symbol of a heroic past, and still a beacon, flickering but alight, to show the way towards the goal which in his youth had seemed impossible to reach.

Slowly the procession rolled along, surging against the houses as an incoming tide swirls up a river, till it reached the Consulate. It halted, and the old Garibaldian, drawing himself up, saluted the Italian colours. The Consul, bare-headed and with tears running down his cheeks, stood for a moment, the centre of all eyes, and then, advancing, tore the flag from off its staff, and, after kissing it, wrapped it round the frail shoulders of the veteran.

[6]These heroes of Italian unification and independence are respectively Benedetto Cairoli (1825–89), Nino Bixio (1821–73), and Garibaldi himself.

COLOMBIA

Editor's Preface to the Colombian Sketches

Colombia is reputedly the land of poets. The story is told of two budding, but down-to-earth, poets who meet in the streets of Bogotá, hands in pocket, clutching papers containing the day's efforts. "I'll not show you mine," says one, "if you promise not to show me yours." "Mirahuano" is the story of one of these poets, but a story with a tragic end, when the topical problem of racial discrimination rears its head.[1] "*Animula Vagula*," or "The Orchid Hunter," is a good example of two literary techniques often used by Graham—the anecdote within the story, and the imaginative re-creation.

[1] See *María* (1867), the romantic novel *par excellence*, of Jorge Isaacs (1837–95), and the anguished poetry of the tragic poet, José Asunción Silva (1865–96), particularly his famous "Third Nocturne" ("*Nocturno III*"), as typical examples of late nineteenth-century Colombian romantic fiction and modernist poetry, respectively.

MIRAHUANO

Why Silvio Sánchez got the name of Mirahuano was difficult to say. Perhaps for the same reason that the Arabs call lead "the light," for certainly he was the blackest of his race, a tall, lop-sided negro, with elephantine ears, thick lips, teeth like a nar-whal's tusks, and mirahuano is a cottony, white stuff used to fill cushions, and light as thistledown. Although he was so black and so uncouth, he had the sweetest smile imaginable, and through his eyes, which at first sight looked hideous, with their saffron-coloured whites, there shone a light, as if a spirit chained in the dungeon of his flesh was struggling to be free. A citizen of a republic in which by theory all men were free and equal by the law, the stronger canon enacted by humanity, confirmed by prejudice, and enforced by centuries of use, had set a bar be-tween him and his white brethren in the Lord which nothing, neither his talents, lovable nature, nor the esteem of everyone who knew him, could ever draw aside. Fate having doubly cursed him with a black skin and an aspiring intellect, he passed his life just as a fish might live in an aquarium, or a caged bird, if they had been brought up to think intelligently on their lost liberty.

The kindly customs of the republic, either derived from demo-cratic Spain or taken unawares from the gentler races of the New World, admitted him, partly by virtue of his talents, for he was born a poet, in a land where all write verses, on almost equal terms to the society of men. Still there were little differences that they observed as if by instinct, almost involuntarily, due partly to the lack of human dignity conspicuous in his race; a lack which in his case, as if the very powers of nature were in league against him, seemed intensified, and made him, as it were, on one hand an archetype, so negroid that he almost seemed an ape, and yet in intellect superior to the majority of those who laughed at him. No one was ever heard to call him Don, and yet the roughest muleteer from Antioquia[1] claimed and received the title as a right, as soon as he had made sufficient money to purchase a black coat.

In the interminable sessions in the cafés, where men sat talking politics by hours, or broached their theories at great length, on poetry, on international law, on government, on literature and art, with much gesticulation, and with their voices raised to their highest pitch—for arguments are twice as cogent when delivered shrilly and with much banging on the table—the uncouth negro did not suffer in his pride, for there he shouted with the rest and plunged into a world of dialectics with the best of them. His Calvary came later, for when at last the apologetic Genoese, who kept the café, politely told his customers that it was time to close, and all strolled out together through the arcaded, silent streets built by the conquerors and stood about for a last wrangle in the plaza under the China trees, as sometimes happened, one or two would go away together to finish off their talk at home. Then Mirahuano silently would walk away, watching the fireflies flash about the bushes, and with a friendly shout of *"Buenas noches, Mirahuano"* ringing in his ears from the last of his companions as they stood on the threshold of their houses, holding the door wide open by the huge iron knocker, screwed high up, so that a man upon his mule could lift it easily.

Beyond that threshold he was never asked except on business, for there dwelt the white women, who were at once his adoration and despair. With them no talents, no kindliness or generosity of character, had any weight. They treated him, upon the rare occasions when he recited verses of his own composition at some function, with grave courtesy, for it was due to their own self-respect to do so, but as a being of another generation to themselves, who had, for so their priests informed them, an immortal

---

[1] A mountainous region in the interior of Colombia, in the northern Andes, whose inhabitants, through long isolation, have gained a reputation for aggressive individualism.

soul, which after death might be as worthy of salvation as their own in its Creator's eyes.

He, though he knew exactly his position, midway between that of the higher animals and man, was yet unable to resist the peculiar fascination that a white woman seems to have for those of coloured blood. Those of his friends who had his interests at heart, and were admirers of his talents, argued in vain, and pointed out that he was certain to bring trouble on his head if he attempted to presume upon his education and tried to be accepted as a man.

His means permitted him to live a relatively idle life, and as he read all kinds of books in French and Spanish, his intellect always expanded, and it was natural enough that he should think himself the equal of the best, unless he happened to take up a looking-glass and saw the injustice which from his birth both God and man had wrought upon him. As now and then he published poems, which, in a country where all write, were still above the average of those his brethren in the Muses penned (for all the whiteness of their skins), his name was noised abroad, and he was styled in newspapers the Black Alcaeus,[2] the Lute of Africa, and a variety of other epithets, according to the lack of taste of those who make all things ridiculous which their fell pens approach.

The Floral Games were due. On such occasions poets write on themes such as "To the Immortal Memory of the Liberator," or dedicate their lyrics to the "Souls of those who fell at Mancavélica," or simply head their stuff "*Dolores,*" "*Una flor marchita,*"[3] or something of the sort. Poets of all dimensions leave their counting-houses, banks, regiments, and public offices, and with their brows all "wreathed in roses," as the local papers say, flock to the "flowery strife." All are attired in black, all wear tall hats, and all bear white kid gloves, sticky with heat, and generally a size or two too large for those who carry them.

Each poet in the breast-pocket of his long frock-coat has a large roll of paper in which in a clear hand are written out the verses that are to make his name immortal and crown his brow with flowers.

Now and again their hands steal furtively to touch the precious

[2] Alcaeus (620–580 B.C.), Greek lyric poet, born in Lesbos.
[3] "A Withered Flower."

scrolls, just as a man riding at night in dangerous country now and then feels at the butt of his revolver to assure himself that it is there, when his horse pricks his ears or any of the inexplicable, mysterious noises of the night perplex and startle him. On this occasion, after the other sports, the running at the ring, the feats of horsemanship, in which men stopped their horses short before a wall, making them rear and place their feet upon the top, the tailing of the bulls, and all the other feats which Spanish Americans love to train their horses to perform, were over, the poets all advanced. In the fierce sun they marched, looking a little like a band of undertaker's mutes at an old-fashioned funeral, and stood in line before the jury, and each man in his turn read out his verses, swelling his voice, and rolling all the adjectives, like a delicious morsel, on his tongue. The audience now and then burst out into applause, when some well-worn and well-remembered tag treating of liberty, calling upon the Muses for their help, or speaking of the crimson glow, like blood of the oppressor, which tinged the Andean snows, making them blush incarnadine, or when a stanza dwelling on alabaster bosoms, teeth white as pearls, and eyes as black as those the Houris flash in Paradise,[4] struck their delighted ears. All read and stood aside to wait, looking a little sourly on their fellow-competitors, or with their eyes fixed on a girl, the daughter of a senator, who dressed in white, sat in a box beside her father, ready to crown the successful poet with a limp wreath of flowers. The last to read was Mirahuano, and the Master of the Ceremonies, after due clearing of his throat, read out his title, "Movements of the Soul." Holding his hat in his left hand, and with the perspiration, which in a negro looks white and revolting to our eyes, standing in beads upon his face, and in the thick and guttural tones of all his race, the poet nervously began.

At first the audience maintained that hostile air which every audience puts on to those it does not know. This gradually gave place to one of interest, as it appeared the verses all ran smoothly; and this again altered to interest as the figure of the uncouth negro grew familiar to them. As he read on, tracing the movements of the soul, confined and fettered in the flesh, lacking

[4] In Islamic religions, the Houris were heavenly female beauties, traditionally created from musk and spices and endowed with the qualities of perpetual youth and virginity.

advancement in its due development owing to circumstances affecting not itself, but the mere prison of the body, a prison that it must endure perforce, so that it may be born, and which it leaves unwillingly at last, so strong is habit, even to the soul, the listeners recognised that they were listening to a poet, and gazed upon him in astonishment, just as the men of Athens may have gazed on the mean-looking little Jew, who, beckoning with his head, after the manner of the natural orator, compelled their silence in the Agora.[5] The poet finished in a blaze of rhetoric after the fashion that the Latin race in the republics of America demands, depicting a free soul, freed from the bonds that race, sex, or conditions have imposed on it, free to enjoy, to dare, to plan, free to work out its own salvation, free to soar upwards and to love.

He ceased, and a loud "*Viva!*" rent the air, and though some of the men of property were evidently shocked at the implied intrusion of a mere negro soul into an Empyrean[6] where their own would soon have atrophied, the poor and all the younger generation—for in America, whatever men become in after life, in youth they are all red republicans—broke out into applause.

Long did the jury talk the poems over, weighing judiciously the pros and cons, but from the first it was quite clear that Mirahuano's composition would receive most votes.

Again the Master of the Ceremonies stood up, and in dead silence proclaimed the prize had been adjudged to señor Sánchez, and that he was requested to step forward and be crowned.

Shoving his papers hastily into his pocket, and clinging to his hat, just as a drowning sailor clutches fast a plank, the poet shuffled up toward the box in which the jury sat, and stood half-proudly, half-shamefacedly, to listen to the set oration which the President of the Floral Games stood ready to pronounce. Clearing his throat, he welcomed to Parnassus' heights another poet. He was proud that one of their own town had won the prize. The Muses all rejoiced; Apollo had restrung his lyre and now stretched out his hand to welcome in the son of Africa. The eternal verities stood once more justified; liberty, poetry, and

[5] Found in Homer, the Agora was the meeting-place, later the market-place, which was the center of their political, religious, social, and commercial activity. The mean-looking little Jew is probably St. Paul.

[6] See note 3 of "Feast Day in Santa María Mayor."

peace had their true home in the Republic. Europe might boast its Dantes and Shakkispers, its Lopes, Ariostos, and the rest, but Costaguano need not fear their rivalry whilst poets such as Mira—he should say as Silvio Sánchez—still raised their paeans to the great and indivisible.

He could say more, much more, but words, what were they in the face of genius?—so he would bring his discourse to a close by welcoming again the youngest brother of the lyre into the Muses' court. Now he would call upon the fairest of the fair, the señorita Nieves Figueroa, to place the laurel on the poet's brow.

Applause broke out rather constrainedly, and chiefly amongst those who, by the virtue of their station, were able to express their feelings easily, really liked Mirahuano, and possibly admired the poem they had heard, that is as much of it as they had understood.

Dressed all in white, with a mantilla of white lace upon her head, fastened high on her hair to a tall comb, shy and yet self-possessed, the señorita Nieves Figueroa advanced, holding a crown of laurel leaves, with a large silver ornament, shaped like a lyre, in front of it, and with long ribbons of the national colours hanging down behind. Her jet-black hair was glossy as a raven's wing. Her olive skin and almond eyes were thrown into relief by her white clothes, and gave her somewhat of the air of a fly dropped in milk, or a blackbird in snow. Clearly she was embarrassed by the appearance of the man she had to crown, who, on his side, stood quivering with excitement at his victory and the approach of the young girl.

Raising the crown, she placed it on the negro's head, where it hung awkwardly, half covering his eyes, and giving him the look as of a bull when a skilled bull-fighter has placed a pair of banderillas in his neck. Murmuring something about the Muses, poetry, and a lyre, she gracefully stepped back, and Mirahuano shuffled off, having received, as he himself observed, "besides the wreath, an arrow in his heart."

From that day forth he was her slave, that is, in theory, for naturally he never had the chance to speak to her, although no doubt she heard about his passion and perhaps laughed with her friends about the ungainly figure she had crowned. Debarred from all chance of speech with her he called the "objective of his soul," dressed in his best, he called each Thursday morning at señor Figueroa's house to deliver personally a copy of his verses tied with blue ribbons at the door. The door was duly opened and the verses handed in for months, and all the town knew and talked of the infatuation of the negro poet, who for his part could have had no illusions on the subject, for from the moment of the Floral Games he had never spoken to the girl except, as he said, "by the road of Parnassus," which after all is a path circuitous enough in matters of the heart.

His life was passed between the little house, buried in orange and banana trees, where his old mother, with her head wrapped in a coloured pocket-handkerchief, sat all the day, balanced against the wall in an old, high-backed chair, watching his sisters pounding maize in a high, hard-wood mortar, with their chemises slipping off their shoulders, and the *Café del siglo*, where all the poets used to spend their time.

Poets and verse-makers were as much jumbled up in people's minds in the republic as they are here, and anyone who had a rhyming dictionary and the sufficient strength of wrist to wield a pen wrote reams of stuff about the pangs of love, the moon, water, and flashing eyes, with much of liberty and dying for their native land. When once they fell into the habit, it was as hard of cure as drinking, especially as most of them had comfortable homes, though they all talked of what they underwent in the Bohemia to which they were condemned. For hours they used to sit and talk, reading their verses out to one another or with their hats drawn down upon their brows to signify their state.

To these reunions of the soul, for so they styled them, Mirahuano came, sitting a little diffidently upon his chair, and now and then reciting his own verse, which, to speak truth, was far above the rest of the weak, wordy trash produced so lavishly. As it cost nothing to be kind to him, for he would never take even a cup of coffee, unless he paid for it himself, they used him kindly, letting him sit and read when they were tired, help them to [choose] consonants, and generally behave as a light porter to the Muses, as he defined it in his half-melancholy, half-philosophising vein.

One night as they sat late compassionating one another on their past luck, and all declaiming against envy and the indifference of a commercial world, whilst the tired waiters dozed, seated before the tables with their heads resting on the marble tops, and as the flies, mosquitoes, and the *vinchucas* made life miserable, their talk drew round towards the hypothetical

Bohemia in which they dreamed they lived. Poor Mirahuano, who had sat silently wiping his face at intervals with a red pocket-handkerchief—for in common with the highest and the lowest of his kind he loved bright colours—drew near, and sitting down among the poets, listened to their talk. The heavy air outside was filled with the rank perfume of the tropic vegetation. The fireflies flashed among the thickets of bamboos, and now and then a night-jar uttered its harsh note.

In the bright moonlight men slept on the stucco benches in the plaza, with their faces downwards, and the whole town was silent except where now and then some traveller upon his mule passed by, the tick-tack of the footfalls of his beast clattering rhythmically in its artificial pace, and sending up a trail of sparks as it paced through the silent streets. Nature appeared perturbed, as she does sometimes in the tropics, and as if just about to be convulsed in the throes of a catastrophe. Inside the café men felt the strain, and it seemed natural to them, when Mirahuano, rising to his feet, his lips blue, and his face livid with emotion, exclaimed, "Talk of Bohemia, what is yours to mine! Mine is threefold. A poet, poor, and black. The last eats up the rest, includes them, stultifies you and your lives." He paused, and, no one answering, unconscious that the waiters, awakened by his tones, were looking at him, half in alarm, half in amazement, broke out again. "Bohemia! Think of my life; my very God is white, made in your image, imposed upon my race by yours. His menacing pale face has haunted me from childhood, hard and unsympathetic, and looking just as if He scorned us whom you call His children, although we know it is untrue. Your laws are all a lie. His too, unless it is that you have falsified them in your own interests and to keep us slaves."

Seizing his hat, he walked out of the café without a salutation, leaving the company dumb with amazement, looking upon each other as the inhabitants of some village built on the slopes of a volcano long quiescent may look, when from the bowels of the sleeping mountain a stream of lava shoots into the sky. His brothers in the Muses missed him from his accustomed haunts for two or three days, and then a countryman reported he had seen in the backwater of a stream an object which he had thought was a dead bullock or a cow. Wishing to secure the hide, he had lassoed it, and to his great astonishment he found it was the body of a negro, dressed in black clothes, as he said, just as good as those worn by the president. Being of a thrifty turn of mind, he had stripped them off and sold them at a *pulpería*, when he had dried them in the sun.

It seemed to him fortuitous that a black rascal who in all his life had never done a stroke of work, but walked about just like a gentleman, making a lot of silly rhymes, at last should be of use to a white Christian such as he was himself, white, as the proverb says, on all four sides.

He added, as he stood beside his half-wild colt, keeping a watchful eye upon its eye, and a firm hand upon his rawhide halter, that as a negro's skin was of no value, he pushed the body back into the stream, and had no doubt that it would soon be eaten up by the caimáns.

ANIMULA VAGULA[1]

"You see," the Orchid-hunter said, "this is just how it happened; one of those deaths, that I have seen so many of, here in the wilderness."

He stood upon the steamer's deck a slight, grave figure, his hair just touched with grey, his flannel Norfolk jacket, which had once been white, toning exactly with his hat and his grey eyes.

At first sight you saw he was an educated man, and when you spoke to him you felt he must have been at some great public school. Yet there was something indefinable about him that spoke of failure. We have no word to express with sympathy the moral qualities of such a man. In Spanish it is all summed up in the expression, *"un infeliz."* Unlucky or unhappy, that is, as the world goes; but perhaps fortunate in that interior world to which so many eyes are closed.

Rolling a cigarette between his thin, brown, fever-stricken fingers, he went on: "Yesterday, about two o'clock, in a heat fit to boil your brain, a canoe came slowly up the stream into the settlement. The Indian paddlers walked up the steep bank carrying the body of a man wrapped in a mat. When they had reached the little palm-thatched hut over which floated the Colombian flag, that marked it as the official residence of the Captain of the

[1] Renamed "The Orchid Hunter" by Tschiffely in *Rodeo*. The title is taken from the opening line of the poem of the Emperor Hadrian to his soul—*"Animula vagula blandula,"* meaning "Sweet, wandering, fleeting soul."

Port, they set their burden down with the hopeless look that marks the Indian, as of an orphaned angel.

" 'We found this "mister" on the banks,' they said, 'in the last stage of fever. He spoke but little Christian, and all he said was, "Doctor, American doctor, Tocatalaima; take me there."

" 'Here he is, and now who is to pay us for our work? We have paddled all night long. The canoe we borrowed. Its owner said that it gains twenty cents a day, and we want forty cents each, for we have paddled hard to save this mister.' Then they stood silent, scratching the mosquito bites upon their ankles with the other naked foot—a link between the *homo sapiens* and some other intermediate species, long extinct.

" 'I paid them, giving them something over what they demanded, and they put on that expression of entire aloofness which the Indian usually assumes on such occasions, either because thanks stick in his gullet, or he thinks no thanks are due after a service rendered. They then went off to drink a glass or two of rum before they started on their journey home.

"I went to see the body, which lay covered with a sack under a little shed. Flies buzzed about it, and already a faint smell of putrefaction reminded one that man is as the other animals, and that the store of knowledge he piles up during his life does not avail to stop the course of Nature, any more than if he had been an orang-outang."

He paused, and, after having lit the cigarette, strolled to the bulwark of the steamer, which had now got into the middle of the stream, and then resumed:

"Living as I do in the woods collecting orchids, the moralising habit grows upon one. It is, as it were, the only answer that a man has to the aggressiveness of Nature.

"I stood and looked at the man's body in his thin linen suit which clung to every angle. Beside him was a white pith helmet, and a pair of yellow-tinted spectacles framed in celluloid to look like tortoiseshell, that come down from the States. I never wear them, for I find that everything that you can do without is something gained in life.

"His feet in his white canvas shoes all stained with mud sticking up stiffly, and his limp, pallid hands, crossed by the pious Indians, on his chest gave him that helpless look that makes a dead man, as it were, appeal to one for sympathy and protection against the terror, that perhaps for him is not a terror after all, but merely a long rest.

"No one had thought of closing his blue eyes, and as we are but creatures of habit after all, I put my hand into my pocket, and taking out two half-dollar pieces was about to put them on his eyes. Then I remembered that one of them was bad, and you will not believe me, but I could not put the bad piece on his eyes; it looked like cheating him. So I went out and got two little stones, and after washing them put them upon his eyelids, and at least they kept away the flies.

"I don't know how it was, for I believe I am not superstitious, but it seemed to me that those blue eyes, sunk in the livid face to which a three or four days' growth of fair and fluffy beard gave a look of adolescence, looked at me as if they still were searching for the American doctor, who no doubt must have engrossed his last coherent thought as he lay in the canoe.

"As I was looking at him, mopping my face, and now and then killing a mosquito—one gets to do it quite mechanically, although in my case neither mosquitoes nor any other kind of bug annoys me very much—the door was opened and the authorities came in. After the usual salutations—which in Colombia are long and ceremonious, with much unnecessary offering of services, which both sides know will never be required—they said they came to view the body and take the necessary steps; that is, you know, to try to find out who he was and have him buried, for which, the heat at forty centigrade, no time was to be lost.

"A stout Colombian dressed in white clothes, which made his swarthy skin look darker still, giving him, as it were, the air of a black beetle dipped in milk, was the first to arrive. Taking off his flat white cap and gold-rimmed spectacles—articles which in Colombia are certain signs of office—he looked a little at the dead man and said, 'He was an English or American.' Then turning to a soldier who had arrived upon the scene, he asked him where the Indian paddlers were who had brought in the canoe.

"The man went out to look for them, and the hut soon was crowded full of Indians, each with his straw hat held up before his mouth. They gazed upon the body, not sympathetically, nor yet unsympathetically, but with that baffling look that Indians must have put on when first the conquerors appeared amongst them, and they found out their arms did not avail them for defence. By means of it they pass through life as relatively un-

scathed as it is possible for men to do, and by its help they seem
to conquer death, taking away its sting, by their indifference.

"None of them said a word, but stared at the dead man, just as
they stare at any living stranger, until I felt that the dead eyes
would turn in anger at them and shake off the flat stones.

"The man clothed in authority and dusky white returned,
accompanied by one of those strange out-at-elbows nondescripts
who are to be found in every town in South America and may be
best described as 'penmen'—that is, persons who can read and
write and have some far-off dealings with the law. After a whispered conversation the Commissary, turning to the assembled
Indians, asked them in a brief voice if they had found the
paddlers of the canoe. None of them answered, for a crowd of
Indians will never find a spokesman, as each one fears to be made
responsible if he says anything at all. A dirty soldier clothed in
draggled khaki, barefooted, and with a rusty, sheathless bayonet
banging on his thigh, opened the door and said that he knew
where they were, but that they both were drunk. The soldier,
after a long stare, would have retreated, but the Commissary,
turning abruptly to him, said: 'José, go and see that a grave is dug
immediately; this "mister" has been dead for several hours.'
Then looking at the 'penman,' 'Pérez,' he said, 'we will now
proceed to the examination of the dead man's papers which the
law prescribes.'

"Pérez, who in common with the majority of the uneducated of
his race, had a great dread of touching a dead body, began to
search the pockets of the young man lying so still and angular in
the drab-looking suit of white. To put off the dread moment he
picked up the pith helmet and, turning out the lining, closely
examined it. Then, finding nothing, in his agitation let it fall
upon the chest of the dead man. I could have killed him, but said
nothing, and we all stood perspiring, with the thermometer at
anything you like inside that wretched hut, while Pérez fumbled
in the pockets of the dead man's coat.

"It seemed to me as if the unresisting body was somehow
being outraged, and that the stiff, attenuated arms would double
up and strike the miserable Pérez during his terrifying task. He
was so clumsy and so frightened that it seemed an eternity till he
produced a case of worn, green leather edged with silver, in
which were several brown Havana cigarettes.

"The Commissary gravely remarking, 'We all have vices, great or small, and smoking is but a little frailty,' told Pérez to write down 'Case, 1; cigarettes, 3,' and then to go on with the search. 'The law requires,' he said, 'the identification of all the dead wherever possible.

" 'First, for its proper satisfaction in order that the Code of the Republic should be complied with; and, secondly, for the consolation of the relations, if there are any such, or the friends of the deceased.'

"Throughout the search the Indians stood in a knot, like cattle standing under a tree in summer-time, gathered together, as it were, for mutual protection, without uttering a word. The ragged soldier stared intently; the Commissary occasionally took off his spectacles and wiped them; and the perspiring Pérez slowly brought out a pocket-knife, a box of matches, and a little bottle of quinine. They were all duly noted down, but still no pocket-book, card-case, letter, or any paper with the name of the deceased appeared to justify the search. Pérez would willingly have given up the job; but, urged on by his chief, at last extracted from an interior pocket a letter-case in alligator skin. Much frayed and stained with perspiration, yet its silver tips still showed that it had once been bought at a good shop.

" 'Open it, Pérez, for the law allows one in such cases to take steps that otherwise would be illegal and against that liberal spirit for which we in this Republic are so renowned in the Americas. Then hand me any card or letter that it may contain.'

"Pérez, with the air of one about to execute a formidable duty, opened the case, first slipping off a couple of elastic bands that held the flaps together. From it he took a bundle of American bank-notes wrapped up in tissue-paper, which he handed to his chief. The Commissary took it, and, slipping off the paper, solemnly counted the notes. 'The sum is just two thousand,' he remarked, 'and all in twenties. Pérez, take note of it, and give me any papers that you may have found.' A closer search of every pocket still revealed nothing, and I breathed more freely, as every time the dirty hands of Pérez fumbled about the helpless body I felt a shudder running down my back.

"We all stood baffled, and the Indians slowly filed out without a word, leaving the Commissary with Pérez and myself standing bewildered by the bed. '"Mister," ' the Commissary said to me; 'what a strange case! Here are two thousand dollars, which should go to some relation of this unfortunate young man.'

"He counted them again, and, after having given them to his satellite, told him to take them and put them in his safe.

" 'Now, "mister," I will leave you here to keep guard over your countryman whilst I go out to see if they have dug his grave. There is no priest here in the settlement. We only have one come here once a month; and even if there were a priest, the dead man looks as if he had been Protestant.'

"He turned to me, and saying, 'With your permission,' took his hat and left the hut.

"Thus left alone with my compatriot (if he had been one), I took a long look at him, so as to stamp his features in my mind. I had no camera in my possession, and cannot draw—a want that often hinders me in my profession in the description of my rarer plants.

"I looked so long that if the man I saw lying upon the canvas scissor-bed should ever rise again with the same body, I am certain I could recognize him amongst a million men.

"His hands were long and thin, but sunburnt, his feet well-shaped, and though his face was sunken and the heat was rapidly discolouring it, the features were well cut. I noted a brown mark upon the cheek, such as in Spanish is called a *lunar*, which gave his delicate and youthful face something of a girlish look, in spite of his moustache. His eyebrows, curiously enough, were dark, and the incipient growth of beard was darker than his hair. His ears were small and set on close to the head—a sign of breeding—and his eyes, although I dared not look at them, having closed them up myself, I knew were blue, and felt they must be staring at me, underneath the stones. In life he might have weighed about ten stone I guess, not more, and must have been well-made and active, though not an athlete, I should think, by the condition of his hands.

"Strangely enough, there seemed to me nothing particularly sad about the look of him. He just was resting after the struggle, that could have lasted in his case but little more than thirty years, and had left slight traces on his face of anything that he had suffered when alive.

"I took the flat stones off his eyes, and was relieved to find they did not open, and after smoothing his fair hair down a little and taking a long look at the fast-altering features, I turned away to smoke.

"How long I waited I cannot recollect, but all the details of the hut, the scissor canvas bed on which the body lay, the hooks for hammocks in the mud-and-bamboo walls, the tall brown jar for water, like those that one remembers in the pictures of the *Arabian Nights* in childhood, the drinking gourd beside it, with the two heavy hardwood chairs of ancient Spanish pattern, seated and backed with pieces of rawhide, the wooden table, with the planks showing the marks of the adze that fashioned them, I never shall forget.

"Just at the door there was an old canoe, dug out of a tree-trunk, the gunwale broken and the inside almost filled up with mud. Chickens, of that peculiar mangy-looking breed indigenous to every tropic the whole world over, were feeding at one end of it, and under a low shed thatched with soft palm-leaves stood a miserable horse, whose legs were raw owing to the myriads of horseflies that clustered on them, which no one tried to brush away. Three or four vultures sat on a branch of a dead tree that overhung the hut. Their languid eyes appeared to me to pierce the palm-tree roof as they sat on, just as a shark follows a boat in which there is a dead man, waiting patiently.

"Over the bluff, on which the wretched little ranchería straggled till it was swallowed up in the primeval woods, flowed the great river,[2] majestic, yellow, alligator-haunted, bearing upon its ample bosom thousands of floating masses of green vegetation which had slipped into the flood.

"How long I sat I do not know, and I shall never know, but probably not above half an hour. Still, in that time I saw the life of the young man who lay before me. His voyage out; the first sight of the tropics; the landing into that strange world of swarthy-coloured men, dank vegetation, thick, close atmosphere, the metallic hum of insects, and the peculiar smell of a hot country— things which we see and hear once in our lives, and but once only, for custom dulls the senses, and we see nothing more. Then the letters home, simple and child-like in regard to life, but shrewd and penetrating as regards business, after the fashion of the Northern European or his descendants in the United States.

"I saw him pass his first night in the bare tropical hotel, under a mosquito-curtain, and then wake up to all the glory of the New World he had discovered for himself, as truly as Columbus did when he had landed upon Guanahani on that eventful Sunday

[2] Almost certainly the Magdalena.

morning and unfurled the flag of Spain. I heard him falter out his first few words in broken Spanish, and saw him take his first walk, either by the harbour, thronged with its unfamiliar-looking boats piled up with fish and fruits unknown in Europe, or through the evil-smelling, badly-paved alleys in the town.

"The voyage up the river, with the first breath of the asphyxiating heat; the flocks of parrots; the alligators, so like dead logs, all basking in the sun; the stopping in the middle of the night for wood beside some landing-place cut in the jungle, where men, naked but for a cloth tied round their loins, ran up a plank and dumped their load down with a half-sigh, half-yell—I saw and heard it all. Then came the arrival at the mine or rubber station, the long and weary days, the fevers, the rare letters, and the cherished newspapers from home—those, too, I knew of, for I had waited for them often in my youth.

"Most of all, as I looked on him and saw his altering features, I thought of his snug home in Massachusetts or Northumberland, where his relations looked for letters on thin paper, with the strange postmarks, which would never come again. How they would wonder in his home, and here was I looking at the features that they would give the world to see, but impotent to help."

He stopped, and, walking to the bulwarks, looked up the river, and said: "In half an hour we shall arrive at San Fulgencio—They came and fetched the body, and wrapped it in a white cotton sheet—for which I paid—and we set off, followed by the few store-keepers, two Syrians and a Portuguese, and a small crowd of Indians.

"There was no cemetery—that is to say, not one of those Colombian cemeteries fenced with barbed wire, in which the plastered gateway looks like an afterthought, and where the iron crosses blistering in the sun look drearier than any other crosses in the world.

"Under a clump of guaduas—that is the name they give to the bamboo—there was a plot of ground fenced in with canes. In it the grave was dug amongst some others, on which a mass of grass and weeds was growing, as if it wished to blot them out from memory as soon as possible.

"A little wooden cross or two, with pieces of white paper periodically renewed, affirmed that Resurrección Venegas or Exaltación Machuca reposed beneath the weeds.

"The grave looked hard and uninviting, and as we laid him in it, lowering him with a rope made of lianas, two or three macaws flew past, uttering a raucous cry.

"The Commissary had put on a black suit of clothes, and Pérez had a rusty band of cloth pinned round his arm. The Syrians and the Portuguese took off their hats, and as there was no priest the Commissary mumbled some formula; and I, advancing to the grave, took a last look at the white sheet which showed the angles of the frail body underneath it, but for the life of me I could not say a word, except 'Good-bye.'

"When the Indians had filled in the earth we all walked back towards the settlement perspiring. I took a glass of rum with them, just for civility—I think I paid for it—and then I gathered up my traps and sat and waited under a big bongo-tree until the steamer came along."

A silence fell upon us all, as sitting in our rocking-chairs upon the high deck of the stern-wheel steamer, we mused instinctively upon the fate of the unknown young Englishman, or American. The engineer from Oregon, the Texan cow-puncher going to look at cattle in the Llanos de Bolívar, and all the various waifs and strays that get together upon a voyage up the Magdalena, no doubt each thought he might have died, just as the unknown man had died, out in the wilderness.

No one said anything, until the orchid-hunter, as the steamer drew into the bank, said: "That is San Fulgencio. I go ashore here. If any of you fellows ever find out who the chap was, send us a line to Barranquilla; that's where my wife lives.

"I am just off to the Chocó, a three or four months' job.— Fever?—oh, yes, sometimes, of course, but I think nothing of it.—Quinine?—thanks, yes, I've got it.—I don't believe in it a great deal.—Mosquitoes?—no, they do not worry me. A gun?—well, no, I never carry arms—thanks all the same.—I was sorry, too, for that poor fellow; but, after all, it is the death I'd like to die myself.—No, thanks, I don't care for spirits.—Good-bye to all of you."

We waved our hands and crowded on the steamer's side, and watched him walking up the bank to where a little group of Indians stood holding a bullock with a pack upon its back.

They took his scanty property and, after tying it upon the ox, set off at a slow walk along a little path towards the jungle, with the grey figure of our late companion walking quietly along, a pace or two behind.

VENEZUELA

Editor's Preface to the
Venezuelan Sketches

These two sketches, written late in life after a visit in 1925, are two of his finest. Though antibullfight, he gives a delightful picture of the simplicity of this Venezuelan *corrida* by comparing it with all that is ostentatious, noisy, and commercialized in a Spanish bullfight. One could not wish for a more picturesque ending to the sketches than the breathtaking sunset, with which he brings the final sketch, and this collection, to a startling, natural climax. Thus the cycle is complete. What began off the coast of Venezuela ends on the plains of Venezuela—a fitting conclusion, naturally and historically.

LOS NIÑOS TOREROS

All the taurine intelligentsia of Caracas was in the bull-ring. They filled the square unpainted wooden boxes, sat on the stucco steps that, as in a Roman amphitheatre, mount to the top of the vast building, and swarmed in the cheap seats that border on the arena, so closely that the poorer of the "intelligents" can strike the bull, if he passes near to them, with their walking-sticks.

The sun turned all to gold. The sand in the arena glistened like gold dust under its fierce rays.

Nature had done her best for the vast amphitheatre. No other bull-ring in the world was situated at the foot of steep descending mountains, cut by the rains into sheer gullies, so deep that the tall trees that fringed their sides seemed to cling to them as lichen clusters on a rock. Tall palm-trees almost overhung the walls, and from the upper seats the panorama of the enchanting valley stretched out, buried in tropic vegetation, with dazzling white houses in the clearings, dotting it here and there like islands in a sea of emerald. The cathedral tower, in the clear atmosphere, appeared so close that you could almost count the stones. The palm-trees, the overshadowing mountains, and the soft tropic sky gave an air of unreality to the whole place. There was no noisy crowd such as throngs the approach to any bull-ring throughout Spain. No gangs of ragged boys hung round to see the entrance of the company at the stage door that so often swallows up a bull-fighter, cutting him off from the public and the world when it was closed. No one cried "*Agua-a-a,*" in the harsh Oriental voice that seems to be an inheritance left by the Arabs to all water-sellers in the peninsula.

There were no *barquilleros*, with their tube-shaped canisters surmounted by a miniature roulette wheel, containing the crisp, rolled-up wafers, called *barquillos*, the delight of children, soldiers, and of nurserymaids in Seville and Madrid.

Nobody sold red-and-yellow paper fans or peanuts. No girl, black-eyed and roguish-looking, with her coarse black hair piled high upon her head, or, if worn short, disposed about her cheeks in curls, sold lemonade, carrying the bottles in the classical wooden *vasera*, with a rose behind her ear.

The wooden boxes held the local aristocracy known to the populace as *el blancaje*, that is, the whites, together with a sprinkling of oil magnates from Maracaibo, whose business seemed to call for their perpetual presence in the capital. The Spanish that they spoke, generally with all the verbs in the infinitive, and with a fine indifference to genders, cases, and the like, for rules of grammar were not surely made for free-born citizens, conserved the accent of the various states from which they hailed. Drawling and high-pitched in the mouth of the New Englander, it suffered a sun-change if the speaker came from further south, till in the mouths of Georgians and Carolinans it became little different from the thick jargon of a plantation negro. With the exception of the aforesaid *blancaje*, and the Americans from Maracaibo, the audience was made up of Indian half-breeds.

These formed a striking contrast, to the people who in Spain fill the cheap seats of bull-fights, in their demeanour. There was no wealth of gesture, no harsh voices raised in dispute as to the merits of their favourite heroes of the ring. Such few women as were present sat quite unmolested. Nobody pinched them; no one remarked upon their charms, in the same way as a dealer chants the praises of his horse. No oaths were heard, still less obscenity. Even the traditional appearance of the mounted *alguacil* to demand the key of the *toril* provoked no jokes, no comment on himself or on his horse. The slight, dark faces showed no expression of impatience at the customary wait, for never under heaven in Venezuela was a bull-fight known to start in time. No one beat on the seats with walking-sticks, drummed with his feet or shouted imprecations on the president as time slipped by, and still the blinding glare fell on the vacant sand of the arena. All was as quiet and as orderly as when in Mexico, before the conquest, the people waited for the human sacrifice, grouped round the terraced steps of the great Teocalli,[1] that reared itself upon the spot where the cathedral stands.

The blending of two races had given the people the outward visible appearance of their Indian ancestresses, but in their blood still boiled the fiercer passions of their forefathers, the conquistadores, ready to break out when they were aroused. All the parade, the pomp, and circumstance of a bull-fight in Spain was lacking. Grouped here and there in knots, the men who should have been all dressed in brilliant costumes stood in old cast-off clothes, bought second-hand, dirty and stained, holding their cloaks that looked like window curtains, no longer serviceable, without a jot of pride. Still in themselves, they were all active, sinewy-looking youths, but evidently country herdsmen, acting as bull-fighters for the occasion, and ill at east on foot, under the public gaze.

The whole scene was more primitive and less rehearsed than it would have been in Spain. The lack of brilliant clothes in the arena, the silent audience, and the absence of the red-and-yellow paper fans that in Spain make a rustling noise, like a flock of pigeons taking wing, as they are ceaselessly shut and opened, made the spectacle more tense, but far less picturesque.

No long procession, with the espada rolled like a sausage in his sash, surrounded by his acolytes scarcely less brilliantly dressed than the chief actor, all swaggering and monkeyfied, but in a way conscious they were the only true descendants of the gladiators, about to risk their lives, defiled across the sand, amidst the plaudits of the crowd. No miserable horses with one eye blinded, and their ears filled with tow, to prevent them hearing the bull's charge, disgraced the show.

Stripped of the adjuncts of bright dresses and the old-world ceremonies, that give an air of picturesqueness in Spain to what is really only a sordid butchery, the stage seemed set for some such combat as must have often taken place in prehistoric times between a man and the wild cattle in a glade of the Caledonian woods. There was no chapel as in Spain, with its attendant priest; no doctor to prevent wounded bull-fighters from dying what would be to them a natural death, with anaesthetics and a battery of instruments. All was reduced to the lowest common

---

[1] Teocalli, in Cholula, Mexico, was the sacrificial site of the ancient Aztecs.

denominator. The sun, the palm-trees, and the soft atmosphere were the only decorations of the bare bull-ring. One group of men and one alone spoke of old Spain, of Seville, and of its classic suburb of Triana.[2]

Behind the barriers, in the full glare of the sun, stood a tall man of middle age, clean-shaven, dressed in the short jacket and tight trousers of the profession, bare-headed, with a red cloak folded on his left arm. He limped a little on one leg, from a wound that had incapacitated him from taking part in his profession as a first actor, but still had left him active and strong enough to face a bull in an inferior capacity.

His face was deadly pale, and now and then his features twisted and beads of sweat stood on his forehead, and ran down his cheeks. In his left hand he held a crucifix, tawdry and cheap, as if bought in a second-hand depository of religious articles. In front of him stood his sons, two boys of fourteen and fifteen years of age. Dressed in the traditional *traje de luces*, all gay in spangles and gold lace, their blue-black hair brushed back and plastered with some inferior cosmetic so closely to their heads that it looked like a cap of pitch, they faced their father, turning their brilliant eyes upon him with the fixed stare of all performers about to risk their lives before the sovereign public. Then they advanced and sank a knee before the image of their Saviour on His cross, knowing He died for bull-fighters, as well as for all other sinners.

Their father signed them with the cross, and when they stood up, strained them to his chest and kissed them. Then the boys drew themselves up and, with their cloaks wrapped round their left arms, strutted into the enormous empty plaza, at the head of their poor, ill-dressed *cuadrilla* with as good an imitation of the best style of Seville or Madrid as they could manage to assume. No blare of music heralded their entrance. The rustle of a thousand fans did not disturb the air. No shouts of welcome encouraged them. The ragged regiment marched out to the middle of the open space. The shabby members of the company took up their places, their gay but tattered cloaks covering their tawdry sweatstained clothes. A cloak hides all deficiencies, says the Spanish saw, and certainly in their case there was a good store of deficiencies to hide. Nearly all stockings had a ladder in them;

---

[2]Triana is famous for its typical character.

some, good honest holes, but darned with cotton. The heel-less pumps that bull-fighters all wear when in full dress were held in place, sometimes with elastic bands across the instep, sometimes with bootlaces. One man, a tall gaunt half-bred Indian, shuffled off his shoes, after having placed them carefully behind the barrier, and in his dirty stockings, torn and sweat-soaked, stood prepared to risk his life to gain his livelihood.

The entry of the two boys, followed by their father with his limping leg, the woeful-looking *cuadrilla*, and the half-filled seats of the vast amphitheatre, was somehow more impressive than the procession of glittering gladiators, who, headed by their leader in his gorgeous panoply of silk and gold, struts into the arena at Madrid or Córdoba.

No blare of music announced the advent of the bull from the *toril*. Two countrymen opened the sliding door, and with a snort a long-horned prairie bull bounded out, receiving as he passed two thrusts from the long ox-goad the herdsmen, who presided at the gate, bestowed either from the joy of life, or from their lifelong habit of goading any animal that came within their reach. A languid shiver went through the audience, as the long-horn, after a minute of amazement at his unfamiliar surroundings, rushed at the ill-dressed scarecrow who was nearest to him. He, though grotesque-looking as to his exterior, had his heart in the right place, and proved at once that he had graduated in some one of the taurine universities of Spain. Drawing himself to his full height, he executed a skilful pass with his ragged cloak, keeping his feet still, in the best style of Ronda or of Córdoba.

A lazy "*Viva*," that sounded like a muffled cry of "Ease her," on a river steamer, floated from the half-filled benches. All the ragged regiment bravely played their part, with their cloaks, but none of them attempted to place the banderillas in the neck of the bull. Then, but without the bugle call that heralds each phase of the *fiesta nacional*, the elder of the two lads stepped into the middle of the ring carrying the banderillas in his hand. He drew himself to his full height of five feet three or four, hollowed his back, threw up his head, and stamping with his foot challenged the bull to charge. The company, who knew their business, crept up behind him, and his father, pale and anxious, stood waiting with his cloak. The long-horn came on gallantly, with his head just in the right position, neither too high nor too low, and the brave lad "planted a pair," as well placed as the best bull-fighter in Spain could possibly have done. Then did the half-bred audience for the first time wake up, and change their attitude of apathy for one of furious excitement and applause, just as a tropic storm breaks out, almost without a sign.

Shaking the darts in the folds of his neck, the bull careered through the arena, the shabby-looking men making some tolerable passes with their cloaks. The younger brother placed another pair, as skilfully as the first had done, but far more easily, so easily that his skill was lost on a Caracas audience, although it would have brought forth thunders of applause in Spain. The father, whose face had relaxed under the influence of the plaudits of the crowd, now braced himself for the last act. After the bull had been drawn into a favourable position by the one real bullfighter in the troop, a dark and sinewy gipsy from Triana, the elder boy advanced to kill. The bull, fresh from the llanos, was still untired, for he had not exhausted himself upon the miserable horses, or been bled white with lance-thrusts and repeated pairs of banderillas, as in Spain. Lighter by far upon his feet than any Spanish bull, taller and heavier, he seemed an elephant opposed to the slight lad who faced him. By this time the audience was all alight, and watched each pass, if not with knowledge, yet with appreciation. Working as quickly as a man of twice his experience, the boy with his sword hidden in the red muleta, executed most of the passes known to the fancy, turning half-round as the bull charged and patting him upon the flank, or, reaching out with the hand that held the cloak, touched him between the horns. Then, advancing on the furious animal, his arm shot out and took him just in the right place above the shoulder-blade, driving his sword up to the hilt. Stopped in his full career, as if struck by lightning, the bull fell dead, blood gushing in a thick dark stream from both his nostrils. The quiet-looking, rather stocky boy had taken him half-volley (*de volapié*), just as a tennis player takes the ball upon the rise.

All the time that the boy had been in peril of his life, his father, pale and anxious, the experience of years overcoming his slight limp, had hovered round him, to draw off the bull, in case his son should fail or lose his nerve.

When the team of mules, not decorated with plumes and tassels, as in Spain, but taken from a cart, with ordinary harness, had pulled the dead bull from the arena, he patted his son on the shoulder, and for a moment his air of tense anxiety relaxed.

His relief lasted but for a moment, for his younger boy had to deal with the next bull. Fiercer and taller than the first, the second was a half-bred zebu, so huge that even the apathetic audience called to the younger lad to leave him to his elder brother, and not to risk his life.

After the regular passes had been gone through and the banderillas placed, the younger lad advanced, perfectly calm and master of himself. Great drops of sweat hung on his father's forehead, and in his agony of mind his limp quite disappeared, and he stood straight and active, despite his fifty years, as when in his last fight at Seville he had received the wound that ended his career.

Three or four times his son played with the bull, escaping his most furious charges as by a miracle, in even better style than that his elder had displayed. Then fixing his feet firmly, he waited till it lowered its head as it charged home, and with a thrust between the horns, pithed him with a stroke just in the spinal marrow. The enormous animal sank like a ship sinks, slowly, when engulfed between the waves, without a struggle, and it is to be hoped quite painlessly. Flushed with his triumph, the boy advanced, and placed his foot upon the neck of his late adversary, standing a moment, like a bronze statuette, amidst the yelling of the crowd, who now, excited furiously, threw off the cold exterior they had inherited from their Indian ancestors. Their triumph and their father's agony were over for the day, and in the dust behind the barrier, after a long embrace that somehow gave the trio an air as of the statue of Laocoön,[3] they kissed the crucifix, and no doubt gave thanks to their own Christ, he of *El Gran Poder*,[4] who from his shrine in the Triana shoots out his lips at all the other Christs in Spain.

---

[3] In Greek legend, Laocoön was a priest of Apollo, but having profaned the temple, he and his two sons were destroyed by serpents while preparing to sacrifice a bull on the altar of Poseidon. Immortalized by Vergil, the pathetic scene is also rendered in sculpture in the famous Laocoön group of the Vatican. Graham's image is very apt, historically and artistically.

[4] The Great Power.

LOS LLANOS DEL APURE[1]

Man has not staled their wildness, and they still stretch out along the Orinoco, the Apure, and the Arauca to the far-distant Meta, just as they first came from the Creator's hand when on the seventh day He rested from a work that He must surely now and then regret. A very sea of grass and sky, sun-scourged and hostile to mankind. The rivers, full of electric eels, and of caribes, those most ravenous of fish, more terrible than even the great alligators that lie like logs upon the sand-banks or the inert and pulpy rays, with their mortiferous barbed spike, are still more hostile than the land.

In the four hundred years the llanos have been known to Europeans, man has done little more than to endow them with herds of cattle and with bands of half-wild horses and of asses that roam upon them, just as their ancestors roamed the steppes of Asia from the remotest times. Islets of stunted palm-trees break the surface of the plains, as the atolls peep up in the Pacific Ocean and also bear their palms. The sun pours down like molten fire for six months of the year, burning the grass up, forcing the cattle to stray leagues away along the river banks, or in the depths of the thick woods. Then come the rains, and the dry, calcined plains are turned into a muddy lake, on which the whilom centaurs of the dry season, paddle long, crank canoes dug from a single log.

The llanos, with their race of half-amphibious herdsmen, but

[1]Renamed "The Plains of Venezuela" by Tschiffely in *Rodeo*.

little differing in features and in hue from their ancestors, the Achagua Indians, have been the scene of great events. They have had their days of glory, when they were almost household words in Europe during the great struggle for the independence of the Spanish colonies, a hundred years ago. At the Queseras del Medio, by their aid, Páez,[2] Prince of llaneros, and almost the last good lance that villainous saltpetre has left to history, broke the cavalry of Spain. Out of the woods, sheltered behind the smoke of the dry grass they had set on fire, the saddleless, wild horsemen, half-naked, with but a rag or two tied round their bodies by a thong of hide, swooped on the uniformed, drilled, disciplined, brave, heavy-handed Spanish troopers, like the riders of the Valkyrie. Páez, himself as wild and savage in those days as any of his men, rode at their head upon a half-tamed colt. Those were not days of tactics, for personal prowess, perhaps for the last time in history, ruled everything. It must have been a glorious sight to see their charge, the flying hair, the tossing manes and tails, the dust, the shrill screams of the attacking horsemen, the answering shouts of "*Viva España*" of the Spanish troops, the frightened taotacos whirling above them uttering their harsh note, while in the sky the vultures sailed aloft, like specks against the sapphire blue, knowing a banquet was being set for them. To-day the llanos that furnished the troops with which Páez so ably seconded Bolívar in his long fight for independence are almost depopulated. No one seems to know the cause.

Though much of the population has gone, enough remains to herd the cattle, the vast llanos' only wealth. Unlike the gauchos and the Mexicans, the Roman Butari, the Arabs of North Africa, the Western cowboy (before fell cinemas made a puppet of him), any old saddle, any clothes, content the dweller on the plains of the Apure. His horse is almost always thin, often sore-backed, and always looks uncared for, while the ungainly pace at which he rides, a shambling *pasitrote*, or tied camel waddle, moving both feet on the same side at once, deprives him of all grace. Still few can equal, none excel, him for endurance. Nothing daunts him, neither the peril of the rivers, with all their enemies to mankind ever awake, to tear or numb the unlucky horseman who

[2]José Antonio Páez (1790–1873), Venezuelan general, first president of Venezuela. He headed the separatist movement from Bolívar's Colombia. See Graham's book *José Antonio Páez*.

may come near their fangs or their electrically charged bodies, or any other danger either by flood and field. He, of all wielders of the rawhide noose, alone secures it, not to the saddle, but to his horse's tail, fishing for, rather than lassoing, a steer, playing it like a salmon with a rope a hundred feet in length, instead of bringing it up with a smart jerk, after the fashion of the Argentines or Mexicans. Abominably slow and tedious in his methods to the eyes of commentators; still it is never wise, in matters of such deep import, to criticise or to condemn customs that use and wont have consecrated.

If the llaneros have changed outwardly, the llano has remained the same. No puffing steam-engine or petrol-reeking car defile its surface. Diligences it has never had, and the sole method for a caballero when he wants to traverse it is on a horse. Some indeed may have ridden mules. Camels and asses, with llamas, yaks, bullocks, and buffaloes, no doubt can carry man upon their backs, but on the horse alone can he be truly said to ride. So the llanero still rides the llano on his pacing horse, the reins held high, the stirrups dangling from his naked toe, his eyes fixed on the horizon, as a sailor on his watch looks out across the sea. The mirage still hangs castles in the air and cheats the eye in the terrific heat with pools of water, always just out of touch, as happiness is ever out of reach in life. The Promised Land is always a day's march ahead of us.

Unchanging and unchanged, the llanos swelter in the sun as they first sweltered at the creation of the world, and as La Puebla saw them in the expedition that Maestre Diego Albéñiz de la Cerrada describes,[3] he who wrote, as it were in a mirage, his observation so minute, his gift of artistry so great, and with his dates, and trifles of that nature, all awry. So distant are the llanos from our vain-glorious, noisy and evil-smelling civilisation, as to be almost unaware that such a thing exists. They await the coming of the thing called progress, just as a girl may dream about her marriage night without exactly knowing what it means.

Meanwhile, through palm woods looking exactly like those of

---

[3] Admiral La Puebla was the first man to navigate the Apure River. His exploits were narrated in the spurious travel accounts of Rafael Bolívar Coronado who, under the pseudonym Maestre Diego Albéñiz de la Cerrada, wrote Los desiertos de Achaguas (Madrid: Editorial-América, 1918?), describing La Puebla's experiences on the plains of Venezuela.

the Argentine Gran Chaco, through jungle and through woods, in dust, in rain, under a sun that blisters, if you touch an iron stirrup, the post of the republic carried in canvas bags on two grey mules accompanied by an apocalyptic horse, trails wearily across the plains. If in their pilgrimage the mules, the old white horse, and the dark half-breeds chance to light on a *velorio*, or a wedding at a rancho on the road, they join in it, for after all to-morrow is another day, and time is certainly not money, under the rule of him whose fellow-citizens style *"El Benemérito."*

Even the garden by the Tigris could hardly have been fairer or more bird-haunted than the banks of the Apure, with its myriads of egrets making the trees as white as is a northern wood after a fall of snow. Legions of aquatic birds as black as jet sweep down the rivers in battalions, succeeding one another as if some feathered general was marshalling them to fight.

Flocks of flamingoes rise from the waters, as Aphrodite rose up from the waves, rosy and beautiful.[4] Piero di Cosimo[5] alone could have dealt with them in paint, and if the painter of the "Death of Procris" had but visited the Apure, among his pelicans, his flamingoes, and his swans, he would have placed new species, as fit to grace his theme and far more gorgeous than the birds of the old world. In the freshness of the dawn, when a white mist bathes all the woods upon the rivers in a thin vaporous haze through which the trees show faintly, as a rich purple or green burnous tinges the fleecy whiteness of an Arab's haik, nature exults in the new birth of day.

The llano for a brief moment turns to a tender green and stretches out like an interminable fresh field of corn. From the recesses of the woods along the river-banks comes the harsh screaming of the parrots, and birds and insects raise their morning hymn of praise. Stilled are the voices of the prowling animals of prey, insistent during night. The jaguar no longer snarls, or whets his teeth against the tree-trunks. The red, howling monkeys start their chorus, sounding as if a lion was raging in the everglades, and the shy tapir, after a night passed feeding on the sedges and the grass, swims to his lair, his head and back just

[4] Aphrodite was the Greek goddess of love who, according to Hesiod, sprang from the foam of the sea that gathered around the severed member of Oranus when Cronos mutilated him.
[5] Piero di Cosimo (1462–1521), Italian recluse artist, who lived in dirt and squalor, and produced abstract paintings of primeval life.

showing, like a river horse, leaving a silvery trail behind him to
mark his silent passage through the stream. Wild cattle troop
back to the woods, before the vaqueros intercept them with their
swift horses and their unerring noose.

Without an interval of crepuscule, the sun rises at once fierce,
fiery, and inexorable, streaking the sky with rays of orange and of
scarlet for an instant, then bursts upon the world like a fell enemy
before whom fly all living things except the saurians, who bask
somnolently upon the sand-banks, immune against his rays. Just
at the break of dawn fish leap in shoals into the air, making the
water boil, their silvery bodies for a moment springing like
crescent moons into the air and falling with a splash into the
deep. His well-greased *lazo* ready coiled in front of his right knee,
his brown, bare toes sticking out through his alpargatas, clutching the light llanero stirrup with its crown-like prolongation
underneath the foot, the llanero scans the horizon as his horse
paces rapidly along, leaving a well-marked trail upon the dewy
grass. He sits so loosely in the saddle that one would think if his
horse shied it must unseat him, but that he also shies. High on
his vaquero saddle, so straight and upright that a plummet
dropped from his shoulder would touch his heel, he reads the
llano like a book.

Nothing escapes his sight, as keen as that of his Achagua
Indian ancestors. Signs on the ground, almost undiscernible, he
marks. If his horse, trippling along at its artificial gait, stumbles
or pecks, he curses it, objurgating its female ancestry, gives it a
sharp pull with the bit, digs in his spurs, interrupts for a moment
the interminable galerón that he is crooning in a low voice, and
pointing with his whip says, "Three horses passed along here
early in the night. One is the big cream colour that always strays,
for he is a little lame in the off hind foot, see where he has stepped
short upon it." With an unerring eye he sights a steer with a
strange brand. "That is one of General Atilio Pacheco's animals,"
he says, and turning to his companion, smiling, remarks, "If he
stays too long in these parts he may stay for ever, for God is not a
bad man, anyhow."

As the sun rises higher in the heavens, the light distorting
everything, magnifying or diminishing, according as its rays are
refracted, dried tufts of grass appear as large as clumps of canes,
and animals on the horizon as small as turkey buzzards. Then the
vaquero heads for home, after assuring himself that no bullock

has been killed by a tiger in the night, or has got wounded from any cause and requires treatment to prevent maggots from breeding in the wound. Clouds of dust rise on the horizon. The morning breeze dies out entirely during the hottest hours, and the plain shimmers in the heat. *Bancos* and *mesas*, those curious sand formations that intersect the llanos like striations in a rock, give back refracted heat to meet the heat descending from above. All nature groans. Only the lizards and iguanas seem to revel in it. Homing vaqueros, their *pelo de guama* hats coal-scuttled fore and aft against the enemy, lounge in their saddles. Their horses plod along, with drooping heads, too weary even to swish their tails against the flies. At the straw-thatched houses the riders get off with a sigh and seek the shade of the caney.

As the heat waxes and the air quivers as if it came from some interior furnace, a deathly silence broods upon the plains. A sense of solitude creeps over everything, as if the world had been consumed by some unlooked-for cataclysm that had destroyed mankind. The weary horses, who endure the burden of their lives either parched with thirst, or forced to live a half-amphibious life during the periodical inundations, exposed year in, year out, to the perpetual torment of mosquitoes, horseflies, ticks and all the *plagas* of the insect world, with the off-chance of sudden death from the fangs of tiger or caimán, seek shelter where they can, under the scanty foliage of the Moriche palms. Cattle have long ago retired as far as possible into the reedy swamps. Nothing is stirring; not a sound breaks the afflicted silence of the sun-cursed plain, but the perpetual calling "Oh, ah ho" of the small, speckled doves. Gradually the heat decreases, a breeze springs up, and nature, after her long struggle with the sun, revives.

The animals, who have passed the hot hours under whatever shade that they could find, recommence eating and birds show signs of life. Parrots scream harshly. Flights of macaws, yellow and red and blue, the great white patches round their eyes making them look as if they all wore spectacles, soar like particoloured hawks, uttering their croaking cry. The interval of freshness is all too brief, for night falls without twilight on the llanos; and the sun dips down under the horizon just as he does at sea.

Before the darkness closes in, flights of birds migrate towards the woods, fireflies dart to and fro among the dark metallic leaves of the jungle fringing the river, and from the recesses of the forests the nightly chorus of the wild animals, silent through the day, breaks out. Then comes the miracle; the miracle of miracles, unknown to those who have not journeyed on those interminable steppes or sailed upon the Apure or the Orinoco. No words can paint the infinite gradation of the scale of colour that leaves the spectroscope lacking a shade or two. Green turns to mauve, then back to green again; to scarlet, orange, and vermilion, flinging the flag of Spain across the sky. Dark coffee-coloured bars, shooting across a sea of carmine, deepen to black; the carmine melts into pale gray. Castles and pyramids spring up; they turn to cities; the pyramids to broken arches, waterfalls, and ships, with poops like argosies. Gradually pale apple-green floods all the heaven; then it fades into jade. Castles and towns and ships and broken arches disappear. The sun sinks in a globe of fire, leaving the world in mourning for its death.

Then comes the after-glory, when all the colours that have united, separated, blended, and broken up, unite and separate again, and once more blend. A sheet of flame, that for an instant turns the Apure into a streak of molten metal, bathes the llano in a bath of fire, fades gradually and dies, just where the plain and sky appear to join as if the grass was all aglow.

GLOSSARY

This glossary is designed solely to help the reader appreciate better the foregoing sketches. It is not intended to be specialist, technical, nor exhaustive, nor does it try to provide all the alternative meanings of the words and phrases listed. Its express function is related only to the sketches treated in this volume.

adobe   unburnt brick dried in the sun.
aguas arriba   upstream.
alazán overo   type of piebald horse (sorrel-colored).
alazán tostado   coffee-colored piebald, parched sorrel.
albardón · rut, hummock; literally "a large packsaddle."
alcalde   mayor, chief of a village.
alfalfa   horse fodder, a variety of lucerne-like clover.
alguacil   constable; officer.
aljibe   container for catching rain (in patios).
alpargata   rope-soled slipper.
alzacuello   clergyman's collar.
ánima   spirit.
anta   tapir.
apachería   apache encampment.
araguán, araguay   tree (Venezuela, Paraguay).
arasá, arazá   fruit tree of the Plate region.
Araucano   language of the Araucanian Indians.
armadillo   little burrowing animal encased in bony armor.
arreador   driving whip of the gaucho.
arribeño   native of the highlands.

arroyo spring, stream.
artillería artillery.
Auca rebel Indian.
azulejo blue and white colt.

bacará, bacaray card game; cf. baccarat.
badillero native of Bahía Blanca.
bagual wild horse (without master).
baile dance.
balsa kind of raft.
balsero man who operates a balsa.
barquillo crisp, rolled-up wafer.
barquillero barquillo seller.
basto part of the saddle, panel, pad.
bayeta fine baize cloth.
bayo a horse (bay).
benemérito title meaning worthy or well deserving.
bicho animal; general name for small insects.
bochinche brawl; row, noisy crowd.
bolas ball-shaped gaucho weapon.
boleada hunt with the bolas.
boleadoras bolas.
boliche dingy little bar; gaming house.
bolsón lagoon.
bombachas wide baggy trousers of the gaucho.
bombilla tube used for sucking the maté.
botillería bar.
boyero oxherd, drover.
bozal muzzle of horse; temporary headstall.

caballada herd of horses.
caballería cavalry.
cabresto lead rope, halter.
cacique chief (usually Indian).
caciquillo minor chief.
cachaza Brazilian rum.
cagatinta derogatory term for a clerk; a "pen pusher."
caimán alligator.
calzoncillos underpants.
camalote thick-growing water lily.
campeando rounding up horses.

cancha   racetrack.
candil   oil lamp, kitchen lamp.
canelo   cinnamon tree.
caney   log cabin (Venezuela).
cangrejal   colony of land crabs.
caña   rum.
capataz   foreman.
capibara   water rodent like the water hog.
capilla   chapel.
caraguatá   narrow, spiky plant, whose leaves are used to make
         clothes.
carajo   sexual organ.
carancho   bird like a hawk.
carlón   a kind of wine.
carne blanca   "white flesh"; condition of a beast.
carnear   to slaughter (beasts).
carona   padding of the saddle; leather nummah.
carpincho   water hog.
cassis   black-currant wine.
catre   wooden folding bed.
caudillo   chief, leader.
cautivo   captive.
cejilla   gadget on guitar used to alter the pitch.
cielito   Argentinian dance.
cojinillo   saddle pad, sheepskin.
comandante   officer in charge.
compadre   casual friend.
cordero   lamb; a meek and mild person.
Correntino   native of the northern province of Corrientes.
cortaplumas   penknife.
coscojo   inside rollers of the horse's bit.
cuadrilla   bullfight team.
cuchilla   range of hills; uneven ground.

chacra   farm, ranch.
chajá   horned screamer, the eagle of the pampas.
chamal   kind of shawl, blanket, to cover the legs.
changango   gaucho slang for the guitar.
chañar   Argentinian tree.
chapeado   adorned with metal *chapes* or plates.
chapetón   newcomer, hence, "bad horseman."

charque jerked beef.
charqui beef cut into strips and dried in the sun.
chasqui messenger, postboy (usually an Indian).
¡che! Argentinian greeting meaning "Hey, there!"
chimango bird of prey.
china girl.
chipá bread made from mandioca flour and cheese.
chiquero enclosure, pen for cattle.
chiripá cloth worn instead of trousers.

dehesa pasture ground.
domador horsebreaker.
doradillo honey-colored horse.

encimera part of the saddle, the top cinch.
enjalma Moorish saddle.
entrepelado piebald horse.
espinillo spiky bush, like the hawthorn.
esquina tavern; literally "a corner" where taverns usually are.
estancia ranch, estate.
estanciero owner of ranch.

facón long gaucho knife.
fandango dance.
fiador part of the rider's harness.
fichú silk neckerchief or headscarf.
fiesta nacional "national feast," i.e., the bullfight.
fonda inn.

galerón popular song and dance.
galpón large shed at side of house, usually for keeping meat and vegetables.
gateado sorrel horse with stripe down his back.
gato Argentinian dance.
gaucho pampas cowboy.
gauchaje pampas cowboys (collective).
gaucho haragán wandering gaucho.
golilla handkerchief worn round the neck.
guacamayo macaw (bird).
guadal plantation of bamboo canes.

gualicho, gualichú   evil spirit of the Indians.
guanaco, huanaco   savage llama of the pampa.
guapetón   brave, daring.
guillapiz   cover cloth worn by Indians.

habanera   Argentine dance.
hesperidina   orange drink.
Huincá   Christian.

iguana   reptile, like the lizard.
indiada   Indian camp.

jabeque   gaucho knife; knife wound.
jacú, yacú   bird that says "yac" sound.
jáquima   headstall of a halter.
jefatura   chief's office (e.g., mayor's).
jerga   part of the saddle (cloth on the horse's back).
jipijapa   (hat) made of straw.

lapacho   hardwood tree.
látigo   whip.
liana   climbing plant in tropical forest.
lobo   wolf.
lobuno   wolf-colored horse.
loma   small hill.

llano   plain of Venezuela.
llanero   horseman of the plains of Venezuela.
llapa   name for the last six feet of the lazo; hence "the twist in the tail."

madrileño   native of Madrid.
madrina   bell mare; small herd; rope tying two horses.
malacara   white-faced horse.
malacca cane   light walking stick made of rattan (Malacca is a state in Malaya).
malón   Indian raid.
mamey   mamee tree.
manada   herd.
mandil   felt nummah.
manea   leather cord used to tie the horse's feet.

maneador rope used to tie horses in rodeo; also the man who uses the rope.

manga swarm.

manguri Argentine dance.

mansos tame (Indians).

mañador long picket rope.

mataco Patagonian hare.

mate maté, Paraguayan green tea; the gourd in which the yerba is served.

matecito cimarrón kind of bitter maté, without sugar.

matra saddle rug.

matrero roaming, fugitive from justice.

matrimonio married couple.

maturrango person who rides badly.

mazamorra food made of maize flower with sugar or honey and milk.

médano sand dune, sandbank.

medio bagualón half-broken (of a horse).

mirador tower; balcony; viewpoint.

molle tree.

monte forest, wood; also, a card game.

mosqueador a "flyflapper"; insult applied to a horse.

novena novena, nine-day service in Catholic church liturgy.

nutria otter.

ñandú bird like the ostrich.

ñandubay hard redwood tree; a kind of mimosa.

naranjada orangeade.

ñato flat-nosed.

ombú shady, umbrella-shaped tree.

orchata drink from crushed almonds.

orejano unmarked (of a horse).

orejones dried peaches (look like ears).

overo negro type of piebald horse.

overo porcelano type of piebald horse.

overo rosado type of piebald horse.

pago village.

paja brava coarse grass.

pajonal   land covered with tall grass.
palenque   hitching post.
pampero   a storm from the south.
pangar   to take out the marrow from the bones (e.g., by birds of
     prey).
pangaré   light bay horse, with a fern-colored muzzle.
paraíso   paradise tree.
parar rodeo   to round up.
pasadores   parts of the stirrup, the card straps.
paseo   walk, stroll.
paso castellano   Castilian pace, i.e., trotting slowly.
patrón   boss.
patroncito   boss (diminutive of affection).
payador   troubadour.
pechada   pushing horse's chest against cattle (in rodeo).
pelo de guama   material for hats made from the guamo tree.
peón   ranch hand.
pericón   Argentine dance.
petizo   little horse; also, short man.
picaflor   hummingbird.
picazo   black horse with white nose.
pickelhauben   spiked helmet worn by German soldiers.
pindó   soft inner leaves of the pindó palm.
pingo   fine saddle horse.
piquillín   tree.
piranha   cannibal fish.
plaga   plague.
poncho   kind of greatcoat worn by the gaucho and the Indian.
por contrapunto   through counterpoint (musical term).
potro   colt, filly; rawhide.
pretal   part of the saddle, kind of leather breastplate.
pronunciamiento   uprising, military revolution.
puesto   booth; breeding stall.
pulpería   pampa store.
pulpero   storekeeper.
puñal   dagger.
puta, pucha   obscene exclamations; literally "whore, prosti-
     tute."

quebrada   ravine, gorge.
querencia   horse's home region.

quirquincho   kind of armadillo.
quitandera   prostitute.

ranchería   group of huts.
Ranqueles   Indian tribe.
rapadura   rolls of sugar done up in plantain leaves.
rastra   gadget to fasten belt.
rastreador   tracker.
rebenque   gaucho's leather riding whip.
recao, recado   sheepskin saddle.
redomón   half-tame horse.
reducción   settlement of Indians converted to Christianity.
refrescos   drinks.
reja   grill, railing.
revés   backhand stroke.
rodeo   roundup.
romería   pilgrimage; gathering at a shrine.
roza   clearing (in forest).

saladero   a place for salting meat (or fish).
salvaje   savage.
sangre mía   literally "blood of mine", a term of affection.
santas tardes   archaic greeting, meaning "good evening."
santero   traveling salesman who sells statues, etc.
sarandí   Argentine bush, shrub.
seguidores   two horses that follow each other.
seibo, ceiba   silk-cotton tree.
sobre paso   crossing a river (applied to horses).
soga   rope.

taba   a game played with a knuckleduster.
tacuará   a kind of hard bamboo.
tala   a large tree.
tamandúa, tamanduá, tamandoa   anteater.
taotaco   bird.
Tape   Guaraní Indian.
tapera   dilapidated house.
tapir   large animal that looks like a swine.
tarumá   tree of the verbanaceous family.
tatú   kind of giant armadillo.
tejón   badger.

teruteru   teru-tero, gull-like bird.
tierra adentro   interior (where the Indians were).
tirador   gaucho belt.
tirón   checking of an animal (in the rodeo).
toldo   tent.
toldería   colony of tents or huts (usually of Indians).
toril   bull pen in the bullring.
trabuco   firearm like the blunderbuss.
traje de luces   literally "suit of lights," costume worn by the
               bullfighter.
Trapalanda   horse heaven of the gauchos.
travesía   vast stretch of desert, waterless land.
triste   sad and amorous song.
tropero   trooper (of horses).
tropilla   little troop of cattle, horses, etc.
trotecito   little trot.
truco   card game like whist.
tucán   toucan (bird).
tucotuco, tucutuco   kind of mole.
tulipán   giant firefly; literally "a tulip."
tupoi   cotton shift (worn by Indian women).
tuviano   piebald horse, black, brown, and white in equal
            patches.

urunday, urundey   tree of the Terebinthus family.

valentón   loudmouth, bully.
vaquero   pampa cowboy.
vasera   box for carrying glasses (of lemonade, etc.).
velorio   wake.
ventana   window.
verbena   herbaceous plant.
vicha   woolen string Indians tie round their brow.
vincha   ribbon, band for the hair.
vinchuca   kind of winged bedbug.
vino seco   thick, yellow, Catalonian wine.
viraró   Paraguayan tree.
viudita   little bird with white plumage and black band on the
            wing.
vizcacha   biscacha, a hare-like animal.
vizcachera   place where the biscacha has burrowed.

yaguané   type of piebald horse.
yatay   very tall palm tree.
yerba   Paraguayan tea leaves.

zaguán   passageway, porch, vestibule.
zaino   dark, chestnut horse.
zamaú   Paraguayan tree.
zebu   bull (Venezuela)

BIBLIOGRAPHY

I. Works of R. B. Cunninghame Graham

This list does not include translations, prefaces to other writers' works, and pamphlets. The books have been listed in order of publication.

Notes on the District of Menteith. London, A. & C. Black, 1895.
Father Archangel of Scotland. London, A. & C. Black, 1896.
Mogreb-el-Acksa. London, Heinemann, 1898.
The Ipané. London, Fisher Unwin, 1899.
Thirteen Stories. London, Heinemann, 1900.
A Vanished Arcadia. London, Heinemann, 1901.
Success. London, Duckworth, 1902.
Hernando de Soto. London, Heinemann, 1903.
Progress. London, Duckworth, 1905.
His People. London, Duckworth, 1906.
Faith. London, Duckworth, 1909.
Hope. London, Duckworth, 1910.
Charity. London, Duckworth, 1912.
A Hatchment. London, Duckworth, 1913.
Scottish Stories. London, Duckworth, 1914.
Bernal Díaz del Castillo. London, Eveleigh Nash, 1915.
Brought Forward. London, Duckworth, 1916.
A Brazilian Mystic. London, Heinemann, 1920.
Cartagena and the Banks of the Sinú. London, Heinemann, 1921.
The Conquest of New Granada. London, Heinemann, 1922.

The Conquest of the River Plate. London, Heinemann, 1924.
Doughty Deeds. London, Heinemann, 1925.
Pedro de Valdivia. London, Heinemann, 1926.
Redeemed. London, Heinemann, 1927.
José Antonio Páez. London, Heinemann, 1929.
Thirty Stories and Sketches (selected by Edward Garnett). London, Heinemann, 1930.
The Horses of the Conquest. London, Heinemann, 1930.
Writ in Sand. London, Heinemann, 1932.
Portrait of a Dictator. London, Heinemann, 1933.
Mirages. London, Heinemann, 1936.
Rodeo (selected by A. F. Tschiffely). London, Heinemann, 1936.

II. Selected Studies—General

Bloomfield, Paul. *The Essential R. B. Cunninghame Graham*. London, Jonathan Cape, 1952.
Haymaker, Richard E. *Prince Errant and Evocator of Horizons*. Kingsport, Kingsport Press, 1967.
MacDiarmid, Hugh. *Cunninghame Graham—A Centenary Study*. Glasgow, Caledonian Press, 1952.
Tschiffely, A. F. *Don Roberto*. London, Heinemann, 1937.
———. *Tornado Cavalier*. London, Harrap, 1955.
West, Herbert F. *Robert Bontine Cunninghame Graham—His Life and Works*. London, Cranley and Day, 1932.

III. Critical Articles on the South American Sketches

Davies, Laurence. "Cunninghame Graham's South American Sketches," *Comparative Literature Studies*, Vol. IX, No. 3 (September, 1972), 253–65.
Walker, John. "R. B. Cunninghame Graham: Gaucho Apologist and Costumbrist of the Pampa," *Hispania*, Vol. LIII, No. 1 (March, 1970), 102–106.